LIONS OF JUDAH

By the same author

Not Ordinary Men

Twice Around the World

Volcano Under Snow

LIONS OF JUDAH

John Colvin

Quartet Books

First published in Great Britain in 1997 by
Quartet Books Limited
A member of the Namara Group
27 Goodge Street
London W1P 2LD

A catalogue record for this title is available from the British Library

ISBN 0 7043 7108 1

Typeset by Intype London Ltd
Printed and bound in Great Britain by C.P.D. Wales Ltd

To Joanna and David

Contents

PART II

PART III

LIONS OF JUDAH

Preface

This is an account of Jewish warriors – in the Old Testament, in the long centuries between Bar-Kokhba in 135 AD and the Holocaust, and thenceforward until the return to the Promised Land in 1948.

Jewish 'passivity' (or, at least, apparent failure vigorously to resist violence and brutality) has been, if not an illusion, only an historically *occasional* phenomenon, for which there are many explanations in Jewish faith and culture. Among the hideous European persecutions of recent times, Nazi genocide provided in our age the most terrible and nearly terminal example but, since the establishment of the State of Israel, the 'phenomenon' may no longer have substantive ground for existence.

Vicious fighting in the millennium before Christ between the tribe of Judah and the Beni-Yisrael or Northern Confederation (Joshua) tribes from Samaria on the one hand and the Philistines on the other – and frequently between the Israelite tribes themselves – was incessant in biblical times, often as mad as were the wars waged by the petty rulers of Western Europe. Only the lowering presence of the Philistines and other hostile tribes may have prevented the Israelites from tearing Canaan to bits, and themselves with it.

Nor was Jehovah/Yahweh, their God who had brought them out of Egypt in devastation and violence, a beacon of peace. He led his people across the Red Sea, cruelly drowning all their pursuers. He led them, through His Messenger, to the destruction of Jericho. Through Gideon, He led them again to victory over the massed hordes of Midian. He led them when Joshua beat the Ammonites and Jabesh-Gilead and when Hezekiah defeated the Assyrians and when Jehoshophat conquered the Syrians without a fight.

Until He ceased to be exclusively a war-god and began to devolve His powers to the prophets and the judges, God might be said to have been the greatest military commander of all. When, as with Eli's sons, He withdrew his support from the Israelites, the latter lost the Ark of the Covenant to the enemy, as well as the battle itself. His people themselves, of course, were men of war – gallant, professional, determined to the last on liberty against even the vast armies of Egypt, Syria, Assyria and Babylon. (From the many campaigns involving Megiddo sprang the nightmare of Armageddon, the battle which would end the world.)

But, once removed by Nebuchadnezzar from a shattered Jerusalem to Babylon, deprived of a state, a homeland, the Temple and hence the presence of their God, the Jews in seventy years of exile began to move towards the compilation of the Law and the Book, toward commerce, trade and a gentler ethos of love, compassion and peace. This process of turning in upon the Torah (the first five books of the Bible) led, far away in the future, to the Hasidic conviction that a Jew was neither permitted to kill another human being, even to save his own life, nor to save another life by causing his own death, not principles suitable for survival in the Holocaust, and thus part explanation for the Jewish role therein.

But such examples as King Zedekiah's revolt in Jerusalem, ending in his blinding, captivity and the death of his two sons at Nebuchadnezzar's hand, did not immediately further this change. Although the Jews effectively gave up war under the Persian rule of Cyrus the Great and under Alexander's Greek Empire, dissidence did not end. In the second century BC, the Hasmonean house, the Maccabees or 'Hammer', defeated the Seleucid Greeks under Antiochus Epiphanus, in 165 BC retaking Jerusalem and in 142 establishing independence. In AD 66, the Zealots and their extremist fringe, the Sicarii or assassins, routed the new occupiers of Palestine. Civil War broke out throughout the country against Vespasian and Titus, until Jerusalem and its Temple fell to the Romans in AD 70. It was, nevertheless, not until the defeat in AD 135 of Simon Bar-Kokhba ('Son of the Star', claiming descent from King David) by Julius Severus, fresh from conquest in Britain, that the Jews forswore war and opted for Pharisaical, rabbinic Judaism with its unparalleled valuation of human life itself.

This abstinence, with the glittering exceptions upon which this work will dwell, lasted for eighteen hundred years, although individual and quite extraordinary Jews, ranging from Trotsky to Hyman Rickover and Two-Gun Cohen, fought with distinction in the nineteenth and twentieth centuries in the armed forces of

Britain, America, France, Italy, Germany, Austro-Hungary, China, Russia and India, up to and after the Second World War. A few, a battered few, are alive today, but Israel's own thunder was hushed until 14 May 1948 when Ben Gurion proclaimed the 'Jewish state in Palestine', shelter for Jews everywhere.

From the eleventh century during the Crusades, then from the fourteenth century onwards in Spain, Italy, England, Germany, Poland, Ukraine and elsewhere in Eastern Europe, most bloodily in nineteenth-century Russia, the winds of anti-Jewishness started to blow. Massacre and pogrom began and spread. Jewish responses excluded force. They included conversion to Christianity, as in the decision of the Spanish *marranos* and the baptism of Jews in nineteenth-century Germany. Flight, when 'conversion' was seen by the authorities to be no more than an attempt at concealment of Jewish identity, or when escape to England and the United States became in the nineteenth century the only hope of refuge from the bestialities of modern anti-Semitism, was the other option. Dispersed, and without the coherent centre that Tel Aviv provides today, the Jews could do no other against states seen as inherently evil, *qua* institutions, as well as evil in aim and execution.

Individual and heartbreaking instances of valour during the Holocaust were manifold. Some Jews, especially in Poland, organised resistance, but much of that was devoted to clandestine emigration to areas where the possibilities, alone or under the Allies, of rebirth and concentration against the Nazis were greater than in the cauldron of Europe, where the Jews lacked arms or military leadership. It has been suggested that, among reasons – including submission to God's will – for Jewish pacifism and the relative absence of structured resistance movements during this time, was a simple Jewish failure to believe that the Germans, whose culture the Jews had admired and respected for centuries, could possibly have agreed to Hitler's Final Solution. The excuse, in other words, so often given for German complicity in the liquidation of the Jews – that they *did not know* about the concentration camps – was almost as true of the victims. Their recent history had been one of negotiation, compromise, conciliation – not resistance or confrontation, seen as suicidal when not impracticable – tactics hopeless against this new German policy designed not for piecemeal punishment and expropriation, but the actual annihilation of an entire race. Nor did their long exposure to oppression fit them for an aggressive or even defensive military role in Europe. Such a role was anyway almost precluded by their religion, physical powerlessness or even culture. Paul Johnson has remarked that no word for war exists in Yiddish.[1]

But in 1915, during the British Mandate of Palestine, two Russian Zionists, one of them – Vladimir Jabotinski – in British uniform, had raised the Zion Mule Corps and three Jewish battalions of the Royal Fusiliers to fight the Turks under British (General 'The Bull' Allenby's) command. The Jewish Legion formed the basis of the eventual Haganah. In 1936, Jabotinski founded the Irgun Zvai Leumi, which war followed by the Lehi (FFI) or Stern Gang, after the Second World War.

To these were added in 1945 after World War II the remnants of the Jewish Brigade, a force formed with Winston Churchill's approval to fight the Germans. So that in 1947, Britain, exhausted by war, occupied by world-wide problems of decolonialisation and harried by Begin's persistent terrorism, laid down the Mandate, departing on 15 May 1948, immediately after Independence.

That same day, Arab armies, some under Glubb Pasha, invaded Palestine but, after initial successes including capture of the old city of Jerusalem, most of Palestine was in Jewish hands, leaving only the West Bank of the Jordan and the Gaza Strip to the Arabs, a victory which owed much to the experience and discipline acquired by the Jewish Brigade.

Arab *fedayeen* assaults followed until, in October 1956, Israel conquered the Sinai, put a stop to cross-border raids, and occupied the Gaza Strip. At the end of the June War of 1967, Israel's military operations had brought her control of the Golan Heights commanding Damascus, and occupation of the Left Bank of the Jordan. In the Yom Kippur War of 1973, Egyptian and Syrian forces achieved surprise and massive breakthroughs: Israel was saved by dashing generalship, but also by US electronic aerial support and by a huge supply of American weaponry flown in in the nick of time. Israeli military endeavour had returned the country to that point in Samuel II, when 'came all the tribes of Israel to David until Hebron . . . "we are thy bone and thy flesh" . . . and King David made a league with them in Hebron

[1] Paul Johnson, *History of the Jews*, Weidenfeld and Nicolson, 1987

before the Lord: and they anointed David King over Israel', an Israel then comprising both Judea and Samaria.

In response to an approach in 1977 by President Sadat of Egypt, Prime Minister Begin of Israel offered territorial and other concessions over the Sinai, Jerusalem and the West Bank, in exchange for Egyptian guarantees of Israel's security. Egypt accepted the proposal for the Sinai, which she reoccupied in 1978. The other Arab States and the Palestine Liberation Organisation (PLO) refused negotiations. Far-reaching discussions, also involving the United States, have subsequently taken place, but Jerusalem, the West Bank and Gaza – as well as the Syrian border – remain unsettled questions and not only because of *Arab* opposition.

What follows is not a work of close scholarship. The Bible, for example, has been followed *in extenso*, but chiefly in the King James' version. It should, incidentally, be remembered that one of the most considerable of modern Jewish scholars himself believes that 'the Bible is no more than a national creation myth or work of imaginative fiction. There is not one piece of empirical evidence that Abraham, Moses or Jacob even existed.'[2] That is but one man's view. It should also not be necessary to remind readers that biblical statistics are almost invariably exaggerated. There is seldom any reliable method of correcting them: archaeology, however helpful, is not an absolute indicator.

[2] Article in *Sunday Times News Review* by Norman E. Cantor (author of *The Sacred Chain*, Harper Collins, 1994)

PART I

1
Ur; Abraham, the first warrior; Lot and Sodom

A Sumerian walled city called Ur of the Chaldees lay in a bend of the Euphrates southwest of the 'Land between the Rivers', the other river being the Tigris. That land, in the fifth to second millennia before Christ, was irrigated and provided fairly rich and fertile country, granting occupation not only to the farmers, but to fishermen, builders and craftsmen.

Today the soil is barren desert broken by mounds and ridges, inhabited by Bedouin nomadising between the ruined, mostly buried, cities in the sands of Mesopotamia at the head of the Persian Gulf. Ur and its sister-cities – Nippur, Erech, Larsa, Eridu – southeast of ancient Babylon were once governed by such as Sargon I, the Sumer monarch and priest of Ishtar, square-bearded, hieratic, with his long robe, ritual wand and high pot-hat, whose death preceded rule by Amorites and Elamites, powerful Semitic neighbours to west and east. They, in their turn, were overthrown in the second millennium by the ruler of Babylon, Hammurabi, the great king, whose infantry, advancing in phalanxes with shield and spear, preceded by chariot charges, carried all before it.

Traffic between the towns, when not overland, was riverine, in long boats with horse-head and other prow figure-heads and high sterns, rowed by up to a dozen oarsmen on double thwarts, navigating the brown stream between green fields – pasture and arable – vineyards, date-palm groves and banks lined with reeds. The rowers and the workers as a whole wore short, practical, almost kilt-like tunics, while officials and others of the upper class wore long skirts not unlike a Sinhalese lunghi, with shawls draped over one shoulder, the other bare.

The mud and asphalt walls of the city were high, and the stepped sides – diminishing upwards – of the ziggurat forming the temple of the Moon Goddess, and the palaces and other brick monumental buildings in Ur were of a formidable grandeur. At the foot of the city walls thrust the small square or oblong houses of the people, on the flat roofs of which they slept in summer, and in which they crouched on cold nights, warmed by camel-dung fires. In the maze of lanes and little streets uniting the centre of the town with the wharves by the river moved ox-drawn vehicles, donkey-carts, sheep, goats, and the populace in grey, brown or sometimes brighter garments, in clamorous and stinking confusion.

The rich, their necks and shoulders laden with jewellery, the women's dresses vivid scarlet, blue, yellow and green, occupied large whitewashed houses with central galleried courtyards hung with tapestries, their walls lined with coloured stone. In the corridors stood statues and pottery, and on dining tables in the open courts were gold vessels of marvellous design, destined to lie unseen for four thousand years until the arrival of Sir Leonard Woolley and the archaeologists. Silver and other metals, including gold, have also been identified in the trappings of Sumerian chariots, axes and swords, together with lapis lazuli, cornelian, marble, amber, obsidian and nephrite in hilts and handles.

Terah, descendant of Noah's son Shem – the progenitor of the Hebrew race – lived in Ur with his family. (Modern archaeologists believe that there was indeed a devasting flood or deluge in Sumeria.) At a time in the second millennium BC, possibly in some relation to the invading Amorites, he moved his family, himself, his son Abraham, the latter's wife Sarah and his nephew Lot, with all their retainers, to a town called Haran about six hundred miles away in the northwest of Mesopotamia, east of Carchemish.

Here Terah died and here Abraham, first patriarch of Israel and ancestor of all the Jews, was called by God: 'Get thee out of thy country and from thy kindred, and from thy father's house, unto a land that I will show thee. And I will make of thee a great nation and I will bless thee, and make thy name great: and thou shalt be a blessing.' The covenant with God had thus been established, tying obedience to God's gift of a land promised to a chosen or elect people. This covenant was later to be ratified several times, initially by Abraham's acceptance of God's terrible demand for the sacrifice of Isaac his son on the Rock of Mount Moriah in Jerusalem, a demand only withdrawn by the Angel of the Lord as Abraham stretched out his hand for the knife.

Abraham and Sarah, with Lot and all their servants, sheep, cattle and goats, and donkeys to carry the baggage and the black goatskin tents, started on the first stage of their long journey as 'the sojourners', nomads known as Habiru or Hebrews, outsiders and wanderers, at some date between the nineteenth and seventeenth centuries BC. They reached Sichem between Ebal and Gerizim, present-day Shechem or Nablus on the west bank of the Jordan, the valley today an intense green broken by the cupola of Joseph's tomb and the white wall of Jacob's Well. (Nablus, in President Nasser's era, was a nest of Palestinian anti-Hashemite monarchical dissidence and, of course, of anti-Zionist and anti-Israeli activity.) Here, after God had reaffirmed the covenant, Abraham built an altar to Him, before moving on to Bethel and Hebron, thence onward into Egypt.

Sarah was beautiful. Abraham feared that the Egyptians would murder him to acquire her. He pretended, therefore, that she was not his wife, but his sister. Sarah was taken into the Pharaoh's house, where she and Abraham were showered with gifts. But God, raging at the trickery, afflicted the Egyptians with plagues until the Pharaoh, resentful at Abraham's deception, drove the family out of Egypt. Hagar, incidentally, Sarah's handmaid with whom Abraham cohabited, was an Egyptian.

Abraham, Lot, their people and herds, both of which had greatly increased over the years, returned to Bethel. Earlier, Abraham had here set up his altar to God before departure for Egypt. As the pasture in that region was thin, too sparse to support their large flocks of animals, quarrels over territory and grass arose continually between the two families and their herdsmen. Abraham decided that, in order to seek greater diversity and a more sensible distribution of land, they must part. Although much older than his nephew, the patriarch generously gave Lot the first choice of grazing ground for his herds. Lot selected the green, well-watered, even lush plain of the Jordan, 'even as the garden of the Lord, like the land of Egypt as thou comest unto Zoar' to the east. When he and Abraham had separated in sadness, Lot to settle near Sodom, probably on the eastern shore of the Dead Sea among the Cities of the Plain, God promised perpetual ownership of all land visible to the eye, north, south, east and west, to Abraham and his descendants. Abraham settled in Mamre near Hebron, later to be King David's capital for many years, where he built an altar and nomadised throughout the length and breadth of the landscape, much of it forbidding, bare, rocky, harsh and of a daunting heat.

Meanwhile, there had been continual fighting in the Valley of the Dead Sea between two groups of kings, among them those of Sodom, Gomorrah, Babylon and Edom, as well as Horites, Amalekites and Amorites. Lot was captured, together with goods and victuals belonging to Sodom and Gomorrah, by the group of four kings, Shinar, Elam, Tidal and Ellasar, and news of his capture was conveyed to Abraham by kinsmen at his residence among the oaks of Mamre. When Abraham heard, he acted not merely as a patriarch, but as the first Hebrew commander, defeating – with his own force – mighty rulers banded together. He assembled his trained men, a complement of three hundred and eighteen slaves born and brought up in his household, and armed them with axes, spears, bows and hurling sticks. 'Drawing out his sword from its sheath', Abraham pursued the enemy nearly to Damascus. Here he divided his men into companies, platoons and sections which fell upon the enemy in the dead of night from separate directions, achieving complete surprise, a tactic to be repeated in other Israelite engagements. Having rescued the captives and restored the captured equipment to the king of Sodom, he refused all reward or even recompense: 'I will not take from a thread to a shoe-latchet . . . lest thou shouldest say, I have made Abram rich.'

Sarah his wife had remained childless. Three visitors arrived at Abraham's tent door in the baking noonday sun. These, who were not ordinary men, but God and His two messengers, told her husband that she was to have a son. Sarah, at her age, laughed in pleasure and unbelief. Of the three men, two then went on to Sodom which, despite Abraham's intercession to God that He might spare that city if only ten righteous men could be found, was destined to be destroyed. Under attack by the mob, the angels took the whole family by the hand and helped them to escape; when, unable to reach the mountains, they had arrived safely at Zoar, Sodom and Gomorrah blew up in 'fire and brimstone', probably exploding bitumen and petroleum as the result of an earthquake in an area submerged after biblical floods. It was then that Lot's wife, nostalgic for the happiness of Sodom, looked backward and was turned into the pillar of salt to which tourist guides today draw the attention of their sceptical or bemused clients.

2
Abraham; Isaac, Esau and Jacob; Joseph

'And thou shalt go to thy fathers in peace: thou shalt be buried in a good old age,' was the undertaking of the Lord in a vision given to Abraham. As the Amorites would not be defeated for another four generations, a period extending to the time of Moses and even of Joshua, Abraham could not cease his wanderings and depart. Nor could the Hebrews inherit the Promised Land until his son Isaac had married – not among 'the daughters of Canaan', which the 'sojourners' now inhabited, but among his own kin.

So that Isaac's wife should be one of their own people, Abraham sent the head of his household back on the long road to Mesopotamia. There, where Abraham's brother Nahor lived, this man stood by the well waiting until the women came out in the evening to draw water. One, Rebecca, a beauty, gave him to drink from the earthen pitcher which she bore on her shoulder, and drew water also for his ten camels; this was the woman, the granddaughter of Abraham's brother, whom the Lord had appointed for his master's son. Isaac at Mamre saw the returning train of camels approach. Rebecca descended from her beast and unveiled. Isaac at once loved her, took her to the tent of his mother, Sarah, and she became his wife, a marriage of love and a link between the Hebrew and Aramaean lines.

Sarah, who predeceased Abraham, lies at rest in the tombs of the patriarchs in caves at Hebron which Abraham purchased from the people of the place, after much ritual hesitation, denial and withdrawal between buyer and seller. Abraham, the founder of Judaism, is buried here with her, as well as Isaac and Rebecca, Jacob and Leah. (The tombs of Joseph and Rachel are not in the caves.) No one has been permitted entry, although Jews might push petitions into the cave by a hole in the thick rock, through which the paper flutters on to the graves below.

Esau and Jacob, also embodying two nations, Edom and Israel ('Two nations are in thy womb'), were the twin sons of Isaac and Rebecca; Jacob, the younger, on delivery holding tightly to the first-born's heel. Esau was 'a hairy man', a countryman and hunter, who married Judith, a Hittite woman, causing pain to his father and mother. One day, returning from a deer hunt, faint with exhaustion and hunger, he was seduced by the scent of his brother's cooking into selling him the elder son's birthright in exchange for the bread and soup of red lentils which Jacob had been preparing and for which he longed. Esau 'despised his birthright'. Jacob, on the other hand, described in Genesis as a 'plain man, dwelling in tents', was a profound intriguer, a warm man, crafty, who exploited, when he could, his brother's open, hearty, careless weaknesses.

Isaac, old, blind and ill, was conscious of his mortality. Rebecca overheard him, as he prepared for death, send his son Esau to shoot a deer with his bow and arrow, as was his practice, so that he might eat venison for the last time before his end and then give to Esau the blessing reserved for the first-born. But Rebecca, who knew how Isaac loved Esau's venison dishes, determined that the Lord's promise to her at the children's birth – that 'the elder should serve the younger' – must be ratified in the interest of Jacob, her favourite. Jacob, before Esau's return, was therefore dressed by her in Esau's clothes and, covered in goatskins to simulate his brother's touch and smell, carried a stew of kid which his mother had hastily prepared, to Isaac where he lay. 'I am,' said Jacob, 'Esau, thy first-born: arise, I pray thee, sit and eat of my venison that thy soul may bless me.' Suspicious at the difference between Jacob's voice and that of his eldest son, and at the speed with which 'Esau' had shot the game and cooked it, Isaac was eventually convinced. After he had kissed and held Jacob/Esau ('the smell of my son is as the smell of a field which the Lord hath blessed'), he blessed him. 'God give thee of the dew of heaven and the fatness of the earth, and plenty of corn and wine: let people serve thee and nations bow down to thee: be Lord unto thy brother . . . cursed be everyone that curseth thee, and blessed be he that blesseth thee.'

The power of the word was believed to carry success, in this instance mastery over Edom/Esau, a triumph not in fact achieved by Israel until King David's time. (Edom lay between the Gulf of Aqaba and the Dead Sea and, if not as rich as Jacob's Canaan, contained much cultivable land.) When Esau returned with the venison which he had just killed, he and his father cried out at Jacob's deception: Esau wept bitterly, swearing aloud to kill his brother. Isaac's blessing to his younger son could not be withdrawn. It was irrevocable, ensuring sovereignty over Israel for Jacob and his descendants. In reply to Esau's pleas and lamentations, however, he rewarded him also with 'the fatness of the earth' and 'the dew of heaven from above'. And, although Esau was bound both to serve his brother as well as to live by the sword in his fighting tribe, he or his seed would, in the end, shake off Jacob's yoke. (Edom, indeed, revolted against Judah, establishing independence in the ninth century BC.) Rebecca, terrified by Esau's threat, dispatched Jacob to her brother Laban in Haran, instructing her son to stay there until Esau's anger had subsided, when she would summon him to return. Apparently, as cover for this edict, she told Isaac that, as Jacob must not make a mistake like that of Esau in marrying Judith 'the daughter of Heth', a family disaster which had caused Rebecca to weary of life itself, she had sent him to her old home to select a more suitable consort, an order with which Isaac agreed and which he ratified.

On the road from Beersheba, at the beginning of the hills to the north, Jacob slept in a valley of stone and rock, a stone beneath his head. In the lonely night, under the bowl of stars, he dreamed that a ladder like a stairway led down from heaven to earth, with angels ascending and descending on God's affairs. Jehovah Himself had come down the ladder to him and stood at his side, repeating His promises made to Abraham of a Promised Land and a great nation that would benefit all the nations of the world. God swore again that He would never abandon Abraham's line or his seed. Jacob then erected in that place which he called 'dreadful' – terrible, full of dread – and also 'the Gate of Heaven', a stone pillar. He named the pillar Bethel or 'home of God'. He promised, in return for Jehovah's assurances, that he would follow God faithfully and of God's gifts return him the tenth.

In Laban, Rebecca's brother, Jacob met his match in chicanery. After falling in love with Laban's daughter, Rachel ('beautiful and well favoured'), Jacob agreed to work for Laban without payment for seven years in exchange for marriage at the end of this term. But, after the wedding feast, the artful Laban insinuated his elder daughter Leah into Jacob's bed without his nephew's knowledge. Jacob had thus been overreached, the biter bit. Laban did give him Rachel as wife after seven days, but Jacob was still required to work for him for another seven years, in the course of which

Leah, Rachel and their handmaids bore him twelve sons, founders of the Twelve Tribes. The Leah group consisted of Reuben, Simeon, Levi, Judah, Zebulun and Issachar; the handmaids' group, Dan, Gad, Asher and Naphtali; Rachel's children were Joseph – whose tribe later divided into those of Ephraim and Manasseh – and Benjamin, born after leaving Haran.

Laban obliged Jacob to work for a further six years, this time on a paid but arbitrarily fluctuating wage. He cheated him to the top of his bent in the numbers of animals permitted Jacob as the family herd, until the angel of God told Jacob to return to his own home in Canaan. Jacob's double-dealing was no less than Laban's and when he stole away clandestinely toward Gilead with his wives and children, he 'had large flocks, and maidservants and menservants and camels and asses'. Rachel, even, stole her father's most venerated image, regarding him as a hard, selfish, grasping and unnatural parent.

In response to a conciliatory message to Esau, Jacob learned with fear and apprehension that his brother was advancing with four hundred men to meet him out of Edom. As a precaution, he divided his entourage into two companies, so that at least one might be preserved if the other was destroyed; furthermore, he sent forward as presents for Esau five hundred and eighty animals, in 'droves' or waves, to make an even greater impression. Jacob prayed to God, without confessing or regretting his actions towards his brother, to seek deliverance from Esau by assiduously reminding Jehovah of promises earlier made and blessings given. He then despatched the entire train across the river, remaining alone in the darkness to ponder and plan for the morrow and devise new stratagems for his own preeminence.

Here, as Jacob waited, someone leapt upon him out of the darkness and wrestled with him, hour upon hour, until dawn when the stranger saw that he was not prevailing. Then He touched 'the hollow of his thigh' (thought to be the sciatic nerve), so that Jacob could not go on fighting, constrained also by the knowledge that he fought against God. Lame, he sought Jehovah's blessing, and God renamed him Israel, 'Perseverer with God'. Jacob was spiritually changed. All his earlier wiliness and deceit gradually fell away. He had met God face to face, and, his natural self powerless, became just, upright, stern and direct. Esau came, and his four hundred men. Jacob bowed seven times before him.

'I have enough,' said Esau; 'my brother, let that thou hast be thine,' and only with reluctance accepted Jacob's presents of cattle. Jacob blessed him and, with his people and beasts, rode on, forgiven, to Shechem where he bought land, erected standing-stones and pitched his tents.

In Shechem, Leah's daughter Dinah was seduced by a prince of a petty tribe (Hivites), 'defiled' in the view of Jacob's sons. These employed guile to persuade the tribesmen that the Jews would accept intermarriage if the prince and his followers were to agree to circumcision. But when the Hivites were still suffering from the wounds inflicted by the knife, Jacob's sons and their adherents treacherously destroyed their cities and expropriated their wives, children, herds and all other wealth, leaving Jacob himself angered and nervous at the possibility of reprisals from other neighbours. The Israelites left Shechem for Bethel, then Ephrath (near Jerusalem) where Rachel died in labour with Benjamin, then to Mamre and Hebron, where Isaac gave up the ghost and was buried.

Because Jacob loved only Rachel, he treated her son Joseph as if he were the first-born of all the Twelve, an attitude symbolised by the gift to Joseph of the coat-of-many-colours, a garment most appropriate to eldest sons. This favouritism, and the naïve arrogance of Joseph in repeating dreams of a future greatness which appeared to denigrate, if not exclude, his brothers, caused the youth deep unpopularity with them. Talking amongst the animals that they were herding, they conspired to kill him, stripping him of the coat-of-many-colours. Reuben, however, who intended to rescue him and return him to Jacob, convinced them to do no more than throw him down a dry well. Judah then persuaded the brothers to sell him to an Ishmaelite convoy 'bearing spices and balm and myrrh, going to carry it down to Egypt'. But in the meanwhile, Midianite traders had kidnapped the boy and themselves sold him to the Ishmaelites who, for twenty pieces of silver, took him into Egypt where he was sold on to Potiphar, captain of Pharaoh's guard. The brothers, to hide their crime, tore Joseph's coat as if a beast had savaged it, and dipped it in goat's blood before showing it to Jacob. Their father drew the 'correct' conclusion and mourned his son, weeping, rending his garments and putting on sackcloth.

The wretched seventeen-year-old, although not dead, seemed

to have come to a miserable end – lonely, far from home and lost to his loving father.

3
Joseph administers Egypt

But Joseph was able and far-sighted. He worked hard and kept his own counsel ('There is none so discreet and wise as thou art,' said the Pharaoh later). Dreading an uncongenial fate and the consequences of inaction, he performed his task well enough to be promoted 'overseer' of Potiphar's household. He was a handsome and attractive man. Potiphar's wife could not long restrain the lust for him that she instantly entertained. He resisted but, one day when they were alone in the house she took him by the sleeve so that when he fled from her demands – 'Lie with me!' – part of his robe came away in her hand. When her husband returned, she angrily showed him the piece of cloth, effectively charging Joseph with attempted rape. Potiphar sentenced him to imprisonment, the end of Joseph's dreams.

In gaol, however, his abilities rapidly secured him the post of supervisor of prisoners. Through divine guidance in the interpretation of dreams, he earned the support and admiration of Pharaoh's butler, then a prisoner but released due to Joseph's efforts. Unfortunately the butler forgot his assurances to Joseph and it was not until two years later, when the Pharaoh was concerned about his own dreams, that the butler advised his master to consult Joseph. Brought before the Pharaoh, Joseph, unkempt and in rough clothes, warned the ruler that his dreams of the lean and the fat kine and the full and the thin ears of corn, foretold seven years of plenty on earth followed by seven years of famine. He counselled that grain should be stored by the state in good years for consumption in lean years. Impressed by his perspicacity, Pharaoh set Joseph 'over all the land of Egypt in vestures of fine linen, a gold chain about his neck'. It was not unusual for non-Egyptians to reach high rank in Egypt, but Joseph was now the Pharaoh's first minister at the age of thirty, married to an Egyptian woman of Pharaoh's choice, the daughter of a priest, and father to Ephraim and Manesseh.

'When there was famine in all lands, in all the land of Egypt there was bread. All countries came into Egypt to buy corn.' Close to starvation in Canaan, Jacob sent his sons, except Benjamin the last-born and son of his beloved Rachel whom he kept with him at home, to Egypt to purchase grain. Once arrived in Egypt, the brothers were brought before the minister. Joseph, dressed in Egyptian robes, long supposed dead, was recognised by none of them. 'They bowed down with their faces to the earth.' The minister, however, knew *them* and, to their bewilderment, at once charged them with exploiting their mission as cover for espionage. But he agreed to sell them grain. His conditions were that Simeon should be left behind in Egypt, and that when they came back again, it should be with little Benjamin as proof of their legitimacy as traders. The brothers returned uneasily to their father Jacob in Hebron. There, in the yards, the sacks which had been filled when they left Egypt were seen to be full but, to the brothers' confusion and dismay, also contained each man's bundle of money which had been intended as payment. Joseph had left them there as a test of those who had so cruelly ill-treated him in the past: their remorse for earlier injustice, reported to him by a planted Hebrew interpreter, had not been enough to convince him of their reform.

'The famine was sore in the land.' Jacob/Israel therefore told his sons – reluctantly agreeing that they take Benjamin with them – to return to Egypt, with double money as well as those sums left in the sacks, together with 'balm, honey, spices, myrrh, nuts and almonds' as gifts. Joseph's steward reassured them concerning the money found earlier and released Simeon, leading them all into the great dining-hall of Joseph's house, with its rugs and hangings. The sight of Benjamin, his only brother by his mother Rachel, caused Joseph privately to weep. Although he astonished the brothers by seating them at table in exact order of age, he did not even then declare himself to them. Covertly placing a valuable silver cup in Benjamin's sack, he despatched them back to Hebron with all the corn they could carry and, again, all their money.

Joseph's steward pursued them on instructions. His men 'found' the silver cup, glistening in the sunlight, in Benjamin's sack; the other brothers with clear consciences protested innocence, swearing that should any one of them be guilty, he must either die or become a bondsman. But brought before Joseph, whose plot had been to discover whether they had really changed from the murderous thugs of the past, their love and concern for

Benjamin and Jacob caused Joseph to break down. He sent his servants out of the hall and at last declared, 'I am Joseph, your brother whom you sold into Egypt . . . but it was *not* you that sent me hither, but God' – the God who had foreseen not only his advancement, but the benefits that it would bring to Israel. With that, and encouraged by the Pharaoh himself, Jacob and many of the sons of Israel, with households and wives and little ones and beasts, came out of Canaan into Egypt. For the Pharaoh had sent wagons to bear them to Hebron and back, with asses, changes of raiment and 'the good things of Egypt'. (Canaan, of course, had itself been an Egyptian province on and off since 2400 BC.) There were yet five years of famine to endure. In Canaan the Israelites would have come to great hardship, poverty and death. In Egypt they would 'eat the fat of the land'.

'And Israel dwelt in the land of Egypt, in the land of Goshen', a wide valley running from the Eastern Nile to Ismailia, 'and they gat their possessions therein and were fruitful and multiplied exceedingly.' (A large number of Israelites had also remained in Canaan with the Jebusites, Amorites and other tribes, without ever settling in Egypt.) So fruitful had they become and such a multitude that, after the eventual deaths of Jacob, Joseph, the brothers and the beneficent Hyksos (Asiatic) Pharaohs of the time, the Hebrew foreigners came to be feared and resented under their new rulers, seen as a sort of internal and external fifth column.

The Pharaohs, or rulers, at the date between the seventeenth and fifteenth centuries BC of the Hebrews' movement into Egypt, were drawn from the Hyksos peoples, Hyksos in Egyptian meaning 'rulers of foreign countries'. Probably Semitic and Indo/Iranian, possibly maritime, they seem to have owed success in mass invasion out of Asia to war chariots, sweeping through Syria and Palestine, reaching Egypt in about 1720 BC. According to an account dated fifteen hundred years later, 'A blast of God smote us and unexpectedly, from the regions of the East, invaders of obscure race marched in confidence of victory against our land. By main force they easily seized it, without striking a blow: and having overpowered the rulers of the land, they then burned our cities, ruthlessly razed to the ground the temples of the gods, and treated all the natives with a cruel hostility.' Their capital was at Avaris, near the residence of the Israelites in Goshen, destroyed after their overthrow by the Egyptian Ahmosis I, and reconstructed by Rameses II whose capital had hitherto been at Thebes, later renamed Tanis.

It was under the Hyksos Dynasty that the Twelve Tribes were made welcome, the Empire period when Joseph was the Pharaoh's viceroy. But after one hundred and fifty years in which the Hyksos conquered Syria and Palestine – traces of one of their castles have been identified at Shechem – the native Egyptians rebelled against the occupiers of Egypt, their own land. The new Egyptian king planned great cities, exploiting the Hebrews as forced labour under *corvée* in the construction of state buildings, palaces and the treasure cities, Pithom and Raamses, which were to store food for trade and against famine and be sources of supply in time of war.

The Jews now became slaves, their main task to make bricks and to drag huge stone building blocks into position; whipped and beaten in the blazing sun, dying as they laboured, the ropes tearing into their wrists and shoulders, they were forced to make bricks but forbidden to use straw. This brutality, conflicting with the need for a continued supply of workers, was meant to reduce Jewish fecundity and limit their lifespan. The Pharaoh's next step, to induce Egyptian midwives to destroy Hebrew boys at birth, failed when the midwives refused to cooperate. The Pharoah then commanded that all Jewish male babies be hurled into the Nile and drowned. One woman, Jochebed, a Levite and wife of a Levite, the priestly caste, gave birth to a son whom she hid for three months. When she could no longer disguise his existence, she made a little ark or boat from bullrushes sealed with pitch and bitumen, into which she put the boy. She then laid the boat among the tall reeds on the bank of a river and instructed his sister, Miriam, to watch concealed nearby. An Egyptian princess, daughter of the Pharaoh, came to the river to bathe, attended by her women. Seeing the ark in the reeds, she sent one of this entourage to bring it to her. When she had uncovered the child, the baby began to cry; recognising that it was a Hebrew child, she took pity on him. His sister, Miriam, came out of the rushes, offering to find a nurse for the boy until the princess should be ready to adopt him. The 'nurse' was Jochebed, the baby's mother, who brought him up until he became 'son' to the princess, being named Moses, 'he who was drawn from the water'. Moses then was raised and grew up in the court as an Egyptian. But when he saw an Egyptian belabouring a Hebrew, he killed him, thinking himself unobserved. But there *had* been a watcher, one of his own race . . .

News of the crime, through this Jewish eyewitness, reached the authorities, who sought to arrest and execute Moses. Moses fled for his life into Midian where, by a well, he drove off shepherds who were harassing the daughters of Jethro, a priest of Midian, and stealing water from their troughs. Moses drew water for these girls and for their flock. The priest took him in, gave him in marriage a daughter, Zipporah or 'Little Bird', who bore him a son, Gershom, 'stranger in a strange land'. Jethro also put him in charge of his flock. One hot summer day, Moses herded the sheep and goats to slopes where the pasture was less bare and desiccated by the sun than in the plains, to Horeb, the mountain of God, called Sinai by the Hebrews.

4
God, Moses, the Plagues and the Reed Sea

'. . . The children of Israel sighed by reason of the bondage, and they cried and their cry came up unto God by reason of the bondage. And God heard their groaning and God remembered his covenant with Abraham, with Isaac and with Jacob. And God looked upon the children of Israel and God had respect unto them.'

That day on Mount Horeb, Moses saw a fire burning in a bush, but the bush was not consumed by the fire. Out of the bush, God called to him: 'Moses, Moses . . .' He had seen the affliction of His people and heard their cries, He would deliver them from the oppression of their Egyptian taskmasters, and lead them into a land filled with milk and honey. Moses protested that he was incompetent and unqualified to be the leader of God's people on earth, or to approach Rameses II, the Pharaoh, and bring the children of Israel out of the land in which they were prisoners and into the Promised Land; for he stammered, was slow of speech, not eloquent, and lacked divine powers. God angrily reminded him of his Levite brother Aaron's eloquence. As for supernatural powers, He turned Moses' staff into a serpent, made his hand 'leprous as snow' and spoke of the first miracle, the transformation of the water of the River Nile into blood. He warned him, however, that Pharaoh would not let His people go until He had punished Egypt, despoiling that country of gold, silver and jewels.

Moses, with Jethro's permission, returned from Midian to Egypt with his wife and sons. He and Aaron, in the name of the Lord God of Israel, called on the Elders, repeating God's promises. The people were overwhelmed with relief, bowed their heads and worshipped. But when Moses pleaded with the Pharaoh for the children of Israel to make a three-day journey into the desert to sacrifice, the king angrily refused, even ordering the foremen to make work more difficult for 'the idle labourers', depriving them again of straw for the bricks, forcing them to gather stubble, then thrashing them for their pains. The people, through Moses' mouth, complained to God that their state was now worse than before, that God's intervention had made them stink in Pharaoh's nostrils and had put a sword against them in Pharaoh's hand. But God swore to the children of Israel: 'I am Jehovah, I am the Lord, I will bring you out from under the burdens of the Egyptians and I will rid you out of their bondage and I will redeem you with a stretched-out arm . . . I will be to you a God and I will bring you into the land which I did swear to give to Abraham, Isaac and Jacob.' But the children of Israel, in anguish and captivity, did not believe.

Moses went again to Pharaoh and again the king refused. Moses then bade Aaron lift his rod and all the waters turned to dark red blood. The fish died, the river stank, and the people could not drink, wash or cook. When Pharaoh hardened his heart, Aaron with his rod this time brought a plague of glutinous, slithering frogs into the Egyptians' houses: hopping in and out of beds, servants' quarters, dining-halls, kitchens, they swarmed everywhere, except in Goshen where the Israelites dwelt. Pharaoh pretended to yield but, when the plague had been lifted by God, did not fulfil his promise. God next sent a plague of lice from the dust of the land to madden the Egyptians and their beasts, then swarms of biting flies, then a vicious cattle disease (murrain) upon the beasts of Egypt. Still Pharaoh continued to deceive, first promising to let the Israelites go, then cancelling the orders when the plagues were lifted.

A plague of suppurating boils followed. Moses said once more to Pharaoh, 'Thus saith the Lord God of the Hebrews, "Let my people go, that they may serve me." ' But Pharaoh did not let the people go, nor was he swayed by the plagues of thunder, hail and fire, 'very grievous, smiting the flax and the barley'. But, on that occasion, he said, 'I have sinned this time, the Lord is righteous, and I and my people are wicked.' Yet he would not yield after the plague of locusts which followed, destroying 'every herb of the land, all the fruit which the hail had left, all the green things in the trees'. But it was the Lord that hardened Pharaoh's heart, so that Pharaoh should comprehend the greatness of God and His own people understand His power. After the next plague, that of darkness, Moses refused Pharaoh's offer (the king, by now, seriously disturbed) to let the Hebrews go, but without their flocks and herds.

Against the next plague 'there [was] a great cry throughout all the land of Egypt, such as there was none like it nor shall be like it any more'. For God had decreed that all the firstborn of men and beasts should die throughout Egypt, from the Pharaoh's child to the maidservant's and the firstborn of the animals. The Angel of Death would pass through Egypt, sparing only Goshen. There each head of a Hebrew family would kill a lamb or a kid and sprinkle with hyssop its blood upon the lintel and doorposts as a sign to God and His angel that they should 'pass over' Goshen, leaving the families unharmed. So was established the absence of leaven, prohibition of work, the Feast of the Passover to be kept forever, the flesh of the Lamb to be roasted and eaten with unleavened bread.

On the midnight, God executed his terrible sentence, smiting all the firstborn of Egypt: the dead were in all the dwellings of Egypt. A horrified, if not panic-stricken Pharaoh, at last, too late and in the dead of night, told Moses to take God's people with their flocks and herds out of Egypt. The Egyptians, as God had prophesied, in their terror and anxiety to see them gone before they were *all* dead men, loaded them with gold and silver and jewels, the Hebrews despoiling the Egyptians as the mixed multitude and their beasts, the hosts of the Lord, moved out of Egypt taking Joseph's bones with them.

Led by God in a pillar of cloud by day and by night a pillar of fire, they did not travel along the main road out of Egypt – 'the Philistine way' – from Memphis and El-ʿArish to Gaza; that route was guarded by Egyptian military posts and, even if they were evaded, would lead eventually to confrontation with the 'mechanised' (chariot-borne) Canaanites. The Israelites took instead the road through the Wadi Tumilat on to the Reed Sea (*not* the Red Sea), near today's Kantara. At this point, between 1270 and 1260 BC, in the shallows of the Bitter Lakes and the Gulf of Suez, there were both strong winds and strong tides. Troops under Xerxes drowned there in the fourth century BC. God had decided to make a final demonstration to Pharaoh of His authority, ordering Moses to take His people forward across the Sea of Reeds. Pharaoh, customarily treacherous and resentful, despite all assurances mustered his infantry, his cavalry and his horse-drawn war-chariots and came at the Israelites out of the desert as they lay helpless in their tents at Etham facing the sea. The Egyptians, in their horsed two-man chariots, with bows,* bronze battle-axes, sickle swords and chain-mail coats, began the advance.

Seeing the massed armies of Egypt driving at them on their flank, the people in their terror blamed Moses for removing them to the wilderness from homes which suddenly seemed almost secure. But Moses told them to stand firm, to be brave: the Lord would fight for them. And God moved the pillar of cloud until it stood between the Egyptians and the Israelite camp, so that the Egyptians were in cloud and darkness, while the pillar of fire gave light to the Hebrews all night. The Lord drove the sea back in the east wind, dividing the waters, making the sea dry land: the children of Israel crossed the Reed Sea on that dry land through a wall of water on either hand, hotly pursued to the middle of the sea by Pharaoh's cavalry.

Yahweh 'troubled the host of the Egyptians', removing their chariot wheels. When He instructed Moses to stretch out his staff in the morning, the waters closed upon the Egyptians, 'the depths covered them, they sank as lead in the mighty waters', the sea swallowed them, chariots, horsemen, and all those mighty battalions. The Lord had fought for the Hebrews against the Egyptian battalions. Indeed, the only fighter *was* God, Moses being accorded divine status as His instrument of Holy War; no human troops engaged the enemy. Later, God and the soldiers joined and fought together in other conflicts, but the Battle of the Reed Sea was exclusively fought by Jehovah without man's help. Unlike in David's battles, Yahweh was the commander here, the Divine Warrior. Moreover, though natural explanations are available for all the plagues, no *human* commander arranged or mounted them.

* These bows were allegedly made from Lebanon cypress, the sinews of oxen, horns from an *ovis ammon*, tendons from a bull.

5
Moses in the wilderness; his death; Joshua

After three days' march out of Egypt, the Israelites had found no water in the wilderness. When they came to Marah, the waters were bitter there, made sweet only when Moses threw a length of wood therein. At Elim was an oasis with palm trees in some quantity, and twelve wells. In the wilderness of Zin, after more than thirty days' march, the people were hungry, complaining to Moses that, whereas in Egypt they had had at least meat in plenty, here after their deliverance from Pharaoh's beatings, they had nothing.

But God sent flocks of quails among them which they caught as the birds rested in the sand, near the black tents. In the morning, He rained manna, or 'what-is-it?', on them, 'a small round thing, as small as the hoar frost', 'white like coriander seed and tasting like a honeyed biscuit'. The people gathered it every day except the Sabbath, 'the bread which the Lord hath given you to eat'. And, even then, the Israelites disobeyed God, some gathering manna on the forbidden seventh day.

Moses chastised the entire congregation. Since God had assured them that He would provide them with food both in the morning and in the evening, their murmurings were not against Moses but against the Lord himself. 'What *are* we? . . .' At Rephidim there was again no water and, despite his reproaches, the Israelites again turned on Moses, blaming him for the thirst which seemed likely to destroy them, their children and their cattle, even taking up stones with which to stone their leader. But Moses, on the command of God, smote the rock of Mount Horeb/Sinai with his staff, drawing forth streams of clear, cool water, enough for all the multitude to drink as it poured out of the stone and down the mountainside.

In the desert wilderness, there were members of other wandering tribes who competed with the Israelites for the few resources that existed in the sands. Among these were the Amalekites, a branch of the Edomites who nomadised south of Judah between Radesh and Hormah. A band of Amalekites imprudently attacked Hebrew stragglers in the great procession moving towards Canaan out of Egypt. (It was precisely this attack against the rear guard that led to the ferocity of Maimonides' injunction against the Amalekites.) Moses had imposed an obligation to bear arms on all those males over twenty years of age able to go forth and battle in their tribes for Israel. Their commanders, 'able men', would become leaders, rulers by thousands, hundreds, fifties and tens, an injunction suggested by his father-in-law, Jethro. Before the clash with the Amalekites, we know only that Moses commanded Joshua, one of his most talented young men, to select warriors, himself standing on the top of a hill with rod held high. Moses was old, but so long as his strength allowed him to keep the staff raised, the inexperienced Israelite soldiers were encouraged, and the battle swung their way, but when he allowed the staff to decline, the Amalekites prevailed over Joshua's nervous troops. So they seated the old man on a stone, while his brother Aaron held one of Moses' arms on high and Hur lifted the other. In this fashion, by dusk, the Israelites cut down the Amalekites, not with stabbing swords, but with scythe-swords, the 'edge of the sword'. Moses built an altar here to his God after the Lord had told him that the memory of the Amalekites would be blotted out forever; he named the altar 'Jehovah, my banner'. After completing his memorial, Moses claimed that the Lord had sworn that He would 'have war with the Amalekites from generation to generation', anticipating the defeat of the Jews by Amalekites when the former came to move on Canaan from Kadesh through Hormah. At all events, while also defending fixed positions and attacking hostile tribes, Joshua's career as an offensive commander had begun.

At Mount Sinai, thick cloud floated on the peak, turned to fire by Jehovah; smoke ascended, the trumpets sounded. God gave to his people through Moses the Ten Commandments, and a mass of lesser, detailed laws and rules to govern their minutest conduct. Moses and the Twelve Tribes of Israel renewed the covenant made with Abraham, promising obedience in return for God's protection and their final settlement in the Promised Land. The people built the Tabernacle and the Ark of the Covenant with rich wood, silk and the sequestrated jewellery of the Egyptians after the Exodus, but promptly broke the covenant in Moses' absence, with Aaron's agreement, by making a golden calf.

Moses in his rage smashed the two tablets on which the Law had been transcribed, and ground the calf to gold dust, which he mixed with water and forced the people to drink. He commanded the Levites to slaughter three thousand of the transgressors: '. . . slay every man his brother, and every man his companion, and every man his neighbour.'

At 'the top of the mount' on Mount Sinai, after accompanying the Lord for forty days and nights without food or water, Moses wrote the words of the covenant and the Ten Commandments on new tablets, which he took down to Aaron and to all the congregation. Jehovah forgave the people – 'My presence shall go with thee and I will give thee rest' – sending His people, their tents folded, out of Sinai into the Promised Land.

From Kadesh-Barnea on the edge of the desert, where the Israelites had bivouacked, Moses sent out spies from each of the Twelve Tribes. A brilliant intelligence brief instructed them to report to Moses on Canaan's land, its quality, forests, herds, crops and fruits, on the strength, quantity and weakness of the inhabitants, on the vulnerability and construction of the cities and defences. When they returned from the valley of Eshcol, although unanimous on the richness and suitability of the land and bringing back fruits to prove it – 'a land of milk and honey' – ten of the leaders advised fearfully against Israelite attack, because of the strength and fortification of the cities and the quantity and size ('giants') of the Amalekites, Hitites, Jebusites, Amorites and Canaanites. Panicked, the congregation ignored the more optimistic counsel of Joshua and Caleb, even proposing a return to Egypt under a new captain, rejecting Moses.

Joshua and Caleb spoke nevertheless to the children of Israel: 'Only rebel not against the Lord, neither fear ye the people of the land; *for they are bread for us*: their defence is departed from them, and the Lord is with us: fear them not.' Jehovah, infuriated at their cowardly disobedience and lack of trust, damned them for their disloyalty, condemning them to forty years in the wilderness. He also demanded the death therein of all their generation other than Joshua and Caleb, and the end of all hope, except for their children, of entry to the Promised Land. Immediate military defeat by the Amalekites and Canaanites right up to Hormah followed. The Israelites, despite their initial submission to the ten hesitant leaders, had made in desperation an attempted invasion of Canaan but, with both the Ark and an angry and frustrated Moses left behind at Kadesh, the expedition lacked divine approval, doomed to defeat by a combined force of desert dwellers and hillmen, led by the king of Arad. Behind that enemy lay Egyptian power still, until 1200 BC, dominating Canaan.

Even Moses and Aaron were included among those who would not pass into the Promised Land. In Moses' case, this prohibition was perhaps caused by Moses' loss of control when he exceeded the Lord's instructions over water and, instead of standing meekly by, furiously struck the rock at Meribah with his staff, indeed producing great gouts of water but disobeying Jehovah, adherence to whose smallest wish was paramount.

After the defeat beyond Kadesh, Moses understood that he could not drive into Canaan from the south. He also realised that he did not yet have the weapons to take walled cities in the Beersheba valley, nor could his untrained men defeat regular soldiers who had war-chariots. He, or Joshua, by then his commander-in-chief, determined on an assault from the east in a circuit through Transjordan, marching on the fringe of the desert. The hill kingdoms of Moab and Ammon were inhabitated by descendants of Lot. Edom, also mountainous, was historically Esau's fief. Canaan had thus been settled by Hebrews before Moses arrived. Moses sought the king of Edom's permission to travel through that country on the King's Highway, a road which still exists today, then running through Bashan (Og), Sihon, Moab and Edom to the Gulf of Aqaba. The king refused. Moses then turned his troops southeast out of Kadesh, possibly as far as the gulf but more probably branching northeast along the western frontier of Edom, east along the brook Zered, then north by the eastern frontier of Moab towards Heshbon. He then sent messengers to the king of Heshbon, an Amorite (i.e. Canaanite) called Sihon, seeking his permission to use the King's Highway through *his* kingdom, promising, as in Edom, not 'to turn into the fields or into the vineyards – nor drink of waters of the wells . . .' But that king too rejected Moses' request, and sent an army against him. As Heshbon had not had time to digest their king's recent seizure of land in Moab, the defences could not withstand the Israelite attack and the result was the first major victory of that race against a foreign power.

Moses' next target was Bashan, under King Og, which lay to

the east of the Sea of Galilee. (The king was immensely large, owning an iron bedstead thirteen feet long and six feet broad.) The Israelites attacked and defeated him, taking all of Bashan, including thirty cities and all the cattle and the spoils of the cities, both walled and unwalled, 'utterly destroying the men, women and children of every city . . . we smote (Og) until none was left to him remaining'.

But when the tribes of Reuben and Gad saw the richness of the earth of Sihon, they sought to remain there with their cattle, on the east bank of the Jordan. They had no desire to join the army's passage of the river into Canaan, wanting to stay in Gilead. (Jehovah had earlier – after the defeat by the king of Arad – felt obliged to set serpents on recalcitrant and complaining Israelites before 'curing' them with the brass serpent that later became the badge of Aesculapius.) When Moses reminded them of the consequences of earlier pusillanimity ('forty years in the wilderness') at the valley of Eshcol, the men agreed to leave their families and flocks behind in Gilead, and fight with their brothers westward, 'every man armed for battle'. Moses, leader, patriarch, and religious constitutionalist had given unity at last to his clans. They had become the Jewish people and nation, the nation and people of Israel, bound together, although often straying, by the Ten Commandments, the web of law transmitted at Mount Sinai and, above all, by their own history. Now, with Hebrews earlier settled on the East Bank, they formed – for the time being – a coherent battery of tribes, waiting to move into Canaan and to fulfil God's promise to Abraham, Isaac, Jacob, Joseph, and to Moses himself. This was at last a people in arms, advancing towards destiny.

The Israelites moved their camp up to the frontier. Hearing this intelligence, King Balak of Moab tried to persuade Balaam, a noted prophet and sage, to curse this 'mighty' threat – 'They cover the face of the earth' – to both Moab and Midian, rather than confront the Israelites militarily. Balaam, after many representations from Balak including direct bribes of bags of gold and silver, defied God's contrary remonstrance. But the ass bearing him to Balak to do the king's bidding could not move from fear at the sight of God's angel with a sword barring the way, no matter how much its rider beat it. Nor could Balaam, commanded by King Balak to damn Jacob and Israel at the place of sacrifice, do other in his speech than repeat God's *blessing* on both. He could not physically 'go beyond the commandment of the Lord, to do either good or bad of mine own mind; but what the Lord saith, that will I speak'.

At the peak of Mount Pisgah where God had sent him, Moses looked down as he died on the Promised Land, the wilderness as well as the fertile Jordan lands which he would never enter, but for which he had striven so long. In a long address in the plains of Moab, just before the invasion of Canaan, to the people whom he had for many years commanded, he reminded them of the joy and sadness of their common times and history, of God's love and care for them, of the covenant, of God's protection at the Reed Sea and thereafter, of the Law and the Commandments, of the people's obligation and obedience to Jehovah and, again, of God's love. He was instructed by God: 'Charge Joshua and encourage him and strengthen him, for he shall go over before this people, and he shall cause them to inherit the land which thou shalt see.'

'And Moses the servant of the Lord died there in the land of Moab, according to the word of the Lord . . . but no man knoweth of his sepulchre unto this day.' Visitors to Petra today are assured by nomads along the Wadi Mussa (Moses) that they, the Bedul as they call themselves, were the original shepherds of the place two thousand and more years ago. Moses was known to their forefathers.

6
Joshua's victories in Canaan

'Canaan' is said to derive its name from *kinakhkha*, an Akkadian word meaning 'reddish-purple' from the purple dye in dust. It had been an Egyptian province. Joshua was summoned by the Lord to lead the Israelites across the River Jordan into Canaan, the Promised Land, which extended from the Euphrates or, at least, the Lebanon and anti-Lebanon mountains, to the wastes of the South. Obedience, Joshua was instructed, would bring victory: '. . . do according to all the law . . . turn not to the right hand or to the left that thou mayst prosper.' Disobedience, on the other hand, led to failure and punishment.

At this time, between 1210 and 1190 BC, the Egyptian occupation, earlier strengthened, especially in the cities of the plain by Canaanite support, had been enfeebled, and the seaborne Philistines were temporarily contained on the coast. Egypt itself was fully engaged with invaders from southern Europe. But whether in Canaanite or Egyptian hands, the strong points in the flat land below the hills were still held by troops equipped with chariots and other weaponry beyond the capacity of Israel's light forces to defeat.

Joshua had a firm base in Gilead, Moab and Bashan where the Israelites, as we have seen, had already begun settlement. The water of the Jordan in that area was often low and fordable particularly opposite the main target, the ancient fortified city and luxurious oasis of Jericho, with its palm trees and wells. (The historian Josephus described it as the most fertile spot in Judaea, rich in palms and in balsam . . .) Joshua determined on a crossing of the Jordan in that latitude.

The spies, or scouts, despatched ahead of the first contingent, visited the house of a woman named Rahab, described as a harlot but, possibly, an innkeeper with that occupation's access to information. 'I know that the Lord hath given you the land and that your terror has fallen upon us . . . all the inhabitants of the land faint because of you' . . . neither did there 'remain any more courage in any man'. She and her customers had heard of the

Reed Sea miracles and, closer to home, of the defeat of Og and Sihon. This was a sound indicator of local morale, determining Joshua to delay his assault no longer. The two scouts, after being hidden from royal counter-intelligence under flax on Rahab's roof, returned safely to headquarters with this and other tactical intelligence, assuring Rahab beforehand of her personal safety in any future Israelite attack.

An earthquake, relatively common in this region and repeated as late as 1927 with an English professor as witness, brought down the cliffs bordering the Jordan, damming it so that no water flowed. 'And the people [forty thousand tribesmen, armed] passed over right to Jericho' on dry land. At this miraculous moment, the Levites bearing the Ark dipped their naked feet into the Jordan to find it suddenly transformed into a hard foothold by today's Damiyeh Bridge. Next day, the army made its base at Gilgal for the Passover, no more eating manna but 'the fruit of the land'. In Gilgal today, sacred circles and battered altar steps can still be traced; *gilgals* are, in fact, conical, one being near Shechem or Nablus̆, close to Jacob's well, another being the Hill of Samaria; and there are others, perhaps including Mount Tabor.

Outside Jericho, over against Joshua, stood a man with a drawn sword in his hand. 'Art thou for us,' asked Joshua, 'or for our adversaries?' The man replied: 'As captain of the host of the Lord, am I now come.' Joseph fell on his face and worshipped him. And then, as they did in England on 'the Longest Day', the regiments went into battle. Led by the priests bearing the Ark, their ram's-horn trumpets blowing, they circumnavigated the ancient citadel once a day for seven consecutive days in the terrible heat of the plain. At dawn on the seventh day, the people shouted, and 'the wall fell down flat, so that the people went up into the city, every man straight before him, and they took the city'. Recognising the scarlet thread marker in her window, the soldiers took out Rahab and all her family to their own camp. No walls stand from the Jericho of that day. Archaeological evidence therefore does not exist, and we should remember the caveat in our preface. Perhaps there was another earthquake. Perhaps the soldiers penetrated through breaks in the aged stone fabric, or climbed into the fortress over the walls, taking everything by the sword, the defenders become lax after the endless circular processions when nothing seemed to threaten any longer. Perhaps it was a miracle.

'Cursed be the man before the Lord, that riseth up and buildeth this city, Jericho,' said Joshua.

Manasseh, Ephraim, Benjamin, Reuben and Dan may have been the most active military tribes. The army, at all events, was inspired by a faith in Jehovah, liberator and saviour, not matched by Canaanites lacking a common unifying faith, most of whose cities were autonomous units, all of them split by divisive geographic features.

Hivite elders of one of these places, Gibeon, a royal city, terrified by Joshua's victories, sought peace with Israel under the pretence that they had walked all the way from 'a far country' not, as was the case, from the near vicinity. Their 'ambassadors', seeking to form a league with Joshua, had arrived in the Gilgal camp, carrying stale and mouldy provisions, torn wine bottles, wearing old shoes and clothing, attributing all this to the length and hardship of the journey. (The Israelites were persuaded by the deception but it took place before Joshua's next campaign, thus securing his rear in advance of the assault on Ai.) In punishment for their trickery, Joshua, although standing by the agreement, made the Gibeonites 'hewers of wood and drawers of water'.

As Joshua did not believe that his lightly armed tribesmen could secure victory against their armoured and more heavily equipped opponents in the plain, he adopted as his first main strategy the penetration and conquest of the Judaean mountain massif. On the fringes of this chain lay Bethel, Gibeon, Gibeah, Jerusalem, even Bethlehem, and from these ranges the Israelites could command the towns of Judah-Lachish, Hebron, Eglon, Debir and so forth. The hills themselves were relatively empty, ready for settlement and unlikely to be vulnerable or even accessible to heavyweight Egyptian reprisal. The men of Israel were highlanders.

His first move was therefore via Bethel towards the watershed. That town itself was strongly defended but Ai, to the south, was a ruin. Israelite scouts from Jericho believed that the position was lightly held and required no more than two to three thousand attackers for success. Ai had, however, because of its strategic advantages, been recently fortified and reinforced from Bethel. Its defenders forced an undignified retreat with loss of life on the first wave of Joshua's infantry, who had had to face a stiff climb of several hours on stumbling mules.

Joshua then moved up to be in the camp with his men, sending a force of thirty thousand to lie in wait 'behind the city' of Ai. He himself at dawn led the main force against the city in the same direction and mode as in the earlier, unsuccessful attempt. But this time, the Israelites' flight was only simulated. The Canaanites, again in triumphant pursuit, left Ai unguarded. The force of thirty thousand 'behind the city' (to the south), and five thousand men whom Joshua had placed in ambush between Bethel and Ai after forced marches up precipitous mountain trails, then sprang the trap. Ai was fired, its few defenders destroyed. When the main Canaanite Ai force saw the smoke rising from their encampments, they found themselves caught between Joshua who now turned his main force right round against his pursuers – 'the Parthian shot' – and the Israelite conquerors of Ai. Those who got away were caught by such men of the five thousand whose task of ambush and of blocking the relief force from Bethel was complete.

In an early example of 'ethnic cleansing' Joshua killed all the inhabitants, destroying later all the kings, tribes and cities his armies encountered, 'making a heap for ever, a desolation unto this day . . . he left none remaining', over and over again.

The conditions of war were not easy. Here among these outcrops of white and grey limestone, against the reds, yellows, purples and blacks of the Jaffa–Jerusalem road, are the great naked ribs and bars of the mountains, like the gigantic stairs of Jacob's dream. By contrast, Roman mosaics, broken capitals, tiled floors can also still be identified under their earth coverings. But much of Judaea is stony land, with only touches of olive green.

Because of Gibeon's treachery to other Amorite kingdoms, including Jerusalem, Hebron, Jarmuth, Lachish and Eglon, the rulers of these cities made war against the delinquent. But Joshua honoured his agreement with the deceiving elders and, after a night march of twelve miles through forested hills, came down from the heights on the Amorite encampments besieging Gibeon. Caught between the Israelites in their headlong rush and the fortifications themselves of the invested city, the Amorites broke and ran down the slope at Beth-Horon where the Maccabees later caught the Seleucids in the first century BC.

Joshua's task was to defeat the enemy before daylight should come to aid their escape: 'Then spake Joshua to the Lord in the day when the Lord delivered up the Amorites before the children of Israel, and he said in the sight of Israel, Sun stand thou still upon Gibeon and thou, Moon, in the valley of Ajalon. And the sun stood still and the moon stayed until the people had avenged themselves upon their enemies . . . And there was no day like that before it or after it, that the Lord hearkened unto the voice of a man: for the Lord fought for Israel.'

In the pursuit that followed, many were killed by the Israelite archers and swordsmen. Some may have been stoned to death by Gibeonite peasants. Some may have fallen to the enemy through delays caused by severe hailstorms. The five kings were found in a cave, then slaughtered and hung by Joshua from trees, left there until nightfall when he had their carcasses put back into the caves: behind great stones, these 'remain until this very day'. The Israelites then moved on to take Azekah, Libnan, Lachish, Gezer, Hebron, Eglon and Debir: 'Joshua smote them with the edge of the sword and utterly destroyed all the souls that were therein. He left none remaining.'

But he did not attack Jerusalem.

To the northeast of Lake Galilee lies the white bulk of Mount Hermon, the patriarch of mountains, where the 'bright cloud overshadowed Jesus'; its snow trails snaking down towards the plains, it is the mountain which commands everything, which sheds 'the dew of Hermon'. To its southwest, near Lake Huleh – today 'the dying lake', a nature reserve – was the kingdom of Hazor and its capital, with a moat eighty metres round and wide basalt-and-stone walls among hills in a golden valley, its gates resembling those of Megiddo. The king of Hazor, and other northern Canaanite kings, joined forces against Joshua, drawn up at the River Merom, west by southwest of Hazor. War-chariots encased in wood, leather and metal (sometimes gold) carried their archers, while on foot ran axemen, javelin throwers and spearmen. But at enormous speed, before the Amorites could be properly deployed, the light infantry of Israel raced down the mountain to the jostling cavalry crammed inextricably in the narrow pass. And there they 'smote them and chased them to Mizpah eastward. So Joshua took all that land, the hills and all the south country, and all the land of Goshen, and the valley, and the plain, and the mountains of Israel, and the valley of the same. So Joshua took the whole land, and the land rested from war . . . Joshua made war a long time with all these kings.' Whether it was he or his successors who won the final victory for Israel over the northerners has been argued. He was, whatever may be said, a forerunner of Napoleon, Wellington, Giap, a great captain,* conquering because he recognised and used his people's virtue, intelligence, panache, cunning and patience.

At Shechem, where Hebrews had probably settled even before the arrival of the Israelites – Abraham and Jacob had both erected altars there – Joshua called an Assembly of the Tribes. (The Vale of Shechem is criss-crossed with tiny streams springing from tens of sources.) At this, the congregation pledged or renewed obligations to Jehovah, received God's law from Joshua and established a Covenant Alliance, a confederacy of the Twelve Tribes, united by religion with consequent political and military bonds, its headquarters and the Ark at Shiloh.

Joshua died and was buried on Mount Ephraim, as was the son of Aaron, and 'the bones of Joseph, which the children of Israel brought up out of Egypt, buried they in Shechem'. Thenceforward, and until the time of Kings, the tribes were governed by judges, non-hereditary leaders possessed of spiritual power, arbiters of legal disputes as well as military commanders.

Moab, meanwhile, its King Eglon as cruel as he was fat, was conquered by the Israelites, whose leader Ehud, after presenting taxes, had sought private audience with the king. A left-hander, his dagger on the right thigh not discovered by the royal guards, he had stabbed the gross king, locked all the doors and fled to the hills. When the crime was discovered, the battle with the Moabite army that followed was won by Ehud, 'and Moab was subdued that day under the hand of Israel'.

* A château near Compiègne has towers dedicated to military leaders, one of them to Joshua.

7
The murder of Sisera; Gideon and Jephthah triumphant

Continual aggression against the Canaanites followed Joshua's death. Jerusalem was taken, fired, its inhabitants put to the edge of the sword. The tribes of Judah and Simeon were particularly active against Canaanites in Hebron, Debir and Hormah. But Israelites elsewhere settled amongst the peoples of the place, adopting their gods, and arousing the anger of God who, in order to 'prove Israel', encouraged Ammonites, Amalekites and Midianites to oppose them.

In Galilee, command of the league of petty Canaanite kings under Jabin of Hazor was given to General Sisera who disposed of, *inter alia*, a force of pikemen as well as 'nine hundred' armoured chariots, a resource of which the Israelites had none at all. Sisera deployed his troops in wooded territory, north of the marshy Jezreel valley. The valley dominated the pass leading to roads towards the east, southwest and the main coast supply route, the Via Maris. The judge of Israel was Deborah, 'a prophetess and the wife of Lapidoth', who lived under the 'palm tree' in Mount Ephraim, there giving judgement to the children of Israel. Conscious that she must principally defeat the enemy's cavalry, she commanded her general, Barak, to concentrate on Mount Tabor, a wooded, conical hill almost impregnable to the war-chariots and commanding movement in the valley. Barak took ten thousand men from the tribes of Zebulun and Naphtali, but not, so Deborah complained in her great song of victory, from the tribes of Reuben or Dan or Asher or Gad. Barak would only obey if accompanied in battle by Deborah, to which she agreed, leading more troops, and they went up together from Ephraim.

Sisera, Deborah had calculated, would try to force Barak down to the plain, once he knew of the latter's arrival on the mountain, in order to overwhelm Israel's less mobile force in a direct confrontation with his chariots, and as soon as Sisera learned that they had reached Tabor, he moved out of his woods in strength. Now a second Israelite division came up from Ephraim in the south to meet him, diverting him from his objective on Tabor, drawing

Sisera's advance away to Taanach where the league's allies had sighted the second division and had begun to engage it. Deborah and Barak now came down with their own forces from the hills and attacked Sisera's main force. At the same time, heavy rains flooded the River Kishon, which swept away or drowned in the torrent many of the enemy's fighting men and horsed chariots. 'From heaven [Yahweh] fought the stars, from their courses they fought against Sisera.' The battle was won by Yahweh, in Holy War.

Sisera alone escaped from the battle. He fled through the mire and went to Kedesh where dwelt Heber the Kenite, a defector from that tribe, who had earlier reported Barak's presence on the mountain to the general. Jael, his wife, saw Sisera running, invited him into the tent, covered him with blankets against the cold. 'He asked for water and she gave him milk; she brought forth butter in a lordly dish.' The marriage of Heber and Jael cannot have been a meeting of true minds: her next action, as Sisera lay sleeping, was not to guard him as he had asked, but to take a nail or tent peg, and hammer the nail into Sisera's temples. 'She fastened it to the ground.' Deborah's song, rather than the prose account, says she actually decapitated him, 'smote off his head'. 'The mother of Sisera looked out at a window and cried through the lattice: "Why is his chariot so long in coming? Why tarry the wheels of his chariot?" '

Gideon was another humble man, chosen by God against his will to be a mighty commander. As a boy, he had threshed wheat secretly – to avoid observation by desert raiders – on a threshing floor near a wine press concealed in mountain caves. Here the Israelites hid, their only recourse against Midianite and Amalekite pirates riding out of the sand into the pastureland, 'as grasshoppers for multitude', on their one-humped camels. Until now, where the raiders had dared to penetrate the Jezreel valley itself, the Israelites could do no other than withdraw into shelter in the hills; until Gideon there had been no organised resistance to these fast dromedary incursions. Gideon, like Moses, pleaded inadequacy. Asking the Angel of God for a sign, he brought a kid, unleavened cakes and broth to him as a present. The broth he poured upon the meat and flour, and the Angel of the Lord caused them with his staff to be consumed by fire. As another sign, the Angel then made a fleece of wool to be wet (Gideon 'wringed out a bowl full of water') when the ground under the fleece at dawn was bone-dry: the next morning another fleece was dry when there was dew on all the ground.

He brought then thirty-two thousand of his fighting men towards the Spring of Harod, in its depression between the Hill of Moreh and Mount Gilboa, east of Taanach where Barak and Deborah, the Israelite Jeanne d'Arc, had defeated the North Canaanites under Sisera. The Midianites were encamped near the well of En-dor, northwest of Moreh and north by northeast of Harod. (Endor today leads to the Crusader castle of Belvoir, but itself contains little except a ruin.) 'On God's instructions', the commander then permitted twenty-two thousand men, 'fearful and afraid', to go to their homes before battle had even begun, leaving ten thousand to stand. This number was still too great for the sort of clandestine night action, emulated centuries later by David Stirling's Long Range Desert Group, that he now intended. The selective test he applied to the combatants was one of common sense adapted to raiding tactics. He brought his division down to the river to drink. The meaning is obscure, but only three hundred men, those that 'lapped putting their hand to their mouth', not as preceding verses indicate 'those lapping as a dog lappeth', nor 'those kneeling', qualified for that night's action, presumably because they would thus have quicker access to personal weapons.

In the evening, Gideon and his soldier servant, Pirah, clambered down the hillside to the fringes of the raiders' encampment, men and camels as 'grasshoppers or the sand of the sea for multitude', black tents everywhere, soldiers patrolling, camels tethered and prone. One sentry told another that he had dreamed of a barley cake which came tumbling down the hill, hit a Midianite tent and overturned. 'That,' said his colleague, 'was the sword of Gideon, for into his hand hath God delivered Midian and all the host.' Gideon, hearing this with joy, mounted a standard Israelite three-company assault at midnight from separate directions, all issued with trumpets and lamps burning inside pitchers. At the blast of their commander's trumpet, on the setting of the middle watch, the men blew their trumpets, broke the pitchers, torches in the left hand, trumpets in the right. In the clamour and the blaze of the torches, the desert raiders panicked, unable to deploy chariot, pike, axe or bow, fighting one another in the livid night, scrambling to saddle, mount and ride away their dromedaries while Gideon's troop – with sword and scimitar and bow – did what damage they could in the darkness, burning the tents with their torches, sparing none, the camels of Midian in their terror completing the confusion.

The general seems, judging by his brutality to those who killed his brothers pre-positioned in a holding force between Tabor and Moreh, to have anticipated a westward move by the enemy, one which forts to the west were intended to prevent. In the event, the Midianites were driven south to the Jordan fords where the Ephraimites, jealous or resentful of not being earlier summoned, fought without great vigour. The rulers of Succoth and Penuel were even more reluctant, so that Gideon felt obliged to tear 'the flesh of the men of Succoth with the thorns of the wilderness and with briars'. In Penuel, he 'beat down the tower and slew the men of the city'. Because his son Jether was too young to carry out his father's order, Gideon himself had to slay the two kings of Midian with his own hand.

Somewhere to the east, on the border between Gilead and Ammon, he 'smote the host'. One hundred and twenty thousand men fell. 'And the country was in quietness forty years.' For the second time, an Israelite commander had used guile, speed and persistence to win ultimate victory in an attack coordinated between his own and allied troops, however lethargic the latter may have proved. But Gideon refused his people's demand that he should accept a throne: 'I will not rule over you, neither shall my son rule over you; the Lord shall rule over you.' He accepted, however, apparently for the public purse, booty gained by his troops: one thousand seven hundred shekels in golden earrings, ornaments, collars, purple raiment from the Midianite kings, and the chains round the necks of their camels. 'Thus was Midian subdued before the children of Israel.'

At the Spring of Harod, not so long ago, the water still poured into the pool from a source hidden by ferns: the stones on the river bed glistened blue.

After Gideon's death, and burial in Ophrah, Abimelech, his son by a maid who had been Gideon's concubine in Shechem, persuaded his mother's family to fund a bid for the kingship instead of submitting to rule by Gideon's seventy other sons. Misapplying the money raised in the temple of Baal Berith, he hired 'vain and light persons' to murder all his brothers except Jotham, the youngest, who escaped and hid. The people of Shechem then crowned Abimelech by a sacred pillar, said to be still standing there.

Jotham spoke in hot protest from the mountain, with a parable of some trees who sought to anoint a king of Trees. The olive refused because it would not give up its luxuriance, the vine because wine cheers men's hearts, and the fig would not waste its sweetness for mere administration. Only the inflammable bramble, signifying fiery destruction for Abimelech and all around him, would agree to the trees' call and that only reluctantly, on conditions. In violent shame for their compatriots' share in killing Gideon's sons, the men of Shechem spoke in drink against the monster Abimelech. But Abimelech with three companies defeated Gaal the rebel commander as Gaal stood at the gate at dawn. The king also attacked the rebels in the fields outside the city, and within it, for the town's garrison was in his pay, burning the main tower and the thousand men inside by lighting branches round its wooden walls. When he attempted the same ruse with a citadel in Thebez, a woman in the tower above him threw down a millstone which broke his skull. Ashamed that he should be thought to have been killed by a woman, he told his young armour-bearer to draw his sword and slay him. 'And his young man thrust him through, and he died.'

The Israelites, for many years after Gideon's death under fairly mediocre judges, diluted their faith amongst other gods, weakening themselves also against the Philistines, and Amorites, blond and tall. The latter were pressing on Gilead to reclaim Heshbon (Sihon) and also preparing to attack the tribes of Ephraim, Benjamin and Judah. In their plight, desperate for a commander, the elders of Gilead sought out Jephthah, son of Gilead by a harlot, who had been thrown out of the family home by his brothers, subsequently to become the chief of a band of mounted outlaws, in which capacity he had demonstrated great paramilitary skill. His agreement to act as 'head and captain' of Gilead's battalions was conditional on becoming permanent 'head' or judge were he to succeed in driving off the Amorites, a clause which the elders accepted. Lengthy diplomatic exchanges took place with the Amorite leadership, Jephthah's claim being based on the historic refusal of the eastern kings to let the Israelites under Joshua pass through their countries, on subsequent conquest by

Israel, and on three hundred years of undisturbed tenure ever since. The Amorites rejected the claim. In the battles that followed, Jephthah captured twenty cities, and 'smote the people with great slaughter in the plain of the vineyards'.

Before engaging, he had vowed to God that, if he were victorious, he would offer a burnt offering to God of whomever came forth first from the door of his house as he returned there. The bargain went wrong, became horrible. His only child, a daughter whom he dearly loved, was the first to come out to him, leading the woman singers who greeted him, singing, dancing, 'laughing with joy' at her great father's return. 'He rent his clothes . . . alas, my daughter, thou has brought me very low . . . for I have opened my mouth unto the Lord and I cannot go back.' 'And she said unto him, "My father, if thou hast opened thy mouth unto the Lord, do unto me according to that which hath proceeded out of thy mouth." ' Jephthah, in agony, sent her away into the mountains, knowing that he must fulfil his vow and sacrifice her. And when she returned after two months with her companions, he 'did with her according to the vow which he had vowed' in this terrible, heart-breaking tragedy.

When the Ephraimites confronted him, complaining that he had not sought their help against Ammon, it was a distraction from grief, if not an end to it. He replied that, in eighteen years, they had never lifted a finger to help him. They then threatened to burn his house down, so that Jephthah had to oppose them. When they tried to flee across the Jordan, the Gileadites stopped them at the single ford: 'Are you an Ephraimite?' 'No.' 'Then say "Shibboleth".' If they said 'Sibboleth', which was their way of pronouncing it, then Jephthah had them killed, forty-two thousand in all the battle.

8
Philistine attack; Samuel and Saul resist

'The People of the Sea', who included the Pulusatu or Philistines, were a warrior-race of tribes from the islands of the Aegean and, even further west, from the Balkans, Macedonia and the Danube, possibly originally from the Taurus Mountains. They settled in Cyprus in the eleventh and twelfth centuries BC, and before that may have been the 'Viking' type of raiders who destroyed the Minoan civilisation in Crete. They may have fought at Troy, and certainly invaded the Nile Delta in the eleventh century BC, when they were eventually defeated by the Egyptians.

Their battle formation consisted of chariots, infantry and, in the rear, a field-train of ox-wagons, which also bore women and children. The chariots were usually drawn by two horses, with crews of three armed with iron-tipped spears and javelins, the infantry with spears, straight (not sickle) swords and shields. Because they fought where possible close up to the enemy, they did not carry bows. They wore armour, a sort of loin cloth, and feathered helmets with chin straps.

After the Egyptian victory, Rameses III appears to have permitted them in the eleventh century BC to settle in domains conquered during the Egyptian invasion of Canaan, chiefly in the coastal plains, as garrison or mercenary troops – in Ashkelon, Gaza and so on. Gaza was already civilised in the third millennium BC, as is seen in the ruined palaces lying above one another down through the millennia, with perfect lintels and doorways, even gold jewellery resembling Celtic design. In the twentieth century, H.V. Morton at Ashkelon observed the feast of Nebi Ayub, or Job, where the Arabs ritually washed their animals and themselves in the white foam of the long, sand beaches, scraping the mud off their dromedaries before shearing them. At Ashkelon, too, by the black ruins of Richard Coeur de Lion's crusader walls and by half-buried statues from Herod's day, were green fields of barley, oats, and onions, *caepa Ascalonia* to the Romans, whence derives *échalote* or shallot.

Egypt's power as a colonial nation was in decline. The Philistines soon sought an independent role, driving inward from their five main fortress cities into Eretz Israel, the Land of the Israelites, founding desert posts into the Negev. Their first advance, strategically obvious, was in Judaea where, not least because of their iron monopoly – the Israelites had, as we know, to come to them even to sharpen their weapons – they had set a garrison at Gibeah with access to Judah and Samson's Benjamin tribe, no distance from Jerusalem itself. The story of Samson, lustful, 'not as others', weak-witted giant and hero, whose intellect allowed him to command no organised force, illustrates the Israelites' dilemma. Mighty even in his fouled ruin, beaten and abused, shorn of his strength, a toy for the gleeful, baiting Philistines, he lifted his poor blinded eyes: 'O Lord God, remember me, I pray thee, and strengthen me, I pray thee, only this once, O God, that I may be at once avenged upon the Philistines for my two eyes.' So he took hold of the pillars, and 'the dead which he slew at his death were more than they which he slew in his life'. They were more than the thirty at Ashdod whom he had stripped, and the thousand men he slew with the ass's jawbone, perhaps more than those that he would have slain had he indeed commanded armies.

Hannah, patient wife of an Ephraimite named Elkanah, was barren, for which she was provoked and abused by Penninah, his other wife, who had children. When the family made their annual visit to holy Shiloh, Hannah prayed for a child at the golden Ark of the Covenant. She would promise it to the Lord for ever. The Lord rewarded her with a boy, Samuel, whom she took to Eli the priest in Shiloh, seeing the child only once a year, when she gave him a new coat and loved him as a mother does, for a little space. But Eli's sons were evil, stealing the burnt offerings, lying down with the women of the congregations, ignoring their father's rebuke, despite God's solemn warnings to Eli of the consequences for his house and family of the sons' conduct. So the Lord revealed himself to Samuel, and established him through all Israel as 'a prophet of the Lord'.

The Israelites then went out against the Philistines of Ebenezer, losing four thousand men. The elders recovered themselves to re-engage with the enemy, this time bringing as holy talisman the Ark of the Covenant from Shiloh itself, escorted by Eli's two scoundrel sons whom the Lord had cursed and already doomed. When it was placed before the army, the soldiers greeted it with a great shout. Terrified by its associations with the crossing of Jordan and other battle honours, and by the actual presence of God, the Philistines, although they feared greatly, fought with even more ferocity. Thirty thousand men, including Eli's two sons, were killed but, yet more disastrously, the Ark was captured. When the old priest heard this news, he fell off his seat backwards, and 'his neck brake, and he died'. His daughter-in-law cried, 'The glory is departed from Israel: for the Ark of God is taken.'

The Philistines, yelling scorn and abuse against the Ark, dragged it within the embattled walls of Ashdod, while the priests of Dagon danced their lewd dances, sang the victory song and made their own sacrifices. They laid it down below the gaze of the fish god's image, and howled with especial joy and triumph for at Eben-ezer they had also destroyed the holy town of Shiloh.

Next morning, grey with drink and lechery, the priests and their bedraggled acolytes came into the temple of Dagon. During the night the god had crashed down from its pedestal before the Ark and lay with its hideous face on the ground. Although nervous, they righted it. But the following day, Dagon had not only fallen again, but its head and the palms of its hands had been removed and were lying at the entrance gate. Only its scaly tail and the stump of its body remained. The great doors of the temple had been barred shut throughout the night. The priests were too frightened to restore the fish god to its plinth, or to try to repair the idol. They left it where it lay. Rumours of shame and catastrophe began to run through all five Philistine cities: the people, in the fear of God, were forbidden entry to the temple at Ashdod.

So long as the Ark stood there, a disease of haemorrhoids, painful and embarrassing, spread through Ashdod and the countryside. The elders, in panic, took counsel of the lords of the Philistines. After much heated discussion, the Ark was hastily bundled off to Gath. The entire population of Gath was soon seized also with agonising piles, so that, in response to angry complaints, the elders of Gath sent the Ark on once more, this time to Ekron. But at the gates of Ekron, the council refused the Ark entry to their city. 'They have brought the Ark of the God of Israel to us, to slay us and our people. For there was a deadly destruction throughout all the city: the hand of God was very heavy there'; no market; houses sealed; the streets empty. Trade and commerce were at a standstill, hunger and thirst widespread. The rulers sent for the priests and diviners, who agreed that the Ark had to be returned to the Israelites. It must, however, they insisted, not be sent back empty but fully laden, with ten magnificent gold images, one provided by each city and each lord of the Philistines, since the 'plague' had been shared among all of them. To resist Jehovah, and to harden their hearts, as did the Pharaoh and the Egyptians, would be useless: they would *have* to let the Lord's people go, before He would lighten his hand on their gods and their land.

So they made a cart of rich woods, and a coffer of the same into which they put the offerings of gold. Into the cart, they put the coffer with its peace offerings by the side of the Ark with its golden rings and gilded staves, its mercy seat of pure gold, the two cherubims of beaten gold, the crown of gold, the pure gold candlestick with shaft, branches, bowls like almonds, its knobs and its flowers, the seven lamps, the tongs and snuff dishes. To the cart they harnessed two milk-white cows whose calves had been taken away from them. 'If,' said the priests, 'the cattle, unbroken to yoke or plough, do no more than stay in the village where they are, or drag the cart helter-skelter to the calves for whom they long, we shall know that the plague was not cast by Jehovah, but by evil coincidence. But if they take the Ark and the offerings from Ekron up the coast road (Via Maris) to Beth-Shemesh, we shall be sure that it was the Lord's hand that smote us, He that did us this great injury.' The cattle, once the drovers had withdrawn, trudged straight on, although mournfully lowing for their young, turning neither left nor right, towards Beth-Shemesh, the nearest Israelite village on the other side of the Philistine border. When they reached the outskirts, the great crowd of Philistines which had followed them turned away and returned home, understanding with Whom they had to deal. Peasants harvesting in Beth-Shemesh saw the cart come into a field where there was a standing stone. In joy at recovering the Ark, they broke up the cart, offering the wood and the cattle themselves as burnt sacrifices to the Lord. The Levites of the place took down the Ark and the coffer with the jewels and put them on the stone. The Ark was subsequently moved to Kirjath-jearim and that became its habitation for twenty years.

The Philistines were thus discomfited, although they wasted no time in buckling on their armour and mounting their chariots and attacking Samuel at Mizpah. Their defeat there owed more to massive thunderstorms than to Samuel's or the Israelites' military skill. Further Israelite victories may have taken place on the coast, 'Ekron even unto Gath', but a temporary peace ensued with the Amorites. Samuel could circuit-judge between Bethel, Gilgal, Mizpah and his own home, Ramah. Peace and victory were, of course, attributed to Israelite revulsion against 'strange gods and Ashtaroth', but, alas, their return to devotion to the Lord in their usual inconsistent way was only temporary.

Samuel's sons, like Eli's, were dishonest and corrupt, interested only in the acquisition of money in their judicial capacities at Beersheba and Bethel, taking bribes in reward for bought judgements, earning hatred and creating discontent. In this, they reflected the general sloth and rottenness of the government, while the Philistines to the southwest, and other enemies, were still powerful enough to present a threat of annihilation to the southern tribes, if not to the whole of Judaea. The people were angry, fearful and distressed.

The elders therefore came to Samuel in Ramah. They used popular resentment of corruption, and insecurity caused by Israelite military weakness, as reasons to persuade Samuel to yield his authority in favour of the new and untried system of monarchy. After Samuel had then unwillingly taken counsel of God, the Lord told him that the people's rejection was not of Samuel, but of Himself: ' . . . hearken to the voice of the people . . . they have rejected *me* from being King over them.' Samuel therefore told the elders that a king would take all power of decision from them and into his own hands, dispose of their children as he thought fit, as charioteers, infantrymen, cooks, bakers, sweetmakers, weaponsmiths. He would make them 'captains over thousands and over fifties', force them to till his land, take a tenth of their seed, fields, vineyards, olive groves, sheep, take their servants, strongest workers, beasts, and put them all to his own work.

But the people, despite Samuel's warnings of tyranny and authoritarianism, sought to 'resemble other nations', of whom they had received good report. 'Nay, but we will have a king over us; that we may also be like all the nations; and that our king may judge us, and go out before us, and fight our battles' – not unlike the French Presidential system, as de Gaulle conceived it. Samuel, despite his warning to them that a monarch, unlike de Gaulle, once installed could not be overthrown, no matter how much his subjects cried out, agreed on the Lord's command to appoint a king.

Meanwhile, a rich grazier named Kish, 'a mighty man of power' from the small tribe of Benjamin, immediately northwest of Jerusalem, had lost his donkeys in what was one of the most arid, barren areas of Judaea. They were not popular, the Benjaminites, but they were, in their tiny, dry pocket of hill and dale, fighting-men accustomed to regular 'border' wars with the Philistines and the Jerusalem Jebusites, struggling also to cultivate their olives and rear their thin hill sheep in the one hundred square miles of sparse land which was their portion.

His son, Saul, born in the village of Gibeah, possessed outstanding good looks, height and physical presence. The Benjaminites, while members of the Northern Confederacy and having adopted Canaanite gods, had, at this time, begun to accept the worship of Jehovah. Samuel, as a Levite, in the face of increasing Philistine aggression achieved a sort of concordat between the Joshuaite Northern Confederacy with their gods, and the tribe of Judah, worshipping Jehovah, to whom the northern tribes had begun to turn. Saul later was grievously to punish and reject the Ashtaroth (Mother) and Bull cults and to persecute as prostitutes the temple priestesses who yielded their bodies to the cult worshippers. As a member of the Benjamin tribe, he was a Joshuaite, but since he worshipped Jehovah and spoke Hebrew, Samuel saw him as a unifying factor among *all* Israelite tribes.

Kish had told his young son to take a servant and go out in search of the family's unbroken donkeys who, without bridles, had strayed from their pastures. After some days' fruitless journey over the harsh sides of Mount Ephraim, in wilderness, and through the gentler valleys of Samuel's own country, their food was all gone. Saul, fearing that his father might now be more worried about their absence than about the asses, proposed to turn back. But his man advised him to consult a prophet, 'a man of God', in the little walled town of Ramah that lay nearby in its own olive groves and barley fields; the servant had only a quarter silver shekel with which to pay him. The prophet was Samuel. Young girls drawing water at the well told Saul that the seer was about to make sacrifice at a hill shrine. (The Lord had already warned Samuel that He had sent to see him 'a man out of the Land of Benjamin', whom Samuel would 'anoint to be captain of my people Israel'.) Samuel then, after giving Saul a shoulder of lamb to eat among the banqueteers, and after Saul had slept on the roof of the house, told him that the donkeys had been found. Later he anointed him in privacy from a vial of oil, and sent him on his way. On the road, as Samuel had prophesied, two men whom Saul met near Rachel's tomb confirmed that the donkeys had been found and that Kish was indeed concerned for his son. In the plain of Tabor, three men on their way to the sanctuary at Bethel, carrying three kids, three loaves and a bottle of wine, gave two loaves to Saul and his servant and – in execution of Samuel's other prediction – a company of prophets came down from the hill of God, near the Philistine garrison, playing a lyre, a pipe, a harp and a tambourine, chanting.

Samuel next called all the people to Mizpah, to which they came in tribes, with tents, mountains of baggage and camel trains, pitching camp before the Lord. Here, before the people and the priests in their linen robes embroidered with pomegranates, golden, scarlet and blue aprons, and the High Priest's brilliantly jewelled golden judgement breastplate, Samuel proclaimed Saul to be the Elected King, renewing history and the covenant in a 'book' which he laid up before the Lord in the Ark. Saul went back to Gibeah with his followers, and 'all the people shouted, and said, God Save the King'. God's injunction to Samuel at Ramah, before Saul arrived and had been anointed – 'He shall save my people from the hand of the Philistines: for I have seen the affliction of my people, because their cry has come to me' – was to be effected at least to some degree.

But for several weeks Saul lived quietly and at peace with his wife and his son Jonathan at Gibeah, working as before in the fields, steadings and vineyards of his father Kish, waiting for the day when Jehovah and Israel should call him to battle.

9
Saul's affronts to God; Jonathan at Michmash

He did not have long to wait. To the northeast, in the city of Jabesh-Gilead in Gad, among those hills and mountains where Moses had defeated Kings Og and Sihon, the Ammonites were besieging and effectively blockading the walled city. Their king, Nahash, which means 'serpent', bent on driving the Israelites out of the rich farmland of Gilead, had almost reduced the city to starvation. Disease and famine had killed as many of the townsmen as had the spears and arrows of the invader.

Nahash told the town's negotiators that he agreed to their offer of surrender, even permitted their survival, and would withdraw his own ferocious troops, provided he first 'thrust out' the right eyes of the entire population, causing them to be shamed throughout Israel. The 'ambassadors' of Jabesh, weak with famine and disease, begged desperately for a seven-day ceasefire. Nahash contemptuously acceded to the plea. That night, messengers stole out of the dark, hungry city to seek help throughout the country from all the other tribes of Israel. One came to Gibeah, where the people wept at the news. Saul, on hearing it, butchered oxen and sent the chopped pieces throughout the land with the threat that the same fate would befall the oxen of whomever did not come to the aid of Jabesh. In this manner, three hundred thousand men of the Northern Confederacy and thirty thousand from Judah mustered at Bezek. A message was sent to Jabesh: 'Tomorrow, by the time the sun is hot, you shall have help.' Meanwhile Nahash slept peacefully, deceived into the belief that, on the contrary, Jabesh-Gilead would actually surrender at noon.

After a long night-march over rocky terrain under the stars, Saul's huge force, deployed as usual in three divisions, assaulted from across the Jordan the sleeping Ammonite camp with its drowsing sentries. Surprise charges from north, west and south between four o'clock in the morning and first light ensured that the enemy had been destroyed or scattered by the time of the noonday heat. 'Two of them were not left together.'

Samuel then led the people to renew the kingdom. They again

proclaimed Saul to be king, this time before the Lord in Gilgal, with sacrifices as peace offerings. 'And Saul and the men of Israel rejoiced greatly.' Samuel in an equivocal, farewell speech – for we know his opposition to monarchy – while praising King Saul, recounted the past sins of the people, Jehovah's repeated forgiveness and deliverance, and warned that only if they served the Lord and obeyed him and did not rebel, then would the Lord not forsake them. 'But if ye shall still do wickedly, ye shall be consumed, both ye *and your King*.' The people were then terrorised by a storm of rain and thunder, unprecedented at harvest time, brought upon them by the Lord at Samuel's clear and explicit call, the sky black as night, whirlwinds, scudding clouds over the mountain tops in the glare and flash of the lightning. The sun returned to the plain, to the aspen and willow leaning over the rushing water of the river. But Saul's sensitivity, black moods, paranoia, depression and insecurity had been reinforced by these unmistakable if veiled demonstrations of Samuel's lack of confidence and trust in him. As the years wore on and his power and success grew, the king's attributes sometimes turned to despotism, rejection of all authority, and overweening arrogance.

But now, confronted by a Philistine military presence of varying strengths throughout his domain, he decided to create a professional standing army of three thousand – pikemen, archers, swordsmen, spear carriers, sling-shot men – lacking only cavalry and charioteers. Two thousand were posted under his own command at Michmash in the Benjamin hills northeast of Jerusalem and at Mount Bethel on the border between Ephraim and Benjamin north of Gibeon. Jonathan led the third thousand, stationed at Gibeah of Benjamin. He initially defeated the Philistine garrison, killing the commander, after which Saul's entire force of three thousand men moved west again, back to Gilgal.

Saul had originally sent the remainder of his fighting men who had won at Jabesh-Gilead and in other engagements into reserve, back to their villages and cities to await, as it were, their recall to the colours. But when the people of Israel learned that the Philistine reaction to Jonathan's victory was the despatch of an expeditionary force numbering six thousand horsemen, thirty thousand chariots and innumerable infantry, the reserve did not flock to Saul's banner. Many of those regulars, furthermore, who had fought with Saul deserted altogether, running off to Gad and Gilead, some even joining the Philistines, while the civilian population fled to 'caves and thickets and [among] rocks and in high places and in pits.'

Saul had disobeyed God and Samuel, and affronted Samuel's authority by giving burnt offerings to the Lord, against the Lord's command and without Samuel's intervention. (Saul's crime was impetuosity, the powerful desire of a commander to get at his enemy.) For the first time, Samuel rejected him for simple disobedience and refusal to follow God's orders to the letter. 'But now thy kingdom shall not continue: the Lord hath sought him a man after his own heart, and the Lord hath commanded him to be captain over his people, because thou hast not kept that which the Lord commanded thee.' Saul, crestfallen, moved with Jonathan in Samuel's footsteps back to Gibeah and then on to Migron. His force now numbered only six hundred men, facing the vast Philistine army corps in Michmash. Worse, because only the Philistines employed blacksmiths, a craft which Israelites still had not mastered, of all Saul's little battalion only he and Jonathan had cutting or stabbing weaponry sharp and in good repair. In the meanwhile, three groups of Philistine raiders destroyed and looted towards Ophrah in the north, to the valley of Beth-Horon in the west, and to Zeboim eastwards; their massacres, cruelty and armed robbery forced yet more peasants – men, women and children – into hiding.

Jonathan's father, despondent at the defections from his forces, sat at Migron, sullen and gloomy under the crimson blossoms of a pomegranate tree, its leather-like, burnished, apple-coloured fruit yet to appear. Here too was his standard. From an eminence near the threshing floor he watched in frustration the overwhelming numbers of the Philistine horde at Michmash opposite – not like a valley but a huge crack in the rocks, hundreds of feet deep – their blocking force poised right across the approaches.

But Jonathan determined to break the stalemate at enormous risk to his life, and without his father's knowledge or permission since, Jonathan knew, Saul would certainly have forbidden his son's daring coup. Confiding only in his young armour-bearer, Jonathan and that devoted soldier moved northwards at night through the mountain valleys and ravines that lay between Migron and Michmash. (Their base had been selected by the Philistines because it commanded the Israelite positions and the latter's communications between the desert and the Judaean hills.) The passage to the enemy camp was covered by high, rugged crags, sharp-pointed rocks on either side known as 'the Berry Bush' and 'the Shining'. Between these rocks patrolled the outer defence guards of the Philistine corps, the blocking force at which poor Saul stared so resentfully through the hot, baking days at Gibeah and Migron.

After a harsh scramble through these wild valleys and stony hills, and down into the ravine, Jonathan and his faithful body-servant reached the base of the cliff at the peak of which the Philistine outpost stood to. Here they deliberately exposed their presence to the garrison's sentries. These abused them, jeering: 'Behold the Hebrews come out of the holes where they hid themselves'; challenging them further: 'Come up to us, and we will show you a thing.' The soldiers' bronze armour, kilts and feathered helmets were silhouetted against the peaks in the moonless night, butts of spear and javelin rattling the loose stones.

Certain that the sentries would believe that the two dimly glimpsed Israelites would have instantly bolted at the very sight of armed men, Jonathan and his companion climbed slowly and cautiously from the gorge of the Wadi Suweinit far below, up the almost vertical face of the cliff looming over them, hand by hand and inch by painful inch to avoid the clatter of dislodged falling rock. Reaching the summit, they rushed the defences from the rear, killing twenty unprepared, sleeping or over-confident men. The survivors, convinced that they had been attacked by a superior force, lost their heads and fled, howling with fear, into the main camp. Their yelling arrival in pitch darkness below coincided with a minor earthquake, high wind and the ground trembling furiously beneath the position. Chaos and panic spread quickly among the garrison, the supply train with its camels, donkeys, oxen and wagons, and among the raiders now returned from pillage. The soldiers turned on one another in the blackness, having assumed that, not two guerrillas, but nothing less than an Israelite battalion had burst upon them. (In 1917, at Michmash, a British brigade rejected frontal assault in favour of the precise route followed by Jonathan.)

Saul and his sentries heard the clamour at Michmash. The king launched his little force, augmented by returned Israelite defectors and Philistine prisoners and by refugees from the fortresses of

Mount Ephraim in a devastating frontal assault. The enemy – each man's sword against his fellow – did not stand, fleeing northwest to Bethel, in general retreat, ambushed all along the route by Israeli farmers and peasants. 'And they smote the Philistines that day from Michmash to Aijalon.' Later, because of this battle which brought the King hegemony in the region at least for a space, 'Saul took the kingdom over Israel, and fought against all his enemies on every side, against Moab, and against the children of Ammon, and against Edom, and against the kings of Zobah, and against the Philistines: and whithersoever he turned himself, he vexed.'

But, although Michmash was a great victory, it was not complete. Jonathan's unwitting disobedience of an order from his father during the battle had led to sentence of death, a sentence which the Israelites would not accept from Saul: 'Shall Jonathan die, who hath wrought this great salvation in Israel?' So his father angrily called off the pursuit of the fleeing Philistines – those that still stood – who then escaped westwards out of Bethel through the pass at Beth-Horon, and down the Via Maris to their own country, to fight another day.

Elsewhere the Amalekites, despite earlier defeat by Saul, were still nibbling at Judah's southern frontiers from tents in their own land and in the Negev Desert (the 'South Country'), west of the wilderness of Zin. Here they had ceaselessly harassed Moses and his people during the Forty Years. These old, dead, dry lands had not improved, canyons of 'lion-coloured' mountain and embattled rocks, like medieval cities, under the hot, blue skies south of the Dead Sea, from whose gorge huge drafts of wet heat emerge. Nothing grows and flies settle in the eye. In Zin itself, the rock is multicoloured, veined with red, green and ox-blood, the ground criss-crossed by wadis dry or flooded according to season, no birds, no trees, no wind, nothing but a rubble-strewn abomination in the sticky, drenching air. Here was a little Table Mountain, the Mountain of Hor, where Aaron died; the Arava, the Makhtesh Hakatan, and the mountains of Edom south of the salt sea.

The Israelites had not forgotten Amalekite malignance during the hard days out of Egypt, nor had they failed to notice the persistence with which that people had stepped up attacks against their settlements during the recent battles with the Philistines. Samuel accordingly ordered Saul, in the words of the Lord, to 'smite Amalek and utterly destroy all that they have and spare them not . . . man and woman, infant and suckling, ox and sheep, camel and ass'. This then was to be a Holy War, 'Yahweh's Battle', with Jehovah personally engaged and in command, calling upon King Saul's devotion, Himself directing the course of the battle. So Saul with 'two hundred thousand' infantrymen from the tribal confederacy and ten thousand men of Judah, lay waiting for the Amalekites in a darkened, secret valley, thence pursuing the beaten foe from Havilah to Shur in the Sinai, east of Goshen in Egypt, where Joseph and his followers had lived all those years ago. Every living human being of the Amalekites, except King Agag, was slaughtered, but the best animals and much gold, silver and jewellery were retained by the Israelites.

Saul had thereby disobeyed the hard and absolute command of God, perhaps for sensible, practical reasons, but using the excuse that he had intended ultimately to sacrifice those things to the Lord. Samuel rebuked him with severity: 'Behold to obey is better than sacrifice and to hearken than the fat of rams . . . Because thou has rejected the word of the Lord, He hath also rejected thee from being King.' Samuel, however, did not reject Saul's plea for forgiveness or refuse his prayer that he be not publicly dishonoured. But he completed the sacrifice by hewing King Agag – who walked delicately – to pieces before the Lord.

The great general, Saul, had too often subordinated submission to the Lord to his own military requirements. At Michmash, he had, firstly, given burnt offerings without authority, then failed to consult the Ark of the Covenant, considering that the coming encounter allowed no time for Jehovah to deliberate. When, after Michmash, the troops sinned by eating the sheep and the oxen with the blood, Saul built his own altar to God without reference to Samuel. As has been shown, in disobeying the Lord's injunction before the Israelite annihilation of the Amalekites, he was guilty of brushing aside Holy War itself, direct treason to Jehovah.

'The spirit of the Lord departed from Saul and an evil spirit from the Lord troubled him.' Seized by dejection and violent remorse at his abandonment by God, as he lay sleepless or beset by hideous nightmares and wilder imaginings, full of loss, fury and terror, he knew that the Divine had rejected him. Though Samuel never ceased to love him, and mourned for him, Saul and Samuel were not to meet on earth again. The Lord therefore commanded Samuel to end his useless sadness over Saul's conduct, to fill his horn with oil and go to Bethlehem, to seek a king to succeed Saul from among the sons of Jesse.

The hills and mountains of Israel have dictated much of her history. Here, in the gorges and among the abrupt peaks, her wars were fought by those highlanders who crowd the Bible. Here her God was worshipped, at Shiloh, Jerusalem or Mount Sinai. Most of her towns and cities lie among them, at the heights or just below them. Judaea itself is one mountain range sliced across by east-west gorges, the Kidron gorge south of Jerusalem cutting the desert. Between Bethlehem and Hebron, the brown valleys are gentler, the land more fecund, at least after the bleak wadis and bare hills just south of Bethlehem, but nearby crags or distant masses accompany the traveller throughout almost all his journeys. Wild flowers are everywhere – cornflowers, poppies, marigolds, scarlet anemones, narcissi, irises – in Samaria of the round grain valleys as well as in Judaea with its cliffs, gorges, hills and mountains.

Bethlehem 'sprawls over hills and saddles', flat roofs and yellow stone buildings, the desert and vineyards surrounding the town all dominated by the grey bulk of Mount Herod. Rachel's tomb, now a domed, square, stone building, lies off the road to Hebron. Once it stood alone in the shade of a single pistachio tree. In the terrible heat, the olives struggle on the terraces while the sun blazes down from a cloudless blue sky. Samuel, the old grey-bearded prophet, and his servant came up from the south, riding on donkeys into the valley where Bethlehem lies among olive and almond trees, vineyards and wheatfields. They brought with them a heifer which it was Samuel's intention to sacrifice as an excuse, to prevent Saul from discovering his true purpose with Jesse. For he feared that Saul would kill him if he knew.

David, he whom the Lord sought, the youngest of Jesse's sons and Moabite by descent, was found at last among the sheep, 'ruddy, and withal of a beautiful countenance, and goodly to look to . . . [Samuel] anointed him in the midst of his brethren: and the spirit of the Lord came upon David from that day forward. So Samuel rose up, and went to Ramah.'

10
David and Goliath; Saul's persecution of David; Saul's death

Unaware of these events, Saul groaned in the shadows of his tent, refusing to see his advisors and courtiers, rejecting food and drink, sleeping fitfully with dreams, feverish, alone and wretched, gaunt, haggard, shunning the light.

His doctors, their skills impotent to cure him, told him plainly that his condition was beyond them, a product of the evil spirit, to be relieved only by music of the harp from ' . . . a son of Jesse, that is cunning in playing, and a mighty valiant man, and a man of war, and prudent in matters, and a comely person, and the Lord is with him'. The son of Jesse, now with his father's sheep, was David, his anointing by Samuel unrevealed to Saul, so that when David played Hebrew melodies, the king raised him up to be his armour-bearer. The evil spirit left him so long as the music endured. Afterwards, the king remembered nothing . . .

Meanwhile, the Philistines once more had gathered their armies, between Shochoh and Azekah in Judah. Against them in the valley of Elah were ranged the Israelites under King Saul in fortified positions blocking any Philistine advance into the Judaean mountains. Without cavalry, chariots or properly honed weapons, Saul was unable to move aggressively out of the hills into the flat country. For these and other reasons, warfare sometimes assumed a pattern of individual duels between picked champions, and not battle between two armies. The fate of nations could thus be settled by solitary combatants from either side.

'If he be able to fight with me, and to kill me, then will we be your servants: but if I prevail against him and kill him, then shall ye be our servants and serve us.' This was the mortal challenge bellowed by the Philistine giant Goliath, swaggering ten foot tall, in the valley between the armies. Every day, he came down into the valley, in brass helmet, brass chain-mail armoured coat weighing five thousand shekels (56,500 grams), brass pads (greaves) on his legs and a brass gorget at his back. His spear was as thick as a 'weaver's beam', the iron spearhead alone weighing nearly seven thousand grams. A soldier, his guardian, preceded him, bearing a shield.

Goliath called contemptuously to the Israelites: 'I defy the armies of Israel this day: give me a man, that we may fight together.' He had spoken in this vein for forty days now. Fear and flight had been the only response in the camp of Israel. But his camp included as conscripts three of Jesse's sons. To them, a routine feature of clan procedures for the commissariat, Jesse had just sent David with corn, bread and ten cheeses for the commander of their thousand. When David arrived at the valley, he asked some soldiers why they permitted Goliath, an uncircumcised Philistine, to defy God's armies. His brothers became angry, accusing him of impertinence and sensation-seeking: why was he there at all? Why was he not looking after his father's sheep? Who was he to speak so to proper fighting men?, and so on and so forth. ('What have I *now* done?' asked David.) But nevertheless, Saul was told about the gallant if pretentious young man and his intention to strike the giant down. Once kneeling before the king, David told him that, since as a shepherd he had killed with his bare hands both a lion and a bear who were stealing lambs out of the flock, 'the Lord that delivered me out of the paw of the lion and the paw of the bear, will deliver me out of the hand of this Philistine . . . Let no man's heart fail because of him.' The king was attracted to strength and, especially, to valour, but it was uneasily that Saul put his armour upon David. The boy could not bear the weight anyway and, casting it off, set out against the giant with only his staff, his sling and five smooth stones that he had taken from the bed of the little burn that flowed down the rocks.

The giant Goliath lumbered towards him. 'Am I a dog that thou comest at me with staves . . . I will give thy flesh to the fowls of the air and to the beast of the field.' And David replied that, although Goliath held sword, spear and shield, *he* was armed by the Lord God of hosts, the God of Israel who fought not with sword and spear but in His own name. Goliath, his hideous face atop brass armour and black tunic, spear lifted to hurl, shield raised, his brutal mouth contorted with rage, continued to come at him. David ran down the cliff-side to meet him, watching him minutely, putting one of the brook stones into the sling which, whirling it round his head, he discharged. The stone hit the Giant just below the edge of the helmet in the middle of his forehead, exactly between the bloodshot eyes, so that it sank deep into the flesh, and 'he fell upon his face to the earth'. David stood upon his body, and with Goliath's own sword, sliced off the Philistine's head and carried it by the hair to King Saul. The enemy, seeing that their champion was dead, took to their heels, fleeing in disorder all the way through Gath to the gates of Ekron, losing many killed and thousands more wounded on the roads and in the hills to the pursuing tribesmen of the confederacy and the men of Judah.

When, however, the Israelites returned later to Gibeah from Philistra, the king's insecurity was further inflamed. Singing, playing music and dancing, the women came out to welcome them from all over Israel, crying, 'Saul hath slain his thousands and David his ten thousands.' Saul's paranoia was quickened: such weighted praise must advance David's supposed ambition, even for the throne. 'And Saul eyed David from that day forward.'

One evening, the evil spirit having once more descended on the king, David was playing to him on the harp when Saul twice hurled his javelin with enormous force at him, David evading the weapon so that it hung quivering in the wall. Then the king demoted him from commander-in-chief to commander of a thousand, today's battalion commander. So modestly did David accept this humiliation that the people loved and admired him the more. Saul then sent him into battle expecting that the Philistines would kill him; he also gave him his own daughter Michal to marry, so that she might betray him. But David again defeated the Philistines and, for her part, Michal fell in love with him. Although the king ordered his servants and even Jonathan, his own son, to kill David, Jonathan reconciled his father with his friend, at least for a little while. For Jonathan and David loved one another as their 'own souls', in token, exchanging robes and weapons, making a covenant.

But after David had secured another brilliant victory with heavy losses to the Philistines, Saul in jealous madness again flung his javelin and again missed the young commander. As a result, David – 'there is but a step between me and death' – fled to his home. Michal let him down through a window and he escaped to Samuel at Ramah, while Michal deceived her father's searchers with a false image in David's bed. Saul, knowing that David and Jonathan had renewed their covenant, believing that his son too would overthrow him, tried to murder even him. David fled to Nob where the priests, assuming him to be on the king's business, armed him with Goliath's sword. For this, Saul's spy Doeg, the Edomite, not only betrayed the priests to the king, but, since the entire court refused the mad king's orders, later massacred all except one of them single-handed, while his Edomites put Nob to the sword.

David had taken leave of his beloved Jonathan, confirming the ties between the royal house and himself for the future and for his future people. 'Go in peace,' said Jonathan, 'the Lord be between me and thee, and between my seed and thy seed forever. And he arose and departed and Jonathan went into the city.' David hurried on to Gath where, to hide his identity, he feigned madness, scrabbling at the gates with dribble down his beard, leaving then for a cave at Adullam in order to raise a force of four hundred men among the discontented and those in debt and distress.

After leaving Jesse and his mother with the King of Moab, David and his band returned to Judah, bivouacking in a forest where Saul discovered his presence, without being able to seize him, either by force or guile. The king, in a flood of self-pity, accused the courtiers – 'there is none of you that is sorry for me' – of concealing Jonathan's collaboration with the hated David. He even charged them with hiding from him that Jonathan was 'encouraging rebellion' against his father. But, twice thereafter, once in a cave amongst the wild goats of Ein-Gedi, and once as Saul lay sleeping in the middle of his armies, David spared the king when he could have taken him at his ease had he wished. On the first occasion, he cut Saul's robe in token; on the second he took the king's spear from Saul's side, blaming Abner, the commander, for not protecting his master. To the king, he said: 'For the King of Israel is come out to seek a flea, a partridge in the mountains as when one doth hunt.' Saul wept: 'I know well that thou shalt surely be king, and that the Kingdom of Israel shall be established in thy hand . . . thou wilt not cut off my seed after me . . . nor destroy my name out of my father's house.' But the king deceived himself and David, for he continued to persecute him, as he had done before, even after David with his small force had delivered Keilah from the Philistines. During David's flight, however, in an act of honour and nobility, Jonathan visited

David in a wood in the wilderness of Ziph, to pledge loyalty to the future king.

Samuel died at Ramah and was laid to rest there, mourned by both Saul and David. David, since the king had taken his daughter Michal from him and given her to another, had married Abigail, widow of 'the Fool' of Carmel, Nabal. (When 'the Fool' had earlier refused to provision David's men, Abigail had herself brought them loaves, wine, sheep, corn, figs and raisins in quantity, to spare her husband's life from David's anger.) David, his wives and his force (now increased to six hundred men) sought refuge from Saul with King Achish of Gath. Achish gave them the fortress town of Ziklag as fief and residence whence, on the pretence of attacking men of Israel, they slaughtered *enemies* of Israel as far as Shur at the edge of Egypt, leaving none alive to tell the tale.

Achish believed him, but when the Philistines went in their strength against David's people, the king's fellow princes forbade David to join them, fearing treachery. So they sent him away and went up to the valley of Jezreel with its oak forests and green hills and marshes. David and his band of knights marched back to Ziklag, but they saw fire and smoke over the city as they approached, and smelled burning: the town was a charred ruin, the wives and children captives of Amalekite raiders. An exhausted Egyptian slave of the Amalekites, whom David hunted across the brook Beser, prompted by a piece of fig cake and two clusters of raisins, guided them to the looters' camp, all the raiders drunk and dancing around the spoils. David 'smote' them, recovering wives, sons, daughters, flocks, herds and all the Amalekites' spoil from Ziklag and other *razzias*, distributing it equally amongst the fighting men and the 'tail'. The rest he sent to Elders and friends in Judah, 'all the places where David and his men were wont to haunt', a judicious step toward kingship.

The Philistines, humiliated by the defeat of Goliath and their subsequent rout against King Saul's columns, revived, and prepared for revenge. After dismissing David's battalion, they had mustered a greatly enhanced striking force at Aphek in the Shephelah to advance northward up the coast through the Plain of Sharon beside the Mediterranean Sea, south of Mount Carmel. Here they turned east through the passes into the Esdraelon valley, 'the great battlefield of the eastern world, blood red in its apparel', so as to penetrate the Judaean mountains at Ein-gannin (modern Jenin) by Mount Gilboa, where they might find Canaanite collaborators in the Philistine/Pharaonic garrison cities.

The Philistines were drawn up at Shunem in massive order and with superb equipment. Saul's army, without chariots and disadvantaged in numbers and in other attributes was laagered at Gilboa; the king, seeing the enemy multitude, was afraid and sought God's counsel. The Lord would not answer him either through the prophets, or in dreams, or by Urim and Thummin, the sacred lot. Although he had forbidden witchcraft and wizardry in his country, Saul and two of his staff in disguise were frightened enough to visit at night a woman with a 'familiar spirit' who lived at En-dor and, fearful for her own security, reluctantly called up the ghost of Samuel. The prophet, when told by the king that the Lord had abandoned him, replied angrily: 'The Lord hath sent the Kingdom out of thine hand and given it to thy neighbour David, because thou obeyedst not the voice of the Lord . . . He will deliver thee and the best of Israel into the hand of the Philistines tomorrow.' The witch, seeing that her visitor was 'sore troubled', compelled him and his companions to eat, 'that thou mayest have strength when thou goest on thy way', killing a fat calf and baking unleavened bread for them.

Next day, the Philistine chariots pursued the Israelites up Mount Gilboa. Their archers, chariot-borne, once on level ground gravely wounded Saul and many of his followers, killing hundreds also, including his son Jonathan, there on the bleak hillside. The king, so that he should not be tortured or mutilated by the Philistines, ordered his armour-bearer to slay him. But the boy, because Saul was the Lord's anointed, could not obey. Saul fell upon his own sword among leafless trees in fading light. The enemy found him in the morning, cut off his head and sent it round the Philistine cities, "fastening" his body to a wall in the garrison of Beth-Shan, laying up his armour in the heathen temple of Ashtaroth amongst the cult prostitutes. But the men of Jabesh-Gilead rescued his corpse and those of his sons and buried them beneath the oak at Jabesh.

'The beauty of Israel is slain upon thy high places . . . Saul and Jonathan were lovely and pleasant in their lives, and in their death they were not divided: they were swifter than eagles, they were stronger than lions . . . How are the mighty fallen in the midst of battle! O Jonathan, thou wast slain in thine high places . . . I am distressed for thee, my brother Jonathan: very pleasant hast thou been unto me: Thy love was to me wonderful, passing the love of women.'

The age of David was beginning.

11
David, King of Israel and Judah; Jerusalem as capital

The magnificent language in which David, 'the sweet psalmist of Israel', lamented the deaths of Saul and Jonathan couched a Churchillian appeal to the people of Judah. At the same time it demonstrated a grasp of reality by incorporating instructions to his staff on the organisation of archery training for the men. Never again should an enemy so easily outgun them.

He had made a name as commander of a band of brothers experienced in defence against raiders and in attack on fixed positions, creating a precedent later followed by King Arthur and Robin Hood. This 'name' was consolidated by intelligent distribution of spoils to non-combatant supporters among kinsmen in Bethlehem and in Judah as a whole. The men of Judah knew that – as at Keilah – they could trust him to protect them while, in more lucrative times, his generosity would put money in their purse. He now left therefore for Hebron, in the heart of Judah, departing with his wives, Ahinoam from Jezreel and Abigail from Carmel, and all his troops and their families at the Lord's command.

Hebron, like Jerusalem, Bethlehem and Shechem, lies on the road which runs along the main mountain chain, down which sheep and cattle were herded in relative safety. It is extremely old, containing in the Cave of Machpelah, today below a Muslim mosque, the tombs of Abraham, Isaac, Jacob, Sarah, Rebecca and Leah, enclosed by Herod within an enormous stone wall. In Edwardian Hebron, Jews were a persecuted minority among the sullen Mohammedans, this in a city identified as the site of Adam's creation and death and as the place where Abel was murdered, where Abraham pitched his tent and bought his grave (which Joshua had destroyed), where Absalom made his headquarters, where Joab killed Abner and where Ishbad's murderers were executed. There were twelve fountains in Hebron. The 'oaks of Mamre', where Abraham lived, and later Isaac with Rebecca and his children, Jacob and Esau, are close by. Solomon's Pools, in rich orchard and fruit land to the north, were the sources of

Jerusalem's water supply. The grapes that Hebron grows best come from the vines found by Moses' spies at the brook of Eshcol (Ain Eskali); 'they cut down a branch with one cluster of grapes and they bore it between two upon a staff, and they brought of the pomegranates and of the figs'. South of the town are buried settlements (tells), brown baked hills and, then, the black tents of the nomad Bedu.

David's formative military experience had been largely as a mercenary with the Philistines. The latter were now triumphant in large areas of the south, exercising tutelage over Judah and over David's people themselves, but there is no evidence, despite Achish's support, that he contemplated full incorporation into the Philistine machine. Soon after arrival in Hebron, he was elected king of Judah, a period of office which lasted over seven years, initially to some extent under Philistine sovereignty. Abner, meanwhile, Saul's military commander, had made Saul's son Ishbaal king over Gilead, Jezreel, Ephraim, Benjamin, the Ashurites and the whole tribal confederacy of Israel.

At the pool of Gibeon, the city which had deceived Joshua into alliance before the battle of Ai, a macabre encounter took place between champions, or 'chosen men of valour', from Saul and from David's royal houses. Twelve men were brought by Abner from Israel, and twelve by Joab, David's general, from Judah. At Abner's proposal, they then engaged around the huge circular rock pool, sixty or more feet deep, in a series of simultaneous duels intended – like that between Goliath and David – to reach a political decision without the losses inevitable in a clash of armies. 'And they caught every one his fellow by the head and thrust his sword in his fellow's side . . .' but because all the duellists were killed, the encounter between armies which the duels had been designed to avoid, *did* take place, 'and there was a very sore battle that day'. The victor was Joab, and the men of Judah; since Joab called off the pursuit, Abner was allowed to escape across the Jordan to his headquarters in eastern Amman. Abner had murdered Joab's brother ('The spear smote him under the fifth rib: and the spear came out behind him') and a blood feud was thus engendered between the generals.

The two houses continued to make war. David, who had found time amongst his exertions to marry six wives and breed from them, gradually achieved preeminence. Abner, on the pretext that Ishbaal had abused him for lying with one of Saul's former concubines, threatened that he would help to establish David as king of Israel as well as Judah, 'even from Dan to Beersheba'; this overt threat of treachery was followed by secret negotiations with King David, authorised by the elders of Israel. David had agreed to talk to Abner on condition that Michal, Saul's daughter and his own former wife, be returned to him, a cunning claim on Saul's dynasty: 'And her [current] husband went with her along weeping to Bahurim', whence he was instantly ordered straight back to Israel. 'Go, return.' Abner, too, came to Hebron, with twenty men, undertaking to deliver all Israel to David. But Joab, bound by blood feud and believing Abner a spy and double-dealer, 'took him aside in the gate to speak quietly with him', only to murder him without the king's knowledge, as Abner had killed Asahel at Gibeon. David wept at the grave, and cried out at the shame of dishonourable death by the wicked nephew: 'Know ye not that there is a prince and a great man fallen this day in Israel . . . the Lord shall reward the doer of evil . . .' In Israel, on hearing this news, two of Ishbaal's captains slew him as he lay on his bed in the noonday heat; hoping for reward, they ran with the king's head to Hebron. David, however, in righteous fury had them executed in turn by his men, cutting off their hands and feet, and hanging them over the Pool at Hebron.* The head of Ishbaal, that weak ruler, he buried in the sepulchre of Abner who had most truly betrayed his master.

All the elders of Israel then gathered at Hebron where they formed a league between Samaria, the tribesmen of the Northern Confederacy, and Judah, anointing David as king of Israel *and* Judah. For the first time, a formally united monarchy of Israel was constituted, to be under David's rule for thirty-three years of military triumph and administrative glory, marred by minor rebellions successfully put down by the king. David secured his southern frontier against marauding tribesmen from the Negev by settling soldiers in Hebron with their families from the force accumulated after Adullam, where he had recruited his original four hundred while evading capture by Saul. In this mode he achieved the double purpose of strengthening Hebronite resistance

* In Beirut during the Civil War, combatants in the 1970s used to display to journalists their enemy's severed hands and feet as evidence of local triumphs.

to the desert raiders, and paying off old retainers through land grants, a policy not unlike Australia's with its soldier-settler schemes in the twentieth century.

The king needed a capital for the new country of Israel, one at the intersection of north-south ('watershed') and east-west road communications. To avoid jealousy between Judah and Samaria, he selected Jebus (Jerusalem) as a site, almost exactly on the frontier between the two tribal entities. The choice has been compared with that of Washington, similarly independent of all other administrative divisions, although it may be thought that Jerusalem's elevation and climate are superior to those of the other noble city. An attempt to negotiate peaceful transfer with the (Canaanite) Jebusites was repelled with the oath: 'Except thou take away the blind and the lame, then shalt thou not come in hither'. This has been interpreted either – placing lame and blind people on battlements – as a deliberate insult to King David, or as a form of curse derived from the Hittites, threatening blindness and physical ruin on the attackers, sympathetic magic.

The grey, battered fortress city of Zion was on an eminence south of the Old City, divided into town and 'citadel'. From the town, a tunnel through the immemorial rock – the Warren Shaft discovered in 1857 by Sergeant Birtles of the Royal Engineers under the Palestine Exploration Fund – ran down to the Gihon Spring, Jebus' source of water, outside the walls at the foot of the hill. (Some travellers profess to have heard the rush of secret waters under the Damascus Gate and a subterranean torrent below the Mosque of Omar.) The tunnel, or 'gutter' as it was called, was steep and far from wide: it would have been difficult for many troops under Joab's command to have used this passage to penetrate the town. That, nevertheless, has been the method by which most commentators have preferred to explain David's ingress into Jerusalem, although there seems to have been a simultaneous penetration into the then 'citadel', by scaling, battering ram or tunnelling, perhaps supported by arrows and slung stones, perhaps by a little treason. And the Hebrew word for 'trident', a weapon common in David's time, may have been incorrectly transcribed as 'gutter', so the channel may not therefore have been used at all for the seizure, the blind and lame being assaulted with tridents, and Joab's prize of becoming David's 'chief and captain' secured on other grounds. If, however, it is accepted that the Israelites *had* breached the citadel, the tunnel troops or others would then have reinforced the town from which Jebusite attention had been distracted by Joab's sudden appearance at the top of the 'gutter'.

At all events, 'David dwelt in the fort and called it the City of David. And built round about from Millo [terrace] and inward . . .' The king took the city using his own household troops, the equivalent of the Brigade of Guards and the Household Cavalry, Jerusalem becoming by conquest indeed the City of David. These men, organised and governed by 'the thirty', originally the commanders from the raiding days, also included Philistine mercenaries, Cherethites, Pelethites and Gittites from Gath, who had formed David's bodyguard and owed absolute loyalty to the king they served; they were professionals (*gibborim*), fast, mobile, highly trained, with the regulations, discipline and tradition of such fighting machines. It was they who took the first shock of any engagement, requiring then a militia army in support.

The existence of this militia army can be demonstrated by David's order to its commander: 'Assemble me the men of Judah within three days, and be then here present. So Amasa went to assemble the men of Judah . . .' The militia units, twelve formations of twenty-four thousand each, were recruited on a tribal basis by quota according to size of tribe, and then allocated by 'the thirty' or some other central body to their formations. Such units served for a month in reserve on rotation, but in emergency all could be called-up simultaneously. As we have seen, in battle they tended to be deployed in three-divisional mode.

Although the claim is made that Solomon, son of David by Bathsheba, commanded fourteen hundred chariots and twelve thousand horsemen, it is doubtful whether his father's first armies, with their guerrilla experience, had any armour or cavalry. Those armed with bows and slings possessed the special (ambidextrous) skill of the Benjamin tribe; shield and buckler were favoured by Gad's mountain troops; shield and spear were particular to Naphtali and Judah. The Zebulunites, alleged incidentally to be the host tribe from whom the Japanese are descended, were all-rounders and kept brilliant 'dressing'. The men of Issachar were expert scouts and reconnaissance troops . . . Judah formed the phalanx, or heavy brigade, supported by spearmen from Judah, Naphtali and so on, using axes or swords at close quarters, lancers and javelin men being deployed elsewhere.

Having established a capital which became also a centre for military operations against the Philistines and the tribes across the River Jordan, David founded a second headquarters to the north-east of the Jordan in the Valley of Succoth, easily defensible, commanding the roads, self-sufficient in food and water, and the eventual launching point for his wars against the Arameans (Syrians). Not all his measures were popular. Forced labour in camps led to tyranny by Solomon's day, and the census instituted for tax as well as for military purposes caused Jehovah to afflict Israel with a three-day pestilence, killing seventy thousand in 'punishment'. In order to embed religion – the personal covenant between the Almighty and David's house – in the temporal state (his palace, civil works, a military presence, good administration, a reformed system of justice), the king took the Ark of the Covenant away from the previous holy city of Shiloh to lodge it on the rock of Mount Moriah in Jerusalem with the tabernacle; to his wife Michal's embarrassment, David joined his people in dancing and leaping to the sound of trumpets before the Ark. The site of the temple to be built later by Solomon was also believed in myth to be the source of the waters of the Flood, and the waters of the Garden of Eden were supposed to rise near the Gihon Spring and the Pool of Siloam.

His immediate military task was to defend the capital, and, indeed, Israel itself, from the attacks of the Philistines. Once that threat could be removed, he and his generals could proceed against the Trans-Jordan states of Moab, Edom and Ammon, followed by the more formidable Syrian forces of Aramea. Thus he would establish an empire of Israel between 'The Great Sea' or Mediterranean, the howling and inhospitable wilderness of Egypt and Arabia to south and east, and the Euphrates river to the north. To the northwest, he intended no aggression, making a treaty with King Hiram of Tyre and his seafaring Phoenicians which secured his maritime flank and ensured supplies of cedar and of fir, floated down the coast. The treaty also provided for carpenters to work the wood, and masons the stone, in order to build 'a house for David' and, when Solomon succeeded, the Temple.

12
David against the Arameans; his adultery with Bathsheba

Alarmed by these events, in particular by the united monarchy and by David's seizure of Jerusalem, the Philistines determined to preempt any further Israelite expansion, mustering a large army with which they invaded Israel in a great sweep through the Valley of Elah south of Jarmuth and north of Adullam. David had assembled his army at Adullam where his first recruitments to protect himself against Saul had taken place. He shadowed the enemy on a parallel course, allowing the Philistines to penetrate fairly far into the mountains of Judaea before assaulting them in the Valley of Rephaim at Baal-perazim, 'the plain of breaches', when they fled, leaving their sacred images behind to be burned by the Israelites.

The Philistines later returned to the attack, again through the Rephaim valley which extends today right into the Holy City itself. David first withdrew, as if running back in fear to Jerusalem, but then concealed his men in mulberry trees, the Bechaim Wood, today a conifer 'forest' bordered by fenced tarmac roads. There are two explanations for his subsequent conduct. The king told his rather outnumbered light troops that the Lord would intervene on their behalf with a mighty but unseen army. When the evening breezes blew through the trees, the soldiers believed the sound to be that of Jehovah's invisible divisions come to their aid, and thus fell confidently upon the enemy, in the conviction of Holy War in its literal meaning; another writer has said that the breeze was at noon and that the main function of the wind was to cover the noise made by the tramping Israelite advance. In either case, surprise was total, the Philistines smitten from Geba 'until thou come to Gezer'.

Victorious against Methegamma in Philistia, his cohorts took Gath, where Achish had given him both sanctuary and the fiefdom of Ziklag when Saul had pursued him in his uncouth, long-haired madness. Philistia was not conquered. That martial race broke out regularly until David's death, frequently in single-combat duels, until David 'waxed faint' and his staff forbade him battle, so that 'the light of Israel should not be quenched'.

Nevertheless, the Philistines were certainly at least more closely contained. Neighbouring Dan had been consolidated for Israel round Gezer; the whole Plain of Sharon was pacified; such of the defeated Canaanites as remained inhabited the Esdraelon Plain, the country's richest, longest and strategically most valuable flat land; the coast was more or less occupied from Jaffa to Gaza. But two hundred and fifty years later, the leper King Uzziah (Azariah) of Judah was still battling the Philistines in Gath and fortifying Ashdod on the Philistine coast, as well as fighting the Ammonites, whom his son Jotham also engaged. Even at the end of the nineteenth century, Arabs still annually raided Asdraelon, fought over for centuries like a sort of Palestinian Flanders, remarkable not for cultivation but as a continual battlefield.

Although 'forbidden' battle, David seems to have commanded troops personally in the successful war against Moab, which rendered that kingdom a vassal state, the ceasefire an occasion for a peculiarly arbitrary division of prisoners between those to be slaughtered and those to be spared. His next victims were the Rehobites of Syria under King Hadahezer of Zobah whom he defeated on the Euphrates, despite Damascene (Aramean) intervention for Rehob. (It seems possible that Joab took operational command of the Israelite forces after either the Moab or Rehob campaigns, certainly at Edom and thereafter, with Abishai his brother as corps commander.) Rehob lost a thousand chariots, seven hundred horses and twenty thousand infantrymen; the Israelites hamstrung most of the horses leaving only enough to draw one hundred chariots with which, by this time, they were at last equipped. Damascus was garrisoned by Joab and, after he defeated the Edomites east of Amalek and south of the Dead Sea, that territory also remained under his control. These victories brought much treasure, gold, silver and brass to the Ark and treasury of Jerusalem.

David in Jerusalem had greatly increased the number of his wives and concubines, by whom he had large quantities of children; his harem, as was only to be expected, became in the end a nest of intrigue, lies and disputation. He did not neglect, however, emotional and other debts to Jonathan, whose crippled son Mephibosheth he placed in his household ('he should eat bread alway at my table, as one of the king's sons'), and to King Nahash of Ammon, whom Saul had defeated at Jabesh-Gilead, after Nahash had threatened to put out the eyes of the people. Nahash's son responded to David's well-meant approaches by shaving half of the king's messengers' beards, 'cutting off their garments in the middle, even to the buttocks' and sending them away, an insult intolerable to the Great King. Conscious of imminent retribution, the Ammonites sought and received the support of four small but militarily effective Aramean kingdoms, most located in today's Golan Heights. These forces, combined with the Ammonites and with 'Mesopotamian' reinforcements, included many chariots and forty thousand men. The Arameans, because the area was suitable for chariots and because they could menace Joab's rear, chose a position at Medeba in Reuben east of the Dead Sea and southwest of Heshbon and Rabbath-Ammnon. Here they contrived to manoeuvre Joab so that their chariots were behind and on the flank of his army, while the Ammonites confronted the Israelites 'before the gate of the city'. Joab thus found himself forced to face powerful armies 'before him and behind', the Ammonites and Arameans (Syrians) respectively. In a reaction which has been compared with that of the Gloucesters in both the Egyptian campaign of 1801 and in the Second World War, Joab divided his army in two, attacking the Syrians behind him with his 'young men', or 'the choice of Israel', and deploying the remainder under his brother Abishai against the Ammonites in front. The battle ended, the chariots slowed by light infantrymen, halted by the heavy pikemen and finally destroyed by both, in a Syrian retreat followed by a rout of the Ammonites, who fled before Abishai and 'entered into the city', a stalemate because Rabbath-Ammon was not *taken* by the Israelites. Joab then departed for Jerusalem, but returned on David's order, this time with the regular army and mercenaries, augmented by the militia. 'David had gathered all Israel together', and when Joab clashed again with the enemy, at Helam in the Edrei Gap, some seventy miles south of Damascus and about the same distance north of Rabbath-Ammon, the Arameans under Shobach were completely defeated, losing seven hundred chariots and forty thousand men, approximately the total of the original allied force at Medeba. 'So the Syrians feared to help the children of Ammon any more.'

David 'tarried' then in Jerusalem, despatching Joab with his staff and the regular and militia armies to eliminate the Ammonites, now deprived of all allies. Joab took the royal Ammonite city or, at least its 'city of waters' or water supply, only calling on David to complete the conquest, with the ominous warning: 'Lest I take the city and it be called after my name.' David complied, putting the defeated population 'under saws, and under harrows of iron, and under axes of iron' and, in a horrifying reverse preview of the Holocaust, 'made them pass through the brick kiln'.

Before the king had even left again for the field, while he yet 'tarried' in Jerusalem as his armies were confronting the Arameans and Ammonites, he strolled out one still moonlit night on the roof of the palace, the dark bowl of the sky punctured with a myriad stars. Across a little valley, on a rooftop close to his own, a woman more beautiful and more seductive than he had ever known, bathed her naked body under the moonlight. His servants told David that her name was Bathsheba, the wife of one of the officers of his bodyguard, Uriah the Hittite, well known to the King and therefore doubly *chasse gardée*. But David had her summoned secretly by his aide-de-camp: 'and she came in unto him and he lay with her', as he did again and again, night after night. For the king loved her, as he believed he had never loved another, certainly not Ahinoam, or Abigail, or the many concubines, not even Michal or Maacah. Bathsheba was soon with child. He would not prevent the birth. He sent for Uriah from Joab's army. The husband could lie with the wife and thus, 'innocently', deflect the blame that would otherwise be cast on the king for what would incontrovertibly be seen as the capital crime of adultery – the penalty for which was stoning to death – and the more 'social' charge of stealing a retainer's wife. On Uriah's arrival in Jerusalem for his interview with David, the latter falsely presented the recall as an occasion to interrogate him on the progress of the war, on Joab's conduct of strategy and tactics, on the role of Uriah himself. Having disposed of this cover task, David thanked him and sent him off to Bathsheba's house, later despatching a rich dinner from the royal kitchens. But Uriah claimed that since his God and his friends were in the field at Succoth facing the foe directly, he could not sleep or eat in his own home or elsewhere than in barracks, so long as his comrades were thus bloodily engaged – a blunt, honest soldier. David, in a desperate effort to persuade him to love Bathsheba for this one vital night, filled him with liquor but, although drunk, Uriah would not go to 'the rank sweat of her enseamed bed'.

The king, all hope lost, sent Uriah back to his regiment, bearing a letter for his commander-in-chief: 'Set ye Uriah in the forefront of the hottest battle, and retire ye from him that he may be smitten, and die.' Joab obeyed, posting Uriah to a unit of the regular army investing the city by the gate where the danger was greatest, the fighting most intense, and the bowmen on the battlements most accurate. When he then ordered a rash frontal attack against the bristling segment, the Hittite fell among his friends in David's bodyguard, slain by archers in the fortress or by the swordsmen, javelin throwers and heavy pikesmen streaming out from the gate into the field to meet the Israelite assault.

When the king heard of his death, he instantly sent for Bathsheba and made her his wife. But Jehovah cursed him: 'Now therefore the sword shall never depart from thy house . . . thou shalt not die, but the child that is born to thee shall surely die.' The child died. David comforted Bathsheba, and she later bore their son, Solomon.

13
'O Absalom, my son . . .'

Amnon was the son of David and of Ahinoam of Jezreel, the king's firstborn, who conceived an obsessive lust for his half-sister Tamar, daughter of David by Maacah, the Arab King of Geshur's daughter. By pretending sickness, Amnon induced a court pander to persuade the king to send Tamar to his bedroom where he lay, and where she might nurse him with cakes and meat prepared by herself. He 'took hold of her . . . Come lie with me, my sister', but she would not, begging 'do not thou this folly'. After he had raped her, he hated her, ordering a servant to put her out and bolt the door behind her. Tamar wept, rending the many-coloured virgin's robe, covering her head with ashes. Absalom, Tamar's brother, learning of the matter, so loathed his half-brother Amnon for it that, having invited Amnon with all the king's sons to a sheep-shearing in the country near Ephraim, he had the half-brother done to death by his entourage. The other sons, shocked and terrified, rode off on their mules for home and Jerusalem, while Absalom escaped to Geshur, where he remained for three years. After a subterfuge arranged by Joab in which a witch acted the part of a widow interceding for *her* son, David was gulled into bringing Absalom back to Jerusalem. But he refused for two more years to see him face to face until, at last, he agreed.

'The king kissed Absalom', but his son was not only very beautiful, with magnificent hair for which he was admired throughout Israel, but treacherous, resenting his lack of power and seeking to rally the people to him to establish himself as an alternative to his father, offering to act as a source of justice. With two hundred men, he set himself up in Hebron, the old religious capital, in a conspiracy that included Ahithophel, David's former counsellor. The king, believing that Absalom had wide Israelite support, abandoned Jerusalem via the Mount of Olives, with his loyal battalion of six hundred men, crossing the brook Kidron on the way to the desert. He sent the Ark back to Jerusalem, where Absalom had proclaimed himself king. David's high priests there organised an intelligence network with a dual purpose: to find out

Absalom's plans and, through Hushai, an ally of David's clandestine action, to frustrate them and to outwit Ahithophel. For the king was aware that much of Israel, particularly the Northern tribal levies, supported his son; there was ill-feeling towards David; Israel/Judah divisions existed in the monarchy. In the wilderness, a wild man, Shimei of Saul's House, cursed David, casting stones at him and his soldiers, hurling dust . . . 'Come out, come out, thou bloody man, and thou man of Belial.' The king's following lay in Judah and with his mercenaries . . .

In Jerusalem, Absalom flung a wounding blow to David's 'face' by lying publicly with the king's concubines, thus confirming a curse uttered by Jehovah after David had murdered Uriah the Hittite. The traitor Ahithophel sagely advised him to pursue David with twelve thousand men, while the king was most weak and despondent and before he could raise more support. His death would collapse the Davidic state and, without a centre, the people would rally to Absalom. But Hushai persuaded the rebel that David and his men were still mighty and valiant, the more dangerous now that they could be compared with 'a bear robbed of her whelps in the field'. Absalom should therefore not accept Ahithophel's counsel, rather gather all Israel to him 'from Dan to Beersheba', and only then attack with maximum force. Ahithophel's advice was rejected in favour of that put into Hushai's mouth by Jehovah: he rode off on his ass, and, after putting his affairs in order, hung himself, knowing that his counsel had been the most correct.

Hushai reported these events to the high priests, who sent a 'wench' to tell their sons to carry the message to David. But a boy had seen the young men and the girl conspiring. Absalom ordered troops after the sons, who fled to a house in Bahurim where they hid down a well; the woman of the house covered the well-head, strewing corn on it, so the sons were not found, the search-party believing the woman's story that they had 'gone on across the brook'. When the sons eventually reached David's tent, their message was that he should not now proceed into the wilderness but across the Jordan. Supporters brought the king's men 'beds and basins, and earthen vessels, and wheat, and barley and flour, and parched corn, and beans and lentils and parched pulse. And honey, and butter, and sheep, and cheese . . .'

David now divided his augmented forces into three in their

thousands and hundreds, under Joab, Abishai his brother, and Ittai the Gittite, a loyal, honourable, even noble captain. The people, because David's death or capture would be too grievous a blow to their fortunes, would not permit the king to take command in the field. So he stood at the gateside as they went out to war, only instructing his commanders to 'deal gently' with his son Absalom, an order heard by the whole host. The army met Absalom's forces in the wood at Ephraim, where Joshua had told the children of Joseph to improve their portion of land by cutting down trees on the mountainside. Fighting took place over the country, as well as in the wood. As many were lost in the wood as in battle, among them Absalom himself who, when riding on his mule under oak trees, was lifted off the animal's back, suspended from a bough by his chin, robe round his knees, sandals ungirt, sword flapping at his side, the mule trotting off. One of Joab's soldiers who observed the scene told the general that, after the king's warning, not even a thousand shekels would have disposed him to raise his hand against David's son, since the king 'knew everything' that happened. But Joab took three darts and thrust them into Absalom's heart while his armour-bearers hacked the pretender to pieces, flinging him into a pit which they covered with stones. When the messengers told the king, he wept and, little considering the victory, cried: 'O my son Absalom, my son, my son Absalom! Would God I had died for thee, O Absalom, my son, my son.'

Shamefacedly, the people started to return to David in Mahanaim, despite the king's mourning and his apparent indifference to his own troops' victory and his enemy's defeat. When the king continued to mourn, Joab harshly reminded him that he was shaming his supporters, loving his enemies and hating his friends, disregarding his own men who had saved his life and ensured his family's survival: if the king did not address his people, they would desert him. So David went out to the gate and all the people came before the king. After David had appealed to them, the men of Judah came to Gilgal, accompanied by half the men of Israel, including the repentant Shimei and dishevelled Mephibosheth, to escort him across the Jordan to Jerusalem. But, on the way, the men of Israel protested, as was always their practice, that they had not been consulted about the king's return. 'We have ten parts in the king . . . and more in David than ye.' But the Judaites shouted them down, proud that they, and not the Israelites, were of David's own house.

Resentment at exclusion from the blood line was one reason why Sheba, a Benjamite of Israel, then raised rebellion, crying, 'Every man to his tents, O Israel . . . we have no part in David.' *All the men of Israel* then joined Sheba, but those of Judah followed the monarch to Jerusalem. Here Amasa had arrived. This officer of dubious probity had previously seceded from the militia to Absalom's cause, but was now made commander of David's army in order to encourage the return of Absalom's Judaite supporters. Joab was black with rage at his demotion. The king ordered Amasa to call up the levies within the three days allowed for emergency but, because the general delayed, Abishai had to muster the regulars, including Joab's men and the mercenaries. These met Amasa at Gibeon. Joab, who hated him for usurping his grandeur, pretended to take him by the beard in friendly mode as if to embrace him. As Joab swaggered stupidly forward, Amasa did not mark the sword under the robe, with which Joab stabbed him just as he had stabbed Abner after that captain had murdered Asahel, his brother. 'And Amasa wallowed in blood in the midst of the highway . . .'

Those seeking to turn their coats and bask in the king's favours now joined Joab and pursued Sheba to Abel Beth Maachah in northern Naphtali, south of Mount Lebanon, where Joab erected a redoubt against the outer city wall from which to batter it down. Persuaded by 'a wise woman' within the city, who opened a covert communication with him, the general agreed not to destroy the town and its people. If Sheba alone could be delivered to his command, the city would be spared, and his army would depart . . . Shortly thereafter, following guilty conspiracy within the walls, the bleeding head of Sheba was thrown to Joab over the battlements.

David recovered the bones of Saul and Jonathan from the Philistines and buried them in the sepulchre of Kish, Saul's father. In his old age, he did not himself go out again with an army, such differences as continued with the Philistines being settled by duels between respective champions; on David's side, himself, Abishai and others and, for the Philistines, giant descendants of Goliath, one with six fingers and six toes on each hand and foot.

There were other companions whom he remembered: Benaiah

who slew a lion in a pit and, himself armed only with a staff, killed an Egyptian warrior bearing a spear; Abishai who killed three hundred . . . And the Lord, he said at the last, who 'teacheth my hands to war . . . who hast given me the shield of salvation, and girded me with strength to battle . . . he hath made with me an everlasting covenant . . . the sons of Belial shall be all of them as thorns thrust away. . . . For by Thee, I have run through a troop: by my God have I leaped over a wall.'

14
Death of David; Solomon and his strategy

The dying King David lay in the arms of a young girl, despatched by the court to restore a measure of heat to his cold, aged body but, although fair and seductive, she could not rouse the King. Bathsheba, his wife, entered the room. Adonijah, son of Haggith and David, had seized the throne, with chariots, horsemen, a company of men, feasting now on oxen, cattle and sheep, supported by many, but not by the prophet, the army commander, the high priest or the bodyguard. Because David had promised the succession, not to him, but to Solomon, his son by Bathsheba, these omissions would cost Adonijah his life. The king immediately ordered the young Solomon to be placed on the royal mule and taken to the spring at Gihon below the walls at Jerusalem where Zadok, the high priest, anointed him with oil from the tabernacle. The trumpets sounded, the people rejoiced with a mighty clamour, the new king reigned. Adonijah 'caught hold on the horns of the altar', begging for mercy which Solomon granted on conditions; Adonijah bowed down to his half-brother the king; the conspirators fled.

Solomon confined Shimei to Jerusalem, only putting him to death at the hand of Benaiah, his new commander, when Shimei broke his parole by going to Gath to recover defecting servants. Abiathar, the renegade priest, because he had borne the Ark, Solomon did not kill, only banished, thinking on the Lord's words about the House of Eli in Shiloh. But he put Joab to death, who had also deserted the old king for Absalom, and had murdered the guiltless Abner and Amasa. Adonijah then, using Bathsheba as intermediary, sought to marry Abishay the Shunnamite, King David's last concubine. King Solomon – enraged, asking why his mother did not also seek the *kingdom* for Adonijah, Joab and Abiathar – caused Benaiah to fall with the sword upon this perfidious half-brother.

King Solomon had made an alliance with the Pharaoh, symbolised by marriage with the king of Egypt's daughter, who, as dowry, brought Gezer, destroyed by her father – the Canaanites slain –

later to be restored by Solomon. In Gibeon, whither he had gone to sacrifice, the Lord then appeared to him in dreams, asking what He could give and what the king sought, delighted that Solomon asked only for understanding and wisdom – 'a little child' who knew not how to lead his people – therefore adding riches, honour and a long life, for none of which had Solomon begged. Solomon then delivered his famous verdict, awarding the disputed child to the woman ready for it to be given to the false mother rather than have it 'equitably' divided by cold steel.

The kingdom was initially united and content from the Jordan to Philistia in the west, to Egypt in the south, from Dan to Beersheba, and east of the Jordan. Solomon's constructions, the Temple of Solomon (of rectangular Phoenician design and housing the Ark), the royal palace of the king, the house of the Forest of Lebanon, the hall of pillars, the throne room, the wall of Jerusalem, eventually the great defended chariot cities of Megiddo, Gezer and Hazor, with their vast stables for thousands of horses, mules and chariots, were all marvels of their time. As to consumption, the king's own household alone required daily provision of thirty oxen, a hundred sheep and deer, game and fowl, thirty measures of corn and sixty of meal, supplied through twelve officers and their staffs on a monthly roster. And 'Judah and Israel were many, [dwelling] safely every man under his vine and under his fig tree.'

Hiram, king of Tyre, son of a widow of the Naphtali tribe whose husband had been a brass worker, brought about the casting of the bronze columns in the Temple, their capitals heavy with lilies and pomegranates, all however cast in the Jordan valley, not in Phoenicia. He built a 'molten sea' reposing on twelve 'oxen', cup-shaped, with lilies, lions, oxen and cherubim': the amount of gold, fir and cedar that Solomon's great buildings absorbed was incalculable. (In payment of a debt, Solomon gave him twenty cities, the design of which displeased Hiram.) The king built a navy at Eilat, today a tourist resort, at the head of the Red Sea. Thence the navy of Tarshish and Hiram's fleet, mostly manned by Phoenicians, sailed on three-year voyages to Ophir in Arabia and Madagascar returning laden with gold, jewels, ivory, apes, peacocks, linen, horses, mules but rarely silver, for silver was little valued in Jerusalem, no more than if it were stone.

When David still ruled over Israel, after he had defeated King Hadadezer of Zobah in battle, Zobah's son Rezon fled from his own land in command of a trained band. With these troops, he overthrew the Israelite regime implanted by David in Damascus, while other northern Aramean states similarly distanced themselves from Solomon's administration. At the same time, Egypt under a new Pharaoh began to show signs of imminent hostility, and it was then that the king began his building programme of military public works against invasion or a break-up of the monarchy.

His strategy was based not on the French concept of fixed desert posts on *Beau Geste* lines, nor on the rigid Maginot Line, but on offensive mobile units with chariots and light infantry operating as today's motorised columns with tanks, self-propelled guns, infantry, the then components being mules, chariots, soldiers armed with javelins, pikes, swords, spears and sling-shots. The concept depended on well-sited bases, equipped with facilities for supply and maintenance of the mobile horsed, wheeled and foot columns, embodying both offensive and defensive functions.

Among fortresses, Beth Horon, at the pass of that name, dominated the Judaean mountain plateau which the Philistines penetrated on their way to victory over Saul at Gilboa. Baalath guarded the outer approaches to the valleys of Elah and Rephaim, where David had routed the Philistine forces in the Bechaim Wood. Not only Philistines, but Egyptians, and the British under Allenby chasing the Turk after Beersheba in 1917, pursued this avenue. Tadmor, today's Palmyra, 'Queen of the Desert', between the Syrian mountains and the Syrian desert, was the great commercial and revictualling post on the trade routes between Mesopotamia and Israel. Solomon had to send troops to the extremities of these regions – to Aram (of the later Second Captivity) and to Hamath on the Orontes – to halt further dissidence after Rezon's successful resistance in Damascus. Hazor, northwest of Jerusalem, triply monitored the Via Maris on its eastward journey through the Esdraelon Plain, the main Jordan Highway to Damascus, and the road to Damascus via the Golan Heights. Tamar, after which Plymouth's river was named, protected Israel's southern frontiers, while Megiddo ('Armageddon') was the shield and buckler of the Carmel Range and the Jezreel valley. Gezer in Dan guarded Jerusalem from any attack on the capital from the Mediterranean coast via Jaffa, or via Jabneh further south, and Lod.

Solomon loved and desired women even more than did his father, David. Other than the Pharaoh's daughter, he married, or took as concubines, women from Ammon, from among the Hittites, from Moab, Zidonia and Edom, many strange women from many countries outside Israel. Even though they may not really have included *seven hundred* princesses as wives, and three hundred concubines, not that there was cultural or legal objection, it is credible that they stole away his heart to the gods of Moab, Chemosh and Molech. He built for them 'high places' with altars, burned incense and sacrificed to them, making Jehovah sad and angry. Solomon ignored the Lord's warning. His conduct at length drove the Lord to pronounce on him the fate of Israel, that his united kingdom should be taken from him, leaving to his son one tribe only, and that only for David's sake.

Meanwhile, Hadad the Edomite who had left Edom with his family as a child when Joab had almost exterminated the people of Edom in battle, had fled to Egypt where he had married the Pharaoh's sister-in-law, receiving land and possessions. When David died and Solomon succeeded, Hadad hurried back to Israel to strike against the king. Jeroboam, a son of one of the old king's retinue, also took against the new monarchy. Ahijah, the prophet, encountering him on the road out of Jerusalem, seized his own robe, tearing it to pieces strip by strip, handing Jeroboam ten segments representing the ten tribes that would leave Solomon on his death when, because the king had betrayed Jehovah with heathen gods, Jeroboam would succeed him as leader of Israel. Only one tribe, and that because of David, would pass to Solomon's son in Judah, as the Lord had prophesied. Jeroboam, leading an army equipped with three hundred chariots, rebelled against the king. Solomon defeated the insurrection, and the beaten and unsuccessful Jeroboam took sanctuary with Shishak, the new king of Egypt, with whom he remained until the death of Solomon after the latter's forty years on the throne. 'And Solomon slept with his fathers, and was buried in the city of David his father: and Rehoboam his son reigned in his stead'; the house of David was to be afflicted, but not for ever.

Solomon's reign had been one of luxury and grandeur, a sort of Edwardian era. It included massive defence expenditure, the whole funded by deficit financing and in the last resort, by forced labour and heavy, unpopular tax increases. These, together with the concentration of religion in Jerusalem and other signs of neglect of the north, in the end brought Israel's resentment to the boil. Solomon, through the sale and purchase abroad of horses, through the production of iron and copper manufactured goods, through his control of trade between the Mediterranean, Africa, Arabia and on into India and the East, probably did run an external surplus. That was not enough to preserve the desert purity of the covenant or the idea of liberty, on both of which the unity of the kingdom depended. Since it was, after all, a very small Middle Eastern polity, compared with the 'rough beasts' eastward, 'slouching toward Bethlehem to be born', unity was a *sine qua non* for its survival. Unemployment, landless peasants, few very rich, but too many poor, added to the mix of wretchedness and division.

'Things fall apart, the centre cannot hold: mere anarchy is loosed upon the world . . .'

15
The end of the united monarchy

The Pharaoh, angrily aware of the united monarchy's ability to halt or at least effectively to delay Egyptian military advance northward, resentful of joint Israelite-Phoenician maritime power in the Mediterranean and Red Sea, of Philistia's relative powerlessness since David's victories, decided to exploit the new instability in the kingdom. King Shishak I of Egypt therefore helped the return to Israel of the exiled Jeroboam – whose earlier rebellion Solomon had successfully quelled – as a means of weakening further the kingdom's uncertain unity, no longer the divided Judah and Israel which it once was, but now a rather insecure 'Israel'.

In 933 BC, King Rehoboam was crowned at Shechem, one of the older shrines, perhaps Israel's deliberate preference over Jerusalem. Jeroboam attended for his own purposes, with Shishak's malign connivance. Together with others in the northern leadership, they sought assurance from Rehoboam that the *corvée* would be stopped and taxation and other impositions reduced: ' . . . make then the grievous service of thy father and his heavy yoke lighter.' But although the king's older advisers counselled that conciliation and fair words would bind the people to him for ever, the advice of his younger officers was that arrogantly passed to the delegates on their return to the king: 'My father chastised you with whips but I will chastise you with scorpions.'

So, once again, the men of Israel cried the old oath: 'What portion have we in David? neither have we inheritance in the house of Jesse: to your tents, O Israel, now see to thy own house, David,' and the united monarchy was at its end, the Ten Tribes of Israel under Jeroboam in Shechem, only Judah and Benjamin in a Jerusalem ruled by Rehoboam. But although Rehoboam refrained from mustering his 'one hundred and eighty thousand' warriors against Israel, Jeroboam – fearing the magnetism of the Ark in Jerusalem – erected two large golden calves in Dan and Bethel, served not by Levites, but by false priests.

A man of God from Judah was sent to warn Jeroboam in Israel of impending doom. He broke a promise of abstinence that he had made to Jehovah and was in consequence slain by a 'lion in the way' who, miraculously, neither fled nor killed the holy man's ass. But Jeroboam made no move to change his own conduct although God, through the prophet Ahijah, cursed him and made his little son to die, in punishment for the false gods and images that the child's father had permitted. Even in Rehoboam's southern kingdom, 'Judah did evil in the sight of the Lord', building altars, images, groves to other Gods than Yahweh 'on every high hill, under every green tree': the abomination of sodomy was widespread in the land. These affronts to stability provoked the opportunistic Shishak to invade, although without apparently attempting occupation. In Israel he captured Megiddo, Taanach, Shunem and Bethshan. In Judah, where Rehoboam had recently fortified Bethlehem, Etam, Hebron, Ajalon, Lachish and other cities, the Pharaoh took all the treasures from the Temple and the Royal Palace, forcing Rehoboam to substitute bronze for gold in his shields. Irrespective of Shishak's depredations, Rehoboam, Jeroboam and their descendants fought one another ceaselessly over these cities and, especially those of Israel, for over a hundred years; the battle between Abijah and Jeroboam, with absurdly huge forces on either side, ended with the rout of an Israelite ambush – 'five hundred thousand' Israelites dead – and the loss of Bethel, Jeshanah and Ephraim.

The Pharaoh had invaded with twelve hundred chariots and, it is said, sixty thousand horsemen, with Nubian, Libyan and Ethiopian infantry. The first thrust seems to have been directed against the naval yards and fort at Ezion-Geber, near Eilat on the eponymous gulf, thence northward through the desert via Gezer and Gibeon, northeast towards Syria and eastwards into Judaea. Here, in the hills and mountains, the terrain was less suitable for 'armour' and cavalry. Shishak had spared Rehoboam on payment of monetary and other tribute, such as the Jerusalem treasures, by then a considerable volume of gold, silver, lapis lazuli and other jewels, rich silks and linen. He did, nevertheless, make a dashing strike across the River Jordan itself, attacking Succoth in the valley, once David's forward headquarters for operations against the Arameans and Mesopotamians. Unlike General Westmoreland in Vietnam, the Pharaoh – in Israel, not Judah – successfully accomplished a 'search and destroy' mission of bases and equipment on a large scale, although, like Westmoreland, he did not consolidate the feat by pacification or occupation of territory. He returned to Egypt west-about via Megiddo and then southward through Israel's coastal cities and the plain.

In the eighteenth year of Jeroboam's reign in Israel, Rehoboam of Judah died, succeeded by his son Abijam who did nothing to reform the religion, but pursued the war with Israel. Asa, who became king when his father Abijam died, was a reformer who banished the sodomites, removed his father's idols, and the queen mother's pornographic symbol, burning that before the brook Kidron. He did not abolish all the 'high places', but he did restore the incunabulae to the Temple. Seeking help and friends against Israel – in that country, Jeroboam had been succeeded by Nadab and Baasha – he sent all the silver, gold and treasure from the Temple and the royal house as a present to King Ben-hadad I of Damascus.

That Syrian Aramean already had his own alliance with the new king of Israel, Baasha, against whom Asa now sought assistance: Baasha had occupied Ramah, Samuel's town, in Israel but only five miles from Judah's capital at Jerusalem. Although Israel had lost territory to the Arameans after she had been weakened by Shishak, Baasha assumed that in moving against Judah, his rear would be secured by the Treaty with Damascus. Nothing could have been further from the truth and, delighted by the naïvety of both his allies, Ben-hadad attacked Israel in strength on the in-and-out lines of the Pharaoh's 'search and destroy' invasion. On this occasion, what was destroyed was the Naphtali line, south of Mounts Lebanon and Hermon, 'Ijon, Dan, Abel-beth-maachah and all Cinneroth, with all the land of Naphtali'. This line of Israelite fortresses probably included Kadesh, and Hazor which guarded, as we have seen, the Via Maris, that being also the function of Cinneroth. The line's purposes were various, to protect Galilee from the lesser breeds across the Jordan, to act as a springboard for action against the Bekaa Valley and northwest Syria, to hold aggressive movement from the Golan Heights and the valley of the Jordan. Nearly all these posts, especially Dan, were employed, long after biblical times, in the First and Second World Wars, in the War of Independence of 1948, and in Israel's subsequent wars against the Arabs.

While Israel and Syria were thus engaged, Asa seized the opportunity to dismantle Baasha's Ramah, using the stones and timber to rebuild the fortresses of Mizpah and Geba in Judah, close to Jerusalem. (For his danegeld, his appeasement of the dangerous and malign Ben-hadad, he was rebuked by a seer: 'because thou hast relied on the king of Syria, and not relied on the Lord thy God, therefore is the host of the king of Syria escaped out of this land'.) Shishak, while hurling his *Sturm und Drang* against Israel, and restricting most of his activities in Judah to the extraction of 'treasure', had also inflicted *some* damage. Asa repaired these 'store-cities' and fortresses, building others with 'walls, and towers, gates and bars', probably Arad, En-gedi, Beth Shemesh. The centres of activity were those to which his grandfather Rehoboam had directed his attention, protecting the Judaean mountains and the central plateau, the ancestral home and natural base of the Judaites, all located close to intercommunicating roads and therefore to one another, while also providing the armed bases from which counter-attacks could be mounted when the moment came. The concept of 'local' defence was as different from King Solomon's wider objective of protecting his territorial gains outside the heartland, as British defence policy of 'home base and NATO' is today in comparison with that of imperial defence.

Invaders could be defeated on these hedgehog 'castles'. Chaim Herzog and Mordechai Gichon give the example of Zerah the Ethiopian, actually a Kushite and Egyptian satrap, commanding three hundred chariots and the ludicrously exaggerated figure of one million men, who invaded Judah from his fiefdom at Gerar in Philistia. Having lost *élan* and momentum by besieging the fort at Mareshah, one of Rehoboam's strongholds renewed by his grandson Asa, he was brought to a standstill and flight by Asa's army manoeuvring in the valley from behind the stronghold. Asa assaulted him in the flank. This body of men, again large beyond belief, numbering 'three hundred thousand' archers of Benjamin and the same number of Judaite pike and spear men, slaughtered half Zerah's army and pursued the rest to Gerah where they looted or destroyed the neighbouring towns.

The Moabites, Ammonites and their allies from Mount Seir in Edom, invaded Judah from En-gedi, their presence first sighted at the edge of the Wilderness of Jeruel. Jehoshophat, Asa's son, now king of Judah, led his troops on the word of the Spirit of the Lord: 'Ye shall not need to fight in the battle . . . for the Lord will be with you.' The singers went out before the army, praising the Lord. At Tekoa, one of Rehoboam's fortresses, south of Bethlehem and east of the Dead Sea, the enemy was ambushed climbing up the steep path of a canyon, possibly by Judaite troops in false uniforms. The men of Moab and Ammon set upon the Edomites, and then fell on one another: three days were needed for Jehoshophat and his people to collect the jewellery, money and other spoils from the bodies of Judah's foes. Jehoshophat, on return to Jerusalem, developed the programme of military construction – 'castles and cities of stone' – with army headquarters and the reserve in Jerusalem, listed with customary hyperbole as a million men *besides* those in the outstations or 'fenced cities' of Judah.

The fortifications of Judah, store-cities, fortresses, signal stations, watch-towers, erected initially on a large scale by Solomon, rebuilt, increased or repaired by Rehoboam and Asa, were the main deterrent to foreign invasion. This came from Israel itself, the Pharaohs, the Arameans, the 'lesser breeds', the Assyrians, even, centuries later, from Napoleon, many of whom did not hesitate to attack Israel, but rejected engagement with the mountaineers of Judaea. Judah survived many threats long after Israel, her northern neighbour and earlier partner, had fallen. There are reasons for her stamina. Of them, beside faith and valour, the lines of defences were an essential component. 'And Rehoboam dwelt in Jerusalem and built cities for defence in Judah. He built even Bethlehem, and Etam, and Tekoa, and Beth-zur, and Shoco (Socoh), and Abdullam, and Gath, and Moneshah, and Ziph, and Adoraim, and Lachish, and Azekah, and Zorah, and Ajalon, and Hebron, which are in Judah, and Bethlehem, fenced cities . . . And he fortified the strongholds and put captains in them, and stores of victuals, and of oil and wine. And in every city he put shields and spears, and made them exceedingly strong, having Judah and Benjamin on his side.' In fact, Rehoboam appointed his sons to command the garrisons, one to act as commander-in-chief: 'And he [Rehoboam] acted wisely, and dispersed all his children throughout all the countries of Judah and Benjamin, unto every fenced city; and he gave them victuals in abundance', an agreeable instance of efficient nepotism, not unlike, but more indulgent than that in the Royal Navy up to the end of the Second World War. Meanwhile, the civilian occupants of towns became part of the garrisons, as much warriors as the regular troops, associating all with the fighting spirit.

Asa refortified Saul's capital of Gibeah, that king's base before the battle of Michmash. Jerusalem was now defended to the north by Gibeah, by Mizpah where Samuel had called the people and proclaimed Saul as king, Gibeon with its two shafts and circular staircases leading to water, and Geba. The Holy City was guarded in the south by Bethlehem, Christ's birthplace, Etam (Ain Atani), Bether, and Beth Haccerem closer in yet. Of the other fortresses constructed in Judah, and listed above as Rehoboam's creations, some formed a western shield for the high Judaean plateau and the road from the Beth-horon pass; others the roads to Hebron, where Abraham's sepulchre lay and where David was anointed, eastward to Mareshah where Zerah the Ethiopian was defeated (north of Adoraim and south of Beth Shemesh), and from Lachish. Some barred the Vale of Elah between Bethlehem and the Mediterranean coast. En-gedi and Ein-el-Turabe watched the western shore of the Salt Sea, supported by Ziph, also the sub-area of defence against nomads from the Negev. Tekoa's role was that of defence against Moab, Ammon and the Bedu of Arabia, while Arad and Beersheba protected the south and the southern headquarters at Hebron from assault out of the Sinai Peninsula by Egyptians or by Amalekites.

16
Ahab and the Assyrians

While Asa was king of Judah, Jeroboam's son Nadab succeeded his father as king of Israel. (It will be recalled that Jeroboam had fled to Egypt after leading a rebellion against King Solomon, returning to Israel only after the king's death.) In 906 BC, Nadab led his armies against the Philistines at Gibbethon, on the Dan/Ephraim border and strategically important for access to Mount Ephraim and its surrounding hills and ridges. This operation was interrupted by Nadab's death at the hands of Baasha of the tribe of Issachar, who then seized power from the house of Jeroboam the Ephraimite, slaughtering all the leaders of that family. In 882 BC, a further regicide took place when Zimri, a captain of charioteers stationed near the capital of Tirzah, assassinated King Elah (son of Baasha) while that monarch was drunk in his steward's house.

Zimri was almost certainly a regular officer whose troops were part of the household, also posted in Tirzah as a component of the main reserve. The militia, under their general Omri, probably with the rest of the chariots, was again besieging the Philistines at Gibbethon. Learning of the murder, the 'people' in the field acclaimed Omri as king of Israel, marching as a body to Tirzah to besiege the usurper; Zimri, seeing that all was lost, went to the royal palace and, in an act of despair, not wholly unlike Samson's suicide, burnt the house down around him after a reign lasting exactly seven days. A period of civil war followed, but for twelve years thereafter Omri reigned – in apparent amity with Judah – from his new capital Samaria which he built on the hill of that name, having purchased the land from its owner Shemer. The town, now called Sebastia, stands today to the west of Gilboa in olive and fig trees within its Roman wall, a forum therein, a stadium and acropolis, six hundred Byzantine columns and the Church of Saint John, as well as the palace of Ahab, Omri's son; in its time, it was a prosperous town, filled with magnificent ivory.

But Omri, although seeking no further divisive tactics between Israel and Judah, was a vigilant defender of Israel's interests and a constant threat to her other neighbours across the Dead Sea in the Ammon and in the blue granite mountains of Moab. Indeed, an Assyrian monument refers to Israel, not by name, but as 'the Land of Omri', while the stele of King Mesha, now in the Louvre, complains about Israelite oppression of Moab. Mesha paid Israel annual tribute of one hundred thousand lambs and one hundred thousand sheep, but Omri was careful to make no unnecessary enemies, maintaining and strengthening Samaria's alliance with Phoenicia.

Ahab was his successor. Earlier persuaded by Omri to marry Jezebel, daughter of his ally the king of Tyre and a byword for lubricious iniquity, Ahab erected a temple to her god Baal. The woman, by her excesses, scandalised the righteous of Israel and their prophet Elijah. (It was Elijah who had been fed by the brook Kerith at the Lord's command by ravens, and who saw that the widow's barrel and cruse were never empty, and who brought her son back to life.) After Jezebel had had the Lord's prophets murdered during a drought, or those of them not hidden in caves, Elijah performed the miracle of fire of which the Baalite priests were incapable: 'Cry aloud: for he [Baal] is a god; either he is talking, or he is pursuing, or he is in a journey, or peradventure he sleepeth, and must be awaked . . . so they cut themselves . . . till the blood gushed out . . .' The people took the Baalites and slew them with swords by the brook Kidron. It was then that 'the little cloud [came] out of the sea like a man's hand'; and the rain came.

So Jezebel had Elijah pursued to Beersheba when, after wind, earthquake and fire, the Lord's 'still small voice' ordered him to anoint Jehu over Israel, Hazael as King of Syria, and to name Elisha as prophet in his stead. The Lord prophesied that those whom Hazael did not kill, would be killed by Jehu, and those still surviving by Elisha.

But Ahab was still alive and king of Israel when King Ben-hadad II of Syria and thirty-two Aramean kings, leading cavalry and chariots, began to eliminate the potential danger to Aramea itself. At first, Ahab was disposed to appeasement, agreeing to Ben-hadad's demands for treasure and women. When, however, the Syrian insisted on sending his officers physically to search and expropriate property from the houses of the king and people of Samaria, Ahab – with the grave concurrence of his senior advisors

– rejected this presumption. Ben-hadad responded with a boast about the numbers of soldiers he would now put into the field in an all-out attack. Ahab replied defiantly, although he had under his command only seven thousand men: 'all the knees which have not bowed to Baal and every mouth which hath not kissed him'. (It has been assumed, nevertheless, that the militia and, probably, a proportion of the regular army, had not been disbanded or disarmed, but scattered throughout the garrisons, unable to break Ben-hadad's screen round Samaria.) Ahab's tactical plan was to send a small force of two hundred and thirty men drawn from the provincial bodyguards, as a diversion or deception plan. Meanwhile the main force, small though it was, exploited the diversion by attacking the Aramean army already drawn up in array, Ben-hadad nominally in command, but in fact drinking with his cronies in their tents. When the assault came in, the Syrian king had no time to escape other than by leaping on to one of the cavalry horses. At least he was not trapped in the general killing that took place on that battlefield, nor in the attacks on his men running back to the Golan from Israelite garrisons among the mountains and from the enraged populace in hill farms and villages. The retreat became a massacre, one which required a post mortem.

The conclusions of Ben-hadad's general staff were, firstly, that cavalry and 'armour' were not suitable for operations in the mountains – 'their [the enemy Israel's] gods are gods of the hills' – and that future engagements should be on the level plain. Their second recommendation was that professional officers should be substituted for kings at the command level, that control therefore should be central, at least corps or divisional, and not battalion or company. The third ruling was that future hostilities between the two countries should be deferred until the Syrian army should be restored to the strength it had commanded before the battle of Samaria. But Ahab struck before these reforms permitted the Syrians to invade, reaching the approaches to Aphek, Ben-hadad's base southeast of the Sea of Kinnereth, where both armies halted for seven days at opposite ends of a steep, narrow gorge, one hundred yards wide. On the seventh day, the Israelites climbed the hills on either side of the gorge by crag and track in the darkness, and then descended from the heights. Ahab fell upon the Arameans from the rear and from both flanks, part of the little Israel force also confronting the bewildered enemy head-on in the defile itself. When the Syrians fell back on Aphek, having lost the usual hyperbolic 'one hundred thousand' infantry, 'twenty-seven thousand' more were killed by 'a falling wall', more probably by inability to manoeuvre within a crowded city against highly trained troops.

Ben-hadad's staff came out of Aphek in contrition, dressed in sackcloth. Ahab, in receiving them, referred to the Aramean king as 'my brother' . . . 'Now the men did diligently observe whether anything would come from him, and did hastily catch it: and they said, "Thy brother Ben-hadad",' whom they then brought to Ahab. The king of Israel, aware of the looming menace of Assyria and of the need for solidarity against that power, pardoned the Aramean king in exchange for the return of Israel's cities taken by Syria in the past and a treaty of trade between the two countries.

Jezebel, meanwhile, had engineered the stoning of Naboth and the seizure of his vineyard into Ahab's possession. For these crimes, Elijah condemned the royal pair: 'In the place where dogs licked the blood of Naboth, shall dogs lick thy blood, even thine . . . I will take away thy posterity . . . the dogs shall eat Jezebel by the wall of Jezreel.' But Ahab humbled himself and was pardoned, although 'evil' was to be brought upon his son's house.

After the battle of Aphek, there was peace for three years between Israel and Syria. During one of the regular consultations between Ahab and his son-in-law, King Jehoshophat of Judah, Ahab complained that Ben-hadad had not returned to him the town of Ramoth-Gilead promised under the Aphek agreement. Despite a warning by the prophet Micaiah that 'Israel would be scattered on the hills as sheep that have not a shepherd', Jehoshophat agreed to join the battle – 'my people as thy people, my horses as thy horses' – an effective military alliance against the Arameans. Before going into battle at Ramoth-Gilead, sure that Ben-hadad's captains would concentrate on him, Ahab disguised himself. The Syrians at first took Jehoshophat in his robes for the king of Israel but, realising their mistake, had broken off the pursuit when a bowman, 'at a venture', pierced Ahab's breast armour, mortally wounding the king who, to deceive the enemy and encourage the allies, had himself propped up in his chariot, although the blood poured from the wound. He did not die until the evening. Then, at sunset, the troops retreated to Israel and

Judah. In Samaria, as they washed the royal chariot, the dogs licked up his blood as Elijah had foretold.

Ramoth-gilead, in fact, took place just *after* the first major clash of arms between the Assyrians on the one hand, and a combined army of Arameans under Ben-hadad, Phoenicians, Egyptians, Israelites, the largest contingent, commanded by Ahab, whose chariots were estimated by the Assyrians to number two thousand, infantrymen from Ammon, camel-men of the Bedu and the risible 'Queans'. The allied infantry numbered nearly fifty-three thousand, plus about four thousand chariots, one thousand camel-men and two thousand cavalry men. These figures are drawn from Assyrian stone texts and were probably not exaggerated. Nothing is known of the Assyrian numerical roll. As to quality, this army was the best and most advanced in the Near East, although comparison with European armies would have been as difficult then as it would be today, at least until the Gulf War illuminated everything. Their infantry bore bows, pikes, 'keyhole'-shaped slings and, sometimes, swords. Cavalry – archers, javelin men and lancers – supported two- or three-man chariots; infantry shields were either convex, or tall and straight. All soldiers were bearded, their facial hair like *guttae*, complex architectural features cut square below their enormous hooked noses. The bowmen's quivers were carried high, either at their backs or between the right arm and shoulder, helmets bandeau-shaped with side pieces fastening round the chin. The stone-slingers wore conical hats, the shape of those affected by the Seven Dwarfs, whereas the helmets of the foot pikemen fitted the head and back of the neck, some with a forward facing metal 'curl' on top. Battering rams, boats and ladders completed the service establishment or train.

The Assyrian commander, Shalmenezer V, progenitor of Tiglath-Pileser III or Pul the greatest emperor of all, was already heir to an empire which extended from the Euphrates and Tigris to the Caspian and Black Seas and included Armenia, Mesopotamia and Media (Persia). It was his intention that it should embrace the territories *west* of the Euphrates as well – Egypt, Israel, Jordan, Arabia. But when he assembled his forces at Qarqar, north of Damascus, the Assyrians met and could not defeat a southern coalition whose accomplishment even in getting there was truly substantial. Yet, for whatever reason, the Bible does not care so much as to mention this great victory in which the Israelites played the most honourable role.

17
Continual warfare

The 'sheepmaster', King Mesha of Moab, 'author' of the stele or Moabite stone found at Dibon south of Medeba, took advantage of Ahab's death and the allies' instability after their relative failure against Ben-hadad at Ramoth-gilead. He rebelled against this Israelite overlord, and his own obligations in sheep, lambs and wool, successfully crossing the River Zered between the Dead Sea and Kir of Moab, taking territory to the south in Edom, tributary of Judah. More worrying for Israel, he simultaneously invaded Gilead across the River Arnon, south of Aroer, a fortress which he strengthened against attack from the north before capturing or burning villages in the tribal areas of Reuben and Gad in Gilead.

As before the battle of Ramoth-gilead, this time because of Mesha's assault on Edom, Jehoshophat agreed – again: 'I am as thou art, my people as thy people and my horses as thy horses' – to join in the attack against Moab organised by the son of Ahab, Jehoram, the young king in Samaria, accompanied by an Edomite force. The approach was not to be across the Jordan and the Arnon, recently fortified and ready for Moabite resistance, but by the southern route through the Wilderness of Edom. This meant a long and disagreeable journey, but one affording access to southern border areas lightly defended because of their apparent unsuitability as invasion sites. The expeditionary force, whose numbers are not accurately calculable, took seven days to arrive from their various bases – southwards from Samaria and Judaea, northwards from Edom – in a region near the Moab/Edom border, where there was no water for the army, its men, horses, camels and cattle. The prophet Elisha, successor to Elijah, was present with the host and, although furiously abusing Jehoram – 'who wrought evil . . . and clove unto the sins of his father Jeroboam' – agreed, because of Judah, to call upon the Lord. 'Ye shall not see wind, neither shall ye see rain; yet that valley shall be filled with water . . . in the morning there came water and the country was filled with water', the wadi flooded from cloudbursts so far away as to be invisible to the stricken army.

Mesha's commanders prepared their units, standing to at dawn. A trick of the early morning light showed the water in the wadi on the other side of the border to be blood red. Edom means 'red', and there is much red sandstone there, but the Moabites took this as a sign that the allies were slaughtering one another and, 'Now, therefore, Moab, to the spoil,' they cried, advancing on the enemy camp. But no such mutual slaying had occurred. The 'Israelites' went forward into Moab. As the Lord had promised through Elisha: 'they beat down the cities and on every good piece of land cast every one his stone and filled it, and they stopped all the wells of water, and felled all the good trees'. When they had done all this, they besieged Kir of Moab (or Kir Hareseth), later famous as the great castle of Kerak of the Crusaders, almost impregnable, proof against assaults from many quarters over centuries. But the stone-slingers now were particularly effective, and it was in desperation that Mesha led a sortie of only seven hundred men, which failed, against the Edomites in the weakest sector of the ring.

At this last, terrible moment, the Moab king offered his eldest son and heir as a burnt offering. His men may have seen the sacrifice as an inducement to victory, endurance *à outrance.* The allies also may have feared it to be so, an act of blind implacability. Or both may have regarded the act as the ultimate Eastern prophylactic against contagious plague. The defenders may have believed that the measure would succeed. The besiegers might have made the same calculation, or that it might fail and the disease would then spread. Perhaps, on the other hand, Ben-hadad in the north was already beginning preparations for war against Israel. In any case, the allies 'departed from [Mesha] and returned to their own land' in another indecisive engagement so close to victory for Jehovah.

The Arameans under Ben-hadad certainly conducted border-raids into Israel, taking slaves and treasure. (One of the captives was a little girl who became maid to the wife of Naaman, commander-in-chief of the Syrian army, and helped him, through the prophet Elisha in Israel, to cure his leprosy by immersion in the Jordan.) In subsequent warfare, the Syrians found that their plans were continually known to the enemy – betrayals which they attributed to Elisha's prophetic powers – passed in detail to King Jehoram, thus enabling that monarch to save his forces from defeat. The Syrians accordingly sent infantry, chariots and cavalry to invest Dothan, Elisha's residence in Israel, north of Samaria. Although some military engagement took place here, it may not have been the one in which Elisha was enabled by the Lord to strike the Aramean army blind, to fill the hillside with ghostly horses and chariots of fire, or to lead Naaman's troops; 'this is not the way, neither is this the city: follow me and I will bring you to the man whom ye seek. But he led them to Samaria.' Then Elisha's intervention in persuading the Israelite king to spare his enemies (which was only one of his miracles, the others being the widow's cruse, conception by the barren Shunnamite and, later, resurrection of her son) led to a period of peace between Syria and Israel.

Syria, however, soon attacked Israel again, this time in the middle of a devastating famine in which the Samarians had begun to boil and eat their own children. Elisha overcame the murderous hatred of King Jehoram, incurred for having encouraged resistance to Ben-hadad. He sought the Lord's aid. 'A noise of chariots, and a noise of horses, even the noise of a great host' so terrified the Syrians that they fled. 'No man there, neither voice of man, but horses tied, and asses tied, and the tents as they were . . . all the way was full of garments and vessels which the Syrians had cast away in their haste . . . so the people went out and spoiled the tents of the Syrians.' An Israelite officer who had earlier doubted Elisha's word, sneering: 'If the Lord would make windows in heaven, might this thing be', was trampled to death by the mob as he stood in the gate.

In Damascus, Hazael of the king's court smothered his master Ben-hadad with a thick cloth soaked in water, and succeeded him as king of Syria. In Judah, later in the reign of Jehoram (Jehoshophat's son, married to Athaliah, daughter of the heathen Ahab and Jezebel), Edom broke away from Judah in a revolt which, initially beaten down, seems to have resulted in Edomite autonomy and a loss to Judah of caravan tolls and Red Sea trade. Against him, too, rebelled 'the Philistines and the Arabians that were near the Ethiopians'. Jehoram and Athaliah's son was Ahaziah, later king of Judah, who fought beside King Joram of Israel once again against the Arameans, now under Hazael, at Ramoth-gilead where Joram was wounded. Joram then went down to Jezreel to be healed, and there Ahaziah joined him.

The prophet Elisha, because he loathed the Baalite culture of the Tyre alliance and the weaknesses and 'evil' of Ahab's house, anointed Jehu, the 'captain of the King's host', at Ramoth-Gilead, and enjoined him to destroy that house. 'The dogs shall eat Jezebel in the portion of Jezreel, and there shall be none to bury her.' When Jehu came in his chariot to Jezreel, the king's messengers recognised him – 'for he driveth furiously' – and Ahaziah and Joram mounted their chariots to meet him in Naboth's vineyard, stolen by Ahab and Jezebel. And Joram said, 'Is it peace, Jehu?' 'What peace,' cried Jehu, 'so long as the whoredoms of thy mother Jezebel and her witchcrafts are so many?' Joram fled . . . 'There is treachery, O Ahaziah.' Jehu shot him in the back with an arrow, flinging his body into Naboth's field. Ahaziah was caught at today's Jenin (from which, on 19 November 1995, the Israeli army withdrew under the Rabin/Arafat agreement), but escaped to die at Megiddo and be buried in David's city.

In Jezreel, Jezebel appeared at a window, painted and adorned, challenging Jehu with the fate of Zimri, who also slew his master but ruled only for a week before Baasha killed him. Jehu shouted: 'Throw her down', and when the eunuchs did so, her blood spattered on the walls and on the horses . . . 'in the portion of Jezreel, shall dogs eat the flesh of Jezebel'; nothing was left of her but palms, feet and head. Jehu then ordered the deaths of the seventy sons of Ahab in Samaria and had their severed heads despatched to him in baskets and arranged in two heaps at the king's gate. Then followed the slaughter of all Ahab's officials, their children, the priests, King Ahaziah's brethren (in the shearing house) and all the Baal worshippers (in their temples) and the destruction of all temples and artefacts. Ahab's house was liquidated, except for baby Joash, son of Ahaziah, who was hidden in the Temple under loyal guard for six years until his coronation, when Athaliah rent her clothes, crying 'Treason, Treason!', and was put to the sword.

Jehu had not followed the Lord. In the ninth century, Hazael of Syria 'liberated' Philistia on the Mediterranean coast through control of the Via Maris, and, eastwards from Jordan, Moab and Edom through seizure of the King's Highway, the main north-south road on the eastern borders of Judah and Israel. All these advances were made despite years of successful, but exhausting, Aramean resistance in the eighth century to the growing might of Assyria under Shalmenezer III. Jehu had made a self-serving alliance with the Assyrian king, which did him little good when Hazael found his own hands free. So complete was the Syrian achievement that the Israelite army was left with only fifty horsemen, ten chariots and ten (perhaps only one) thousand infantry. Hazael took Gath, moving on to Jerusalem until King Joash of Judah bribed him to desist with treasure from the Temple and the palace. Jehoash of Israel, in more chivalric mode, three times defeated Ben-hadad, Hazael's son, 'and recovered the cities of Israel', to some extent because these victories coincided with Syrian preoccupation over the westward progress of Ramman-Nizeri III of Assyria into their territories. But, urged by Elisha on his death-bed, Jehoash's victories were real, mounted from the Jordan watershed road in central Israel against the flanks of those positions which Hazael had captured in his earlier offensive. Aphek in the Golan, where Ahab had defeated Ben-hadad V, was the first step to Israelite triumphs at Karnain, Lo-debar (both mentioned by the prophet Amos), Damascus, Hazor, Megiddo, Ramoth-Gilead, Moab and Ammon, under the leadership of Jehoash and his son, Jeroboam II.

But Judah, ruled by Amaziah and fired by the same 'evangelism' as Elisha was almost simultaneously advocating in Israel, was the first to strike. Amaziah's army was drawn from Judah and Benjamin, perhaps thirty thousand men over the age of twenty, trained in the use of spear and shield. (He had rejected, to Ephraim's fury, a contingent of ten thousand Ephraimite mercenaries.) This force attacked Edom, Esau's country, falling upon the enemy in the Valley of Salt, killing a thousand men from Mount Seir and taking the capital, now the site of Petra in Jordan, 'rose-red city, half as old as time'. Judah's trade with the Red Sea, Egypt and the Eastern Mediterranean could begin to proceed to her benefit once more. But jealous of this, Jehoash accused Amaziah of boasting. In contemptuous rage, he compared Judah to a thistle and Israel to a cedar. They fought, Israel prevailing and Amaziah slain in Lachish for apostacy to Edom's gods.

Amaziah was succeeded by Uzziah, and Jehoash at his death by Jeroboam II when, as we have seen, Israel expanded its borders into Syria as far as the River Orontes. Damascus was already occupied, and all the old Samaria regained. But it was in this otherwise Golden Age that the prophet Amos spoke against luxury, ostentation and warfare: 'Your trading is upon the poor, and ye take from him burdens of wheat . . . they afflict the just, they take a bribe, and they turn away the poor from the gate . . . By the good life of Jacob, Yahweh has sworn, I will never forget any of their words.' And the high priest of Bethel could only say, 'O, thou, seer, flee thee away into the land of Judah and there eat bread and prophesy *there*.' Amos' counsel would – in the priests' view – break up Israel, bringing victory to its enemies the Assyrians, a fate foretold by the Lord, just as he foretold the final restoration of the tabernacle of David and Israel's return to its own land.

There were nineteen monarchs in Judah in the three hundred years between Rehoboam in 933 and Jehoiachim in 597 BC. Of them all, the most considerable ruler was indeed Uzziah who nevertheless secures only minor references in the Book of Kings – 'he built Elath and restored it to Judah' – under the name of 'Azariah, son of Amaziah'. He was a commanding, ultimately tragic figure, serving God, but condemned to leprosy for burning incense to the Lord in the Temple, a prerogative of the priests, who then watched the leprosy rise in his face. 'They thrust him out from thence; yea, himself hasted also to go out, because the Lord had smitten him', and he lived in sad isolation thereafter, under the regency of his son Jotham.

He had been a great statesman, reigning in Jerusalem in concord with Jehovah for fifty-two years. His first victories were over the Philistines, overcoming but not destroying the defences of Gath, Jabneth and Ashdod, constructing settlements and garrison-castles for Judaean troops near Ashdod on the coast and throughout Philistia. The castles comprised towers, often in pairs, providing enfilading fire from the heights, crenellated battlements, casemate or curtain walls, moats and traditional glacis, ports and so on, manned by bowmen and sling-shooters, the left-handed Benjaminites. 'He prepared for them throughout all the host shields, and spears, and helmets, and habergeons (mail), and bows, and slings to cast stones . . . engines to be on the towers and upon the bulwarks to shoot arrows and great stones . . .' He strengthened also the defences of Jerusalem, the Holy City. His army numbered three hundred and seven thousand men, led by 'two thousand six hundred mighty men of valour', *gibborim*, the landowner knights, most in helmets and chain-mail. (In fact, there were probably only a tenth of those numbers.) When on active service, they are said to have marched in four corps of three divisions each, the corps headquarters astern of the first division, the train consisting of equipment from battering rams to 'field kitchens', the tabernacle between first and third divisions.

Edom had already been subjugated by his father, Amaziah, and, although the united monarchy was not reconstituted, the alliance between Judah and Israel certainly functioned with benefit to Israel as well. Uzziah reconstructed the port and naval base at Eilat, then opened the Negev through conquest of 'the Arabians of Gur-baal'. In the Negev, he combined military defence ('towers in the desert') with civilian settlement, including wells for cattle, in a mutually supporting relationship as in modern Israel, to absorb surplus population, create security and make the desert bloom. Through control of the King's Highway, newly wrested from the Syrians/Arameans, he defeated Ammon, which he held in tribute. He did not destroy the treacherous Philistines, preferring to exploit their own trading interests to support Judah's own. 'And his name spread abroad, even to the entering in of Egypt' itself by the Via Maris at a point not far from Kantara, the site of Exodus where the story had begun. Nor were pastoral and agricultural responsibilities neglected, cattle, crops and vines grew on hill and dale from Karmel to Negev.

Uzziah, via Philistia, Negev, Ammon, Edom, Sinai and Egypt, acquired mastery over the Mediterranean, Arabia and the entire Red Sea commercial trading nexus, a visionary political feat.

18
Babylon; the Persians and the Greeks

Assyria, lying between the Tigris and the Euphrates rivers, cannot easily be differentiated from Babylon of which it was, more often than not, a province: '. . . and the beginning of his [Nimrod's] kingdom was Babel, and Erech, and Accad, and Calneh in the land of Shinar. Out of that land went forth Asshur and built Nineveh, and the city Rehoboth and Calah . . .' Culture, religion, language, race, art and science were common to both, mostly deriving from Babylon. Nevertheless, although nominally Babylon's vassal, the Assyrian Shalmeneser I conquered the Hittites and seized Babylon in the thirteenth century BC, forming an empire which endured for hundreds of years.

The second empire was founded by Tiglath-Pileser III and supported by a huge standing army with two- and four-wheeled chariots. In Israel, both Amos and Hosea prophesied destruction explicitly, in the case of Hosea by Assyria. In Judah, Isaiah and Micah also foretold doom, demanding adherence to Yahweh as the single, unique God: Hosea's themes too were carried south to Jerusalem. In Israel, King Menahem was forced to pay one thousand talents of silver to King Pul (Tiglath-Pileser) who had already invaded Syria in 738 BC. Pekah, 'a captain of the host' or army commander, overthrew Menahem's successor and with Rezon of Syria made war against Jerusalem, then under King Ahaz of Judah, Jotham's son. Ahaz, guided by the prophet Isaiah – '. . . fear not, neither be faint-hearted for the two tails of these smoking firebrands' – repulsed the attack but rejected Isaiah's other advice, yielding treasure and fealty to the Assyrians in total subservience. In 734 BC, taking advantage of Judah's appeasement, Tiglath-Pileser drove down the Syrian/Israeli coast as far as Egypt, in 733 BC taking all Syria with Damascus, Galilee, Gilead and all Transjordan, shipping out the Jewish élite to Assyria and replacing them with Chaldeans and other Babylonians. The Negev, Philistia and Edom fell under Assyrian control, Judah's loss.

Israel was now confined to geographical Samaria. The new king, Hoshea, his territories largely provinces of an alien conqueror, still tried in desperation to represent the permanent spirit of freedom, conspiring with King So of Egypt and, in the process, neglecting to pay his annual tribute to Pul's successor, Shalmeneser V. The Assyrian imprisoned him, depriving the little country of its leader. Even without him, the Israelites, in a resistance whose endurance exceeds even that of Stalingrad or Carthage, held out in Samaria for three years, finally being conquered by Sargon II in 720 BC. 'The king of Assyria took Samaria, and carried Israel away into Assyria' (twenty-three thousand Israelites, chained and half-naked, according to Sargon) 'and placed them in Halah and in Habor . . . and in the cities of the Medes . . . so was Israel carried away out of their own land.' Once again, the Assyrians replaced these Jews, in the broken rubble-strewn cities of Samaria, Megiddo, Shechem and Hazor, with their own Arameans and Chaldeans. Some Samaritans escaped into Judah, some hung on to their faith in exile but, in Israel itself, most of such faithful as remained intermarried with Baalites. It may be that not a hundred Samaritans survive today, while the Ten 'Lost' Tribes of Israel were simply submerged in the culture of Assyria and Babylon, lost not in Japan, Britain, Tibet and other fanciful destinations, but to Jehovah.

Hezekiah, king of Judah, earned the Lord's approbation in almost all things. After Israel fell, however, he disregarded Isaiah's advice – ' . . . if a man lean [on the reed of Egypt] it will go into his hand and pierce it' – by joining Egypt in an internal Assyrian revolution, even attacking the Philistines in Gaza. By 701 BC, Sennacherib had crushed the rebellion, defeated the Egyptians in Philistia, and seized forty-six 'fenced cities' (fortresses) in Judah, including Lachish, taking two hundred thousand prisoners. The clay 'prism' of Sennacherib boasted that he had 'shut up Hezekiah like a caged bird in Jerusalem, the royal city', Isaiah comparing Judah isolated and alone with 'a booth in a vineyard, like a lodge in a cucumber field'. But the king, although his army was greatly inferior to the Assyrians', had improved his city's defences and secured the water supply. Isaiah counselled Hezekiah that, because Jerusalem was the city of David and 'the place of the name of Yahweh of hosts', Judah must resist Sennacherib.

Now the Assyrians sent an army under Marshal Tartan out of Lachish against Jerusalem. The commanders 'stood by the conduit of the upper pool which is in the highway of the fullers' field', and were met by Hezekiah's advisers. Rab-shakeh, Sennacherib's deputy, threatened the Jews with destruction, bribing them also: 'I will deliver thee two thousand horses, if thou be able . . . to set riders upon them . . . and I come and take you away to a land like your own land, a land of corn and wine, a land of bread and vineyards, a land of olive oil and of honey . . . that ye may live and not die, and hearken not unto Hezekiah.' The Assyrian delegation, square-bearded to a man, thunderous and menacing in their red robes, round, pointed brass helmets on their heads, greaves on their legs, buckled cross-belts, swords, circular shields, spoke in Hebrew. The Judaites begged them to talk in Aramaic so that the people would not understand, but they refused.

Through Isaiah, the Lord again told Hezekiah to hold fast against Sennacherib: 'I will send a blast upon him, and he shall hear a rumour, and shall return to his own land . . . he shall not come into this city, nor shoot an arrow there . . . by the way that he came shall he return.' Next morning, far from coming down like Byron's 'wolf on the fold', the Assyrian lines were empty, one hundred and eighty-five thousand dead therein, 'by the Angel of the Lord'. Whether bubonic plague from rodents had struck the invader, or dissent had spread even to within the field armies, or Sennacherib had lifted camp to deal with an Egyptian attack against his forces elsewhere, or with a further outbreak of revolution (the 'rumour') in Babylonia, is unknown. (Sennacherib himself was murdered in Nineveh by his sons.) But Hezekiah was rebuked for later exhibiting his wealth unnecessarily to a Babylonian embassy, Isaiah foretelling that all those riches would be carried one day to Babylon and that the king's sons would become eunuchs in the palace of the king of Babylon. Dying, Hezekiah was granted by Jehovah fifteen extra years of life, to be authenticated by the ten degrees retardation of the shadow of the declining sun on Ahaz's dial-staircase. (The shadow went backwards ten degrees.) After his eventual death, his sons Manasseh and Amon reverted to magical and other Baalite practices. Under their successor, the holy Josiah, the Torah was 'discovered' by the Levites during repairs to the Temple. The Law, together with the teachings of Isaiah and Hosea on love, monotheism, repentance, punishment and redemption, led to major reforms, the revival of the Temple and a change for the better in the people's ethos and morale, attracting support in Judah from peasants and from newcomers to Israel.

Egypt had been almost completely occupied by the Assyrians in the mid-seventh century BC, but Egyptian power had temporarily revived. The Pharaoh Neco, seeing the successful assaults on Assyria by Scythians, Medes, Persians and, above all, by Babylonians, whom the Egyptians most feared, moved on the Euphrates front against the Assyrians, the ancient enemy and destroyer of Thebes. Josiah's army stood against the Pharaoh in 609 BC, not in Judah nor on the Via Maris by the coast, but between Megiddo and the Jezreel valley, falling back on Megiddo after the Egyptians had killed Josiah in his war chariot and defeated his army. Neco then seized his successor, extracting tribute before exiling him to Egypt where he died, succeeded in Jerusalem by another puppet of the Pharaoh and the last Davidic ruler of Judah. But in 605 BC, Nebuchadnezzar of Babylon defeated Egypt at the Battle of Carchemish, Judah becoming Babylon's, not Egypt's tributary, as the prophet Jeremiah had insistently predicted in the visions of the boiling cauldron, the broken pot and the linen waistcoat and in explicit warnings of the Babylonian invasion to come. Yahweh's patience was exhausted: 'Your ways and your doings have brought this upon you. This is your doom and it is bitter. It has reached your very heart.' Jeremiah had heard Jerusalem's death cry.

King Jehoaikim in 600 BC, after three years tutelage, rebelled by refusing to pay tribute. Nebuchadnezzar sent in his Chaldean, Aramean, Moabite and Ammonite raiders against Judah. Egypt and her former possessions from the Nile to the Euphrates were now in Babylonian hands, powerless to help the little kingdom of David. In 598 BC, Nebuchadnezzar invaded with his regular army: King Jehoiachim, Jehoiakin's successor, surrendered in 597 BC, agreeing to his own exile in Babylonia and that of ten thousand nobles, statesmen, warriors, the *gibborim*, administrators, craftsmen and artisans, leaving nothing behind in Judaea but 'the poorest sort of people of the land'. In Babylon, Ezekiel attributed the catastrophe to Hebrew sin, but prophesied their return and the rebuilding of the Temple. Jeremiah fled to Egypt, against his will, wishing only to stay with the downtrodden. The treasures of the palace and the Temple were seized and Zedekiah was made king of Judah by Nebuchadnezzar. But after many years, that Babylonian choice rebelled against his master, with Egyptian assistance, leading his wretched subjects against the might of Nebuchadnezzar. For two years, until famine and superior numbers drove the Judaic army 'by the gate between two walls, by the king's garden' and out of the now ruined city, the Jews resisted the besiegers, being finally trapped in the plain of Jericho.

Here the invader executed Zedekiah's two sons before the king's own eyes, blinding him and carrying him bound to Babylon. The First Temple and the city as a whole were utterly destroyed by fire . . . 'And the pots, and the shovels, and the snuffers, and the spoons and all the vessels of brass . . . the gold and silver . . . the captain of the guard took away' – treasure presumably to contribute to the Babylon ziggurats, hanging gardens and all Nebuchadnezzar's public works, among the seven wonders of the world, made with prisoners' labour. Nebuchadnezzar later thought himself to be an animal, although a herbivore, his nails transformed to claws.

The exile or Diaspora in Babylon lasted seventy years, the caravan road of six hundred miles the only link between Babylon and Jerusalem. The teachings of the Unknown Prophet, the Deutero Isaiah, gradually transmuted the cause from the wrath of the jealous God of Yahweh into the Almighty's doctrine of suffering as the destiny of Jews. Redemption under the Zadok house of Levites, the priests or *cohens*, the *rabbis*, *nasis* (princes), was the other theme. The Jews also, in even less fruitful agricultural land than Palestine, became bankers and merchants. They employed the funds and treasure which Nebuchadnezzar had permitted them to bring to Babylon in enterprises flourishing as far east as today's Calcutta and even further. So that, however heartbreaking, Psalm 137 was not, for everyone, the literal truth:

> By the waters of Babylon we sat down and wept: when we remembered thee, O Sion . . .
> If I forget thee, O Jerusalem: let my right hand forget his cunning . . .

When, indeed, Cyrus the Great formed the Persian Empire with his cavalry, some of the Jews of the Diaspora, military or other collaborators, helped him to add Babylon to his conquests. In return, the Persians under Cyrus and Darius I permitted the Jews' return to Jerusalem. When, in 538 BC, a few tens of thousands under Zerubbabel – some of the original exiled families augmented by Babylonian converts – took up his offer, they found an empty ruined city savaged by Beduin pirates and wild animals, less of it standing than the little that had been left in 597 BC when Nebuchadnezzar ransacked it: no walls, looted, an open city. (Many, if not most, exiled Jews had preferred to remain in the comfort or luxury of Babylon.) Hardly any rebuilding took place until a Jewish noble, Nehemiah, cup-bearer to the Persian king Artaxerxes, received the king's authority to return to Jerusalem with a cavalry unit. He reconstructed the walls and gates of the palace, the pool of Siloam by the garden, the fountains, stairs, the second Temple itself, its timber, silver and gold, restoring throughout Judah the wells, vineyards, olive groves, orchards, refounding the militia and, with the help of the priest or Cohen, Ezra of the Zadok house, rebuilding the city wall as well as contributing a moral and administrative infrastructure. The families started to return to the rejuvenated state, an initial population of one hundred thousand at the most, occupying the city and perhaps two hundred square miles of land.

Artaxerxes, to whom Nehemiah was cup-bearer, was the successor of Xerxes I (the Ahasuerus of the Bible), the misdeeds of whose prime minister Haman led to the brutal massacre – through the intervention of Esther, Xerxes' lovely wife – of seventy-five thousand non-Jews, instead of the extermination planned by Haman of all Jews living within the imperial boundaries. Under the Persians, Jews enjoyed considerable liberty and were pre-eminent in loyalty and good faith.

A new force now burst upon Palestine. At about the era of Exodus, the Greeks' ancestors had begun to move out of Anatolia into the Aegean. By the seventh century BC, the entity which we think of as 'Ancient' Greece had already founded Athens and Sparta, and by 490 and 480 BC, at Marathon and Salamis, had repelled Persian might. It was not, however, until Alexander the Great, Philip of Macedon's son, that the Greeks moved to destroy the Persian Empire and establish their own. After the battles of Granicus and Issus, Barius III surrendered: Greek cities began to rise all over the Middle East. The phalanx, lines of armoured men with huge overlapping rows of heavy spears, different in degree if not kind from the Judaic equivalent, triumphed throughout the empire, in the case of Judaea against only a tiny Temple guard in uniforms as fancy as those of the sentries outside modern royal and presidential palaces, and as ineffective.

As Alexander moved on Palestine and on Jerusalem itself, the high priest, in gold and hyacinth robes, came out to meet him attended by his synod and by all the great men in white. Alexander was deeply shaken, believing that success in his Asian conquests had been promised him by a similar apparition. He kissed the high priest, spared Jerusalem, and permitted the Jews to settle in Alexandria with rich privileges and rights; that city then became the capital of Jewish Hellenism and was inhabited by the Saducees, as opposed to the Pharisees, who remained in Hebraic Jerusalem. Later, under the Seleucid Antiochus, similar immunities were granted to Jews in the Holy City, and to Babylonian Jews given land in Phyrygia and Lydia.

At Alexander's death, Antigonus governed Greece and the islands. Ptolemy ruled Palestine and Egypt but Palestine was later taken (198 BC) by the Syrian Seleucid king, Antiochus III the Great, who also commanded Asia Minor and Syria, administering the Jews of Palestine through their high priests, and granting them liberty and immunities. Jewish anti-Hellenism, representing belief in Mosaic law and in the Davidic succession, grew and became institutionalised in the Hasidic sect and party, opposing both the Seleucid dynasty and Greek or Hellenistic Jews. Meanwhile, 'outside' the former empire of Alexander, the power of Rome began remorselessly to grow and spread, initially into Egypt from which the Seleucid ruler rapidly withdrew his invasion force.

Under Antiochus IV Epiphanes, sacrilege, desecration of the Temple, blasphemy, reintroduction of the Greek pantheon, laxity, interference with the rural economic base, taxation, all provoked dissent among the Pharisees. Circumcision proscribed and the Sabbath outlawed, the Jews took to the hills and to their weapons for the first time in well over three hundred years, driven thither by torture, burning of the sacred writings, massacre, and slavery abroad.

19
The Seleucids and the Maccabean revolt

As well as rebuilding the city and the state, Nehemiah and Ezra had instituted reforms: the enforcement of Jewish law in Judaea, the propagation of the Pentateuch (translated into Greek as the Septuagint), Mosaic Law, the concepts of Atonement and of the Messiah. These, which over the centuries have formed the basis for rabbinical Judaism, were opposed by the 'rationalisation of paganism', by Greek gods and observances, even by Platonism, but were not – are not – as rigorous, pietist or fundamentalist as today's Hasidism. They were a response to undue dilution, even degradation of the Judaic faith and the Jewish ethos, a syncretic 'corruption' to which Hellenised Jewish aristocrats contributed, as rich native subjects have usually done in analogous circumstances.

Then the high priests' abolition of the Mosaic Law, their dedication of the Temple to Zeus or Jupiter Olympias, their fondness for the 'Abomination of Desolation' or pig sacrifice, plus taxation of the farmers to fund a mercenary army, brought these differences to confrontation point. Meanwhile, the Seleucids built and fortified a citadel on a hill opposite to and higher than the Temple in Jerusalem.

Elsewhere, great blocks of stone lie on the hills east of the coast at Tel Aviv, near the village of el-Mikiye or Modiin ('Intelligence' in Hebrew), tombs of the Maccabees. The name Maccabee was derived from the Hebrew word for 'hammer' or, perhaps, from a contraction of their war-cry, 'Who is like unto thee, O Lord.' The village is southeast of the Yargon springs and of the winding River Yargon, banked by citrus orchards and arable fields, north of the River Ayalon over which is a beautiful stone bridge with arched Roman and Mameluke *biberas*, Arabic 'grill' and adjacent lions. Nearby is the site of the ancient town of Lod, olive groves and fruit trees, destroyed by the Romans after they had at last defeated the Zealots in AD 70, and the new towns of Petah Tikva and Ramla. Sycamores, cypresses and casuarinas line the roads and top the hills. (There is a forest here with magnificent vistas, where people from Tel Aviv picnic nowadays.) In biblical times, these hills were terraced and nurtured, the villages not much more than a kilometre apart.

In 166 BC, a Syrian Greek tax collector named Apelles set up an altar in Modiin and ordered an old Jewish Pharisee priest (*cohen*), Mattathias, of the Hasmonean family, to sacrifice and even eat a pig. Mattathias refused, and when a Jew stepped forward to obey, the priest killed both him and Apelles. This happened at a time when Jews of the strict Hasidean party had only recently celebrated a (false) rumour of Antiochus' death fighting the Romans, by throwing the king's priests and officers from the walls of the Temple. This, in turn, led to the massacre of Jews by Antiochus and to the other measures already described. The villagers therefore, after killing the tax-collector's team, formed the nucleus of a resistance movement which fought history's first guerrilla and, then, first main-force war against an occupying power. They struggled for much the same length of time as did the Viet Minh more than two thousand years later. 'And he [Mattathias] and his sons Jochanan, Simon, Jonathan, Eleazer, and Jehudah, or Judas, Maccabeus – the "hammerer" – fled into the mountains and forsook all that they had in the city . . .'

They fled to the rugged heights of the Gophna Hills to the east, pierced like Giap's Cao Bang Hills in Vietnam with caves and grottoes. In the Gophna, as in the Cao Bang, the people fed and watered them, tolerated, then accepted, then listened to them; attracting first a few devoted groups, then the rest of the people, they formed intelligence networks in the surrounding hills and valleys, with good views over the approach roads. Their first efforts were concentrated on compulsory circumcision, destruction of 'Baalite' altars, restoration of the Mosaic Law, punishment of Hellenists, ugly harassment and persecution of the equivalent of the class enemy and, above all, on the creation of a united Judaean guerrilla and, eventually, main-battle army. The first troops were equipped chiefly with slings, maces, swords and shields; there were bowmen, but not mounted archers before the purification of the Temple or even before the time of the Maccabees. There were probably no more than two hundred to start with, none of them with military training, six hundred by 166 BC, to face Apollonius' two thousand when Judas in the first engagement killed the enemy commander, taking his sword and employing it always himself thereafter.

The Seleucid armies, like all 'Greek' units, were deployed in rigorous array. Their core was the heavy infantry, the phalanx, built up from the *syntagma*, sixteen columns totalling two hundred and fifty soldiers, through the *chiliarchia* of one thousand men, to the *strategia* of two hundred and fifty columns and over four thousand troops. Ten *strategiai* counted forty thousand men in an area two and a half kilometres wide, while two *chiliarchiai* (two thousand) made the smallest known battle formation. 'The splendour of their equipment . . . spread dread; the shining brilliance of the arms, marvellously decorated with gold and silver, and the hues of the tunics of the Scythians and Medes blended with the gleam of copper and iron . . . a frightening play of fire . . .'

Each man was equipped with *sarissa* (pike), sword, helmet, shield and greaves and heavy metal or leather body armour. The front five rows of each *syntagma* carried their pikes forward, those behind held theirs upright, a unit on the march looking like a glittering hedgehog. The 'hedgehog', because of the weight of armour and because two hands were required to wield the pike, was sometimes cumbersome, with only difficult access to swords in hand-to-hand fighting. Like a tank, however, which it more or less resembled, it carried immense shock and force. Light and heavy cavalry were deployed on its flanks, and light infantry (the Greenjackets, as it were) in the van. Elephants – illegal under the rules of war negotiated with Rome – and occasional chariots, scythed and otherwise, completed the order of battle, a glorious sight with its gold, silver, yellow, blue, scarlet and white shields and uniforms. Artillery, throwing cannon balls, rocks and arrows, was too static for battlefield use: it was used in siege, sometimes mounted on wheeled towers.

The first success of Judas Maccabeus, who had succeeded Mattathias when the old man died, was a brilliant ambush. With only six hundred fighters he trapped two Seleucid *chiliarchiai* in close order climbing the Levona Ascents. This battlefield was a narrow defile which the Maccabees were able to block, attacking the heavy column from south, west and east, shutting the northern entrance as well. Jammed into this stifling gap, unable to get clear in their heavy mail, the Macedonians and their native allies – their commander dead – were liquidated, with severe losses in arms and equipment then sequestrated by the guerrillas. Morale rose in the Hasmonean camp and so did recruiting figures. Judas then led another ambush, this time with about one thousand men, against a *strategia* of four thousand under General Seron marching slowly up to Jerusalem through the Beth-horon pass. Apollonius' sword in hand, Judas led the assault on the front ranks and on the general himself, at terrifying speed, supported on the flanks by slingsmen and archers . . . In the enemy phalanx 'those behind cried "Forward!" and those before cried "Back",' so that after the swordsmen went in, eight hundred Seleucids, including Seron, were dead, the remainder running towards safety on the coasts of Judaea. Surprise and the prompt elimination of the enemy leader had again brought victory to the Hasmoneans.

By the time of the major battle of Emmaus, Judas probably disposed of a force of six thousand soldiers. Antiochus had appointed a viceroy who selected three generals, Ptolemy, Nicanor and Gorgias, to deal with these turbulent rebels. To avoid further catastrophe in the Judaean hills, they settled into a base camp at Emmaus, their forces estimated at between twenty and forty-seven thousand men, intended to seal the Jews into the mountains or destroy them if they came down into the plain. Judas, his troops apparently organised in 'modern' battalions, companies, platoons and sections, formed the men into four groups of fifteen hundred men at Mizpah, each under a Hasmonean brother, himself, Simon, Jochanan or Jonathan, their presence 'announced' to the Seleucids by religious ceremonies and bonfires. The ruse deceived Gorgias. At dusk, the general moved to attack the Jewish camp. Judas, forewarned, had already flown the coop with three thousand men, making for the main Seleucid camp. He left behind a decoy company which, in ostensible retreat toward Jerusalem, harassed Gorgias. At Emmaus itself, one Maccabee unit of fifteen hundred men was placed north of the imperial camp, while Judas attacked the main garrison in its vast phalanx with his own paltry three thousand. 'Fear ye not their multitude, neither be ye afraid of their onset. Remember how our fathers were saved in the Red Sea . . .' Judas, although outnumbered, had the advantage of the hills – and of military genius – attacking the waiting phalanx *in the flank*, piecemeal, in hand-to-hand combat, while his northern battalions burst into the camp itself. In the chaos, Nicanor's troops escaped to Gezer (Gezara), to Idumea, Ashdod and Jabneh. When Gorgias returned from chasing will-o'-the-wisps, he found his camp ablaze, so fled to the coast with his men, leaving gold, silver, purple uniforms and saddles behind. Seleucid authority was in question. The Maccabeans controlled and occupied most of Judaea outside Jerusalem.

At Beth-zur, Judas again took on an army superior in numbers and armaments, still largely Greco-Macedonian but now with fairly significant quantities of half-trained oriental mercenaries, all under the personal command of Viceroy Lysias. Once again, he trapped his over-burdened enemy, this time from the steep, sloping banks of a gully, whence they fled to Beth-zur, whose garrison joined the retreating units in flying on to Hebron to conserve local strength against contingencies elsewhere in the empire. The Hasmoneans, although they did not assault the citadel, now entered Jerusalem, rededicating and purifying the Temple. It was on this occasion that the little cruse of oil – 'enough' only for one day – burned for eight days in the *menorah* or sacred candelabrum, the origin of Hanukkah, festival of lights. Troops under Judas and his brothers Simon and Jonathan moved to towns in Galilee and Gilead across the Jordan to defeat the persecutors, from Acre, Tyre and Sidon, of Jews in the outback. At Dathema and Raphon they defeated Seleucid forces about to enter both cities over the wall.

Judas then besieged the citadel, a strategic error, since it led to the hurried return from Antioch of Lysias in command of another large army, boasting elephants, chariots and cavalry as well as light and heavy infantry. The indirect approach, guerrilla tactics, hit and run, now had gradually to yield to larger and heavier units, some knowledge of siege warfare, conventional frontal and large-scale action on plain as well as mountain, with Jewish forces now amounting to as many as twenty thousand men and more, at least after the taking of Jerusalem. Not all these troops were employed in every battle, but they were in place, as was their potential for recruitment in Judaea, a contrast to the relatively limited pool of military settlers available to the Seleucids. The latter were also restricted by imperial commitments elsewhere, and by their reluctance to incorporate many 'orientals' in the front line.

On the way northwards to Jerusalem via Beth-zur, Lysias fought the Jews from the high ground as well as on the plain. The Seleucids had learned something of mountain warfare by this time and, at the fight at Beth-zechariah, they also had the alarming psychological advantage of lumbering elephants to add to the effect of the phalangites' implacable forward advance. (Judas' brother, Eleazer, was killed by a falling royal elephant, which he had stabbed in the stomach from below.) Judas broke off the battle, falling back through Jerusalem to the Gophna, leaving a small garrison around the Temple to hold out until Lysias offered a peace treaty. Judas, in guerrilla mode, then ambushed General Nicanor at Kfar Shalem and a much larger force at Adasa, where Nicanor was slain, his troops retreating to the coast, harassed by villagers and soldiers as they went. 'And the land of Judaea was tranquil for a few days' – not surprisingly perhaps in the light of the public dismemberment of Nicanor: 'They cut off the thumbs of his hands and feet and hung them at the gates of Jerusalem . . . a mouth that used to speak arrogantly and hands that used to be brandished at Jerusalem.'

King Demetrius I of Syria, learning of a treaty between Judas and Rome, sent twenty thousand infantry and four thousand horsemen under Bacchides to stamp out the Hasmonean rebellion for good and all. In the more relaxed circumstances in Judaea after the earlier Maccabean peace with Lysias, Judas could put only three thousand men in the field, of whom all but eight hundred deserted after seeing the vast army of the Seleucids. His men, seduced by home life and the 'piping' days of peace, were 'sore afraid, and many vanished from the camp'. Judas' 'heart broke . . . let us go up to our enemies, perhaps we will be able to fight them'. The men urged shelter in the hills, not running away but living to fight another day when numbers would have recovered, but their commander refused: 'If an end is near, let us die bravely for our brothers, and we shall not leave behind us an offence to our honour.'

The enemy horsemen were in two massive formations. The slingers and archers were in front of the phalangites, Bacchides' phalanx on the right. Both sides blew their trumpets. Judas, as was his practice, led his little band hell-for-leather at the commander, breaking the right-wing phalanx, pursuing the enemy into the foothills, although in turn pursued and harried from the rear by the left phalanx. Bacchides, grasping this change, turned his fleeing force to face Judas. Judas, caught between the two superior bodies from behind and in front, was killed, the Hasmoneans defeated. 'And Jonathan and Simon carried Judas, their brother, and buried him at Modiin: How is a hero fallen, the saviour of Israel.'

Like Giap, he had constructed a powerful army with the impelling requirement of 'freedom and independence', using terrain on his terms, mastering surprise, mountain warfare, night tactics, guerrilla warfare, flexibility and, finally, embarking on successful main force action. His army did not fade away, but, in the end, was strong and large enough to wrest independence from the empire. He *was* a great captain.

But four of Mattathias' sons had been killed, before Simon – who led the army which Judas had made – accepted in 143 BC the Seleucids' offer of independence. In 139 he renewed also the peace treaty which his elder brother had signed with Rome. The Hasmonean Dynasty was established, to rule the Second Kingdom of Judah for seventy-six years. They entered the citadel 'carrying palms, to the sound of harps, cymbals and zithers, chanting hymns and canticles, since a great enemy had been crushed and thrown out of Israel'. This 'great enemy' was, of course, not so much the Seleucid conqueror, but the moderate Hellenist Jewish reform movement.

20
The Jewish surrender to Rome

Simon was murdered by his son-in-law in 135 BC and his son John Hyrcanus was installed as ethnarch and high priest in his place, ruling for thirty years with the intention of unifying Judaea and Samaria under Jewish rule, part of the inheritance of King David. Hyrcanus, employing mercenaries from Macedonia and assisted by Parthian cavalry – originally raised in the former Persian Empire – not only destroyed the Syrian Seleucids but conquered and *converted* the Galileans, Samarians and the Idumeans (Edomites) south of Judaea in the Negev and elsewhere, the old Edom.

Hyrcanus' succession had itself been hideously marred by the lashing, torture and final murder by his son-in-law, before his eyes, of his mother and brothers on the battlements of Jericho. The fate of his own victims was little more agreeable, although less appalling than that of those slaughtered by his monstrous son, Alexander Hannai, massacring, crucifying and driving into exile the persecuted Pharisees, bringing the great Hasmonean dynasty to an end in civil war with the Sadducees. Thus was the gate opened to Pompey in 63 BC and, thereafter, to the eventual triumph of Rome. Pompey behaved well, not laying a finger on the golden lamps, lampstands, tables, cups, censers, or the spices and sacred money in the sanctuary. Hannai, on the other hand, crucified eight hundred prisoners, forcing them to watch the butchery of their wives and children. After Pompey's defeat at Pharsalia, Caesar assumed power in Judaea, first through the Idumean, sly Antipater, then the latter's son (the Roman selection as 'King of the Jews'), exterminating all but one of the Hasmonean dynasty. The survivor was Antigonus who recaptured Judaea, expelled the Romans, and once more declared Jewish independence, himself biting off the ears of his uncle, Herod's brother, in Jerusalem. In 37 BC, Antigonus was overthrown by Herod and he and the whole Sanhedrin put to death. 'If ever a man was full of family affection,' Josephus wrote, 'that man was Herod.'

Despite the paranoid Herod, Palestine – now centred in Galilee and governed from Caesarea rather than Jerusalem – flourished under the dynamism of the Jews, guided by the wise Hillel who said: 'To love thy neighbour as thyself. That is the whole law, and all the rest is commentary,' adding, about self-esteem, 'If I am not for myself, who will be for me? And if I am only for myself, what am I?' To Herod, desolate that no tears would be shed at his, 'the Great King's', death, a crony proposed the coincident murder of Hillel, when *all people everywhere* would mourn.

But under the Roman procurators, Greek-speaking gentiles, governors in name but thievish tax-farmers in fact, the rage and misery of the small landowners and the looted aristocracy broke out in a series of 'small' rebellions including that of Spartacists. These, it is fair to say, did not occur under Herod's rule, with its superb programmes of public works in Palestine itself. (In the Diaspora, six million Jews now trebled those in the motherland.) Mob risings took place in AD 6, in AD 44, and in AD 54, and were mainly apocalyptic. 'The end of days, when the heavenly host will give forth in great voice, the foundations of the world will be shaken, and a war of the mighty ones of the heavens will spread throughout the world [and] the people shall be delivered . . . And many of them that sleep in the dust of the earth shall awake, some to eternal life . . .' On the whole, Pharisees and Sadducees accepted foreign rule or, at least, compromised, even sometimes collaborated with it; while the Essenes totally withdrew from communal life into monasticism at Qumran, source of the Dead Sea Scrolls. But other Jews, the Zealots, saw salvation in revolution, independence, allegiance only to God and certainly not to the Emperors of Rome, following, as it were, Hasmonean traditions, in a campaign of grumbling guerrilla warfare and subversion, beginning as early as AD 6 under Judah of Galilee.

For these Jews, apart from all the other issues described, Greek–Jewish animosity, even hatred, was now an additional factor in the demand for revolution against a Roman military presence which was itself Grecophone, and against other anti-Semitic Hellenised Jews monopolising the administration and the board rooms, vulgar, incompetent and brutal. This party of rebels, the Zealots, was itself divided between its original components – dispossessed farmers, bandits, religious fanatics, murderous paranoiacs, assassins, xenophobes. In the end, the movement died of its own divisions but, in the beginning, the Roman legions under Vespasian suffered widespread defeat by an ably led force of Jewish dissidents. The latter's success was aided by the relative absence from Jerusalem of Roman troops, the main cantonments being in the equable climate of the Mediterranean coast with its Grecophone settlements.

The triggers for the rising were pulled in Jerusalem when Procurator Florus mocked the Jewish faith and its accoutrements, and in Caesarea where the Greeks mounted a pogrom against the Jewish quarter, the Roman garrison failing to intervene. Florus then demanded vast sums in 'protection' money from the Temple, the Romans attacked and robbed the Upper Town, Hellenists assaulted other Jewish centres, and the Zealots – with accretions now from Sadducees, Pharisees, Christians, even Essenes – at last mounted full-scale attacks against the Roman garrisons throughout Palestine, unity once more achieved. The Roman soldiers in Jerusalem were driven out or massacred to a man and the commander of troops in Syria, Cestius Gallus, advancing on the Holy City via Acre, was repulsed in the outskirts of Jerusalem, his force of six thousand men cut to pieces in the subsequent rout.

The Zealots were originally, in the main, small farmers in the intensive terraced agricultural economy to which we have referred, dispossessed by greedy tax-farming procurators from little vineyards, grainfields, steadings with a few cattle, goats, sheep and chickens in the green valleys of Galilee and all over fertile Judaea. The Negev, Idumaea and Transjordan, harsh, often desert land, offered little alternative. Their ranks included the Sicarii, called after their murderous daggers (*sicae*) employed against Jewish trading caravans or the Romans or in broad daylight among crowds in the open Knesset of the day. Later, operating from Masada under Menahem and Eleazar, they abandoned their roles as highwaymen and political assassins to bind together in small 'armies'. In this, they were aided by the Edomites or Idumeans, converted to Judaism by Hyrcanus and thus subjected to the brutalities of Herod and the Arabs, and by those Palestine Jews who, although victimised by the Sicarii themselves, found hope and safety only in armed revolt against Roman rule.

The Roman emperor, Nero, despatched Vespasian, his most successful commander, to Judaea with four legions under his hand. This general, aided by 'treachery' among Jewish notables such as the historian and former military captain, Josephus, recaptured within three years most of the fortresses taken by the Jews in AD 66 in Judaea and on the coast. He had deliberately waited before attacking Jerusalem, on Montgomery's principle of preponderance of force and, possibly, on a calculation that the Jewish revolutionary alliance might eventually become self-destructive. In AD 69, Nero died and Vespasian assumed the purple, an event already prophesied to him by a Pharisee, Jochanan ben Zakkai, in whose honour Vespasian permitted the foundation of a Jewish academy or *yeshiva.* (Jochanan had been smuggled alive out of the dying Jerusalem in a coffin, his bearers alleging plague.) Vespasian then appointed his son Titus as his successor with the favourable odds of eighty thousand Romans against ten thousand Sicarii in the Upper City and much of the Lower, two thousand 'non-Sicarii' Zealots in the Antonia and the Temple, five thousand converted Edomites and six thousand men led by John of Gischala, some of the latter in exclusive support of the Sicarii, nearly all of them no more than untrained peasants and shepherds.

Under Titus, their commander (the ultimate irony) was a Jew devoted to the Romans, Julius Tiberius Alexander, Nero's governor of Egypt who, like a Hapsburg, placed the empire above his own people and took only five months to accomplish the fall of Jerusalem. Like Lord Samuel, the British Jew appointed by the British as high commissioner of Palestine during the Mandate, so was Tiberius appointed by the Romans to be 'their' procurator of Judaea.

Inside the Holy City, the wretched and unhappy residents were forbidden to leave. Hungry and even starving, their plight was worsened by the arrival of miserable and homeless refugees from all over Palestine. The Romans had laid waste the land, seizing all domestic animals, destroying the terraces, eroding the precious soil, wrecking the forests, at the precise moment when, in Jerusalem, the Sicarii took the mad decision to burn the food stocks. Now communal fighting began in Jerusalem, Zealots and Sicarii, later aided by Idumeans, against Pharisees and Sadducees alike, stiffened by dispossessed Samaritans. The city burned and ran with blood, helpless against anarchy; the Sicarii had massacred the Pharisaic militia and the Levite Temple guard.

> It was as if, to oblige the Romans, they were destroying all that the City had laid up against a siege and ham-stringing their

> own powers . . . the bodies of natives and aliens, priests and laymen, were piled on each other, and the blood of men and beasts formed lakes in the sacred courts . . . old men and women [even] prayed for the Romans to come.

But, Julius Tiberius Alexander did not attack, although for three or four days he staged an enormous and glittering military parade of infantry and cavalry round the walls, battering rams in readiness. Still the Jews did not surrender. He then assaulted the city directly, first with 'guns', hurling vast white and black rocks weighing half a hundredweight each, and then breaking down the north wall with battering rams. Yet, once in the breach, the Romans were driven out repeatedly by the Jewish garrison who also, by subterfuge, destroyed the tall Roman bombardment platforms. Titus' troops were reinforced by Antiochus' Macedonian-trained units, himself deciding, however, that the better part of valour was to complete a supply blockade of the Jews by means of an impenetrable wooden wall built by Tiberius. In the meanwhile, some of his troops were caught opening the bellies of Jewish deserters to extract gold coins secreted in their intestines. A total of six hundred thousand Jewish 'paupers' were thrown out dead from the city gates, while their corrupt commanders melted down the vessels in the sanctuary. 'The innumerable corpses were a revolting sight and emitted a pestilential stench.'

A small Roman legion unit then took Antonia, without being able to hold the sanctuary, although the army built a road to the Temple. In the city, 'open-mouthed with hunger, like mad dogs, the desperadoes stumbled and swaggered along, hammering at the doors like drunken men and in their helpless state breaking into the same houses two or three times in a single hour'. One woman, Mary of Bethezub, roasted her baby son, eating half and offering half to others. The sanctuary itself was soon fired, the Temple hill a sea of flame. The Romans took the Lower City, burning it to Siloam, then seized the Upper City from platforms, while the Jews fled into the sewers or to the citadel. Tiberius destroyed the whole city, leaving only the massive towers intact, the Temple obliterated for the second time, the town for the fifth in its long history. Terrible crimes were committed by the victors – rape, carnage, looting; prisoners were despatched into slavery, or to make a raree-show in the Colosseum, or to be hurtled for a laugh from the Tarpeian Rock. The Jews had been great fighters, not unworthy losers, defeated not by superior courage, but by greater numbers and heavy equipment: the expulsion by Titus of the majority from their country was an act of horrid vengeance, even if they were largely absorbed by kinsmen in the Diaspora.

Some Zealots and Sicarii under Eleazer bar Yair escaped from Jerusalem to join a Jewish group who had, in AD 66, taken from the Romans the vast honey-coloured rock of Masada, thirteen hundred feet high on the edge of the desert, with a vertical fall to the Dead Sea. From this base, the rebels continued harassing operations against the Romans for two years until the fortress wall lay open to the Tenth Legion under Flavius Silva. Looking defeat in the face, Eleazer and the other nine hundred and sixty defenders decided to take their own lives by cutting one another's throats in this astonishing mountain outpost, fortified by Herod the Great seventy years before. Eleazar said: 'I cannot but esteem it as a favour that God hath granted us, that it is still in our power to die bravely and in a state of freedom which hath not been the case with others who were conquered unexpectedly.' All were dead, except two women hiding in a cave, when the legion broke in next morning through the breach made by its battering ram.

> And so met the Romans with the multitude of the slain, but could take no pleasure in the fact, though it were done to their enemies. Nor could they do other than wonder at the courage of their resolution, and at the immovable contempt of death, which so great a number of them had shown, when they went through with such an action as that was.

Today's Israeli army recruits spend their last night of training in this tragic fortress.

Further Jewish rebellions broke out, this time in the Diaspora – Cyprus, Egypt and Antioch – which took the emperor (Trajan) three years from AD 113 to suppress. The cause of these risings was partly the anti-Semitism of the authorities: the later decision of the emperor (Hadrian) to build a temple to Zeus in Jerusalem was, perhaps, the identifiable trigger for the last revolt of all, that of Simon Bar-Kokhba, which endured from AD 132 to 135.

The Jews had sought a messiah. Bar-Kokhba never referred to himself as 'the Messiah', but he was so designated ('son of a star') by the great scholar Rabbi Akiva: 'This is the great Messiah.' (Others believed differently, reading his name as 'son of a deceiver'.) Not even all the rabbis followed Akiva, Johanan ben Torta commanding: 'O Akiva, grass will sprout between your jaws, and the son of David will still not have come.' Certainly, excavations on the west coast of the Dead Sea indicate that he was a secular administrator, a *nasi* or prince of Israel, hard, direct, authoritarian, a practical man commanding orthodox Jewish followers devoted to Mosaic Law and custom, like the nationalist revolutionaries of 1948.

Hadrian sent Julius Severus, victor in Britain. Even he, with greatly superior forces (twelve legions), was unable to defeat Bar-Kokhba or reverse his territorial gains in open combat. It was not until Severus adopted a policy of siege, wedded to aggressive scorched earth – killing everything that breathed, and burning everything that did not – that the Jews surrendered, all Judaea a desolation. Both the leader and the rabbi were tortured to death, the flesh torn from Akiva's body by iron combs; very few prisoners were taken, most survivors fleeing to Parthia; the Holy City – other than the Wailing Wall – was henceforward forbidden to all Jews. But when Hadrian reported his 'triumph' to the Senate, he had to omit the usual address: 'I and the legions are in health.'

The Jewish state was finished. The Jews renounced war and, with the exceptional 'mercenaries' we shall now encounter, lived without that bloody institution for over one thousand eight hundred years.

21
Diaspora

The history of the Jews in the Diaspora is punctuated by terrible persecutions that went largely unresisted. But alongside these persecutions there is a parallel history of assimilation. In the face of anti-Semitism, Jews often adopted the aspirations of the nations that became their adopted homes, they began to make their mark in all areas of government and public service, the arts and sciences. This history, to this point recounting the prowess of the Jewish people, will become a record of individuals.

Rome, the Imperial City, was taken and sacked in AD 410 by barbarian tribes out of Asia and the North. Elsewhere, under the Sassanid Empire of former Persia and Babylon, the Jews of the Diaspora gradually formalised Jewish thought, including the Torah, in the Talmud, its legal, ethical and scientific exegesis. In Palestine, the 'new' name for Judaea and Israel, the Greek Orthodox Byzantines of the Second Rome, who had there succeeded to Rome's sovereignty, imposed anti-Semitic persecution on the Jews, as well as generally oppressing Christian minorities. In AD 614, the Persians took Jerusalem, the Byzantines returning to massacre the Jews in 629 before themselves being overwhelmed in Palestine and Syria by the armies of Mohammed out of Arabia.

Into Arabia, where isolated Jewish communities had lived for centuries, Jewish immigration substantially increased after the massive Sassanid-Byzantine struggles of the fifth and sixth centuries. Date cultivation, jewellery fabrication and, eventually, international commerce were introduced. Arabia, Syria, Palestine, Egypt, the North African littoral, parts of the Byzantine Empire, Africa, Spain and France all fell to Islam, until Martel held the Muslims at Tours. As 'People of the Book', at least after the Prophet's death, the Jews shared in these advances, contributing to science, medicine, philosophy and mathematics under their Islamic masters. But Islam was not monolithic. It was divided by the profligacy of its individual rulers, split between the Shia followers of Ali and the orthodox Sunni, separated between the Fatimids in Egypt, the Abbasids in the Levant and the Ummayads in

Damascus and, later, in Spain. The Seljuk Turks, the Tuareg, the Almoravids threatened them, and the Mongols were even closer to destroying them. From the West, the storm gathered which presaged invasion by the Crusaders – Christian knights with their forward 'base' in Constantinople – of the Holy Land and of the Holy City of Jersualem itself.

The Crusades began with pogroms of Jews in Hungary by the French Peter the Hermit, looting and atrocities against Jewish communities in Germany in order to raise cash for the journey, and massacres by German crusading bully-boys in Prague. During the siege of Jerusalem in the First Crusade, the Jews in the synagogue were burned alive in an outburst of ethnic cleansing to accompany the slaughter of Muslims in the al-Aqsa mosque, mistaken by the Crusaders for the Temple of Solomon to which they believed themselves heirs. To raise money for the Second and subsequent Crusades, further bloodshed and extortion were necessary among French, German and Central European Jews, seen often as the Antichrist; Jerusalem itself became almost emptied of them, their Talmud execrated. Later, during the European religious wars, Luther preached anti-Semitism – 'On the Jews and Their Lies' – advocating destruction of property, suppression of faith, slave labour, thus accelerating Jewish refuge (first in Venice) in ghettos, and in an exodus out of Germany on the roads to Poland and Eastern Europe. In Germany, including Cologne and Frankfurt, the Jews were not quite passive in the face of massacre, defending themselves when they could.

By the seventh century, the Jews of the Diaspora had settled in the Persian Empire, in Egypt, in Phoenicia, Spain, perhaps even in Cornwall, later throughout the Greek and Latin worlds, in France and in Germany, often with their own synagogues. By the ninth century, the Jews – frequently barred from agriculture – had secured a brief but almost complete mastery of the intercontinental trade, by land *and* sea, between Europe, the Middle East, India and China; Khazaria, stretching from the Don to the Volga, that kingdom of steppe warriors converted to Judaism, remained in the faith for nearly three hundred years until defeated by the Duke of Kiev. By the Middle Ages, Jews had established themselves in England, the Netherlands and yet more widely throughout Germany, until gathering anti-Semitic opposition forced them eastwards into Poland, Lithuania, the Ukraine and Russia, a view admittedly challenged by the Khazar theory, to be outlined later.

Spanish persecution and pressure to convert to Christianity, coupled with attacks from Berber and Almohad invaders had driven even the 'secret Jews' – *conversos* or *marranos* – whose contribution to the Ummayads had been so large, to flee Spain for Portugal, the Americas, Turkey and Greece. Their choice had been baptism or extermination. By 1478, they had begun to be deprived even of that. When in 1492, Christopher Columbus, himself sometimes thought to be of Jewish birth, sailed westwards, most of the Spanish Sephardic population had been thrown out of the country, a residual total of two hundred thousand. The loss in skill, vision and culture was as much a disaster for Spain as it was for the Jews.

The Ashkenazi, Yiddish-speaking Jewish refugees from the horrors of armed German brutality, became most comfortable and influential in Poland where, indeed, they fought with the Poles against the Turkic tribes. Certain rights were guaranteed them by the Statute of Kalisz, extended eastwards when the powerful Polish state conquered Galicia, Transylvania, Belorus, Lithuania and the Ukraine, a happy solution diminished by the spreading influence of German traders and the Catholic Church united in militant anti-Semitism, as opposed to the decency of the royal and aristocratic families. But for one hundred and fifty years, the Jews under the Jagiello House (1386–1572) were a force in Poland, with their own courts, schools and partial self-government. Their role, however, as administrators and bureaucrats in the occupied territories, led to the Chmielnicki massacres by Ukrainian Cossacks in over seven hundred Jewish villages. It has been estimated, probably wildly, that between a quarter and half a million Jews died in those dark, snow-bound, icy wastes. There may have been fewer, but the circumstances were no less cruel.

Jews were excluded from Tsarist territory until the partitions of Poland in the eighteenth century, when they were restricted to the Pale. The Austrians expelled them from Prague in 1794, but readmitted them in 1798. French Jews were granted emancipation by the National Assembly in 1791, and further encouraged by Bonaparte for his own reasons. In London, the revolutionary Lord George Gordon, popularly known as The Honourable Israel bar Abraham Gordon, hung the Ten Commandments on his Newgate prison wall. Earlier in England, about five thousand Jews had been expelled in the thirteenth century, a ban lasting until the seventeenth century. In the eighteenth century, Holland became the first country to admit Jews to Parliament. Jews in Scandinavia, particularly in Sweden, had had for long a strong commercial presence. In Venice, they were initially confined to the Giudecca and, then, to a ghetto in the Cannareggio, which stands today. Under the Hapsburgs, in the German principalities, and under Bismarck, they had been frequently treated in the eighteenth century in civilised mode, achieving both position and prosperity even after the failure of 1848.

Russia inherited the Jewish populations after the Polish partitions, ill-treating them ignorantly but systematically, peasants, bankers, landowners, scholars, traders alike. (The Pale covered twenty-five Tsarist provinces in former Poland, White Russia, Ukraine, Bessarabia, Crimea, and outside it only a very few privileged Jews could move without special permission.) Jews were forbidden residence and employment in the villages, to run village inns, to wear the skull cap, to participate in a whole range of humble trades hitherto open to them. They were continually and humiliatingly harried by police measures over residence codes, even over their own appearance. With effect from 1887, they were banned from branches of the public service and from officer status in certain armies. The state incited other minorities against them, forced them towards baptism and, to add to harassment over education, conscription and residence, organised (in Elisavetgrad, Kherson, Kiev and Odessa) murderous pogroms accompanied by massive expulsions. The Jewish response to these measures was the great voluntary exodus from Baltic ports of over two million Jews to the United States, of hundreds of thousands to Western Europe including Britain, and of thousands to Palestine. Millions more had to stay where they were under Alexander III, whose solution to the 'Jewish problem' was 'one third conversion, one third emigration and one third starvation'.

But, in Germany and some other countries of Western Europe, the Industrial Revolution had now produced a class described by one observer as the 'frayed-white-collar class', insecure and as open to anti-Semitism when the capitalist was the bogey-man as when the communists were the Aunt Sally. These wretched people, theorised upon by Gobineau, Nietzsche, Céline, Houston

Stewart Chamberlain and so on, were manipulated by Hitler and the Fascist demagogues to present Jewry as scapegoat for society's ills and as battlecry for Fascist ambition, culminating logically in the real aim and intention of extermination. 'Kill the Jews' was the single-minded executive programme, ending in Belsen, Auschwitz, Treblinka, Ravensbrück and Dachau. Besides that project, Jewish contributions in science – Einstein, Fermi, Niels Bohr; in finance – the Rothschilds, Hambros, Samuel Montague; Spinoza in philosophy; such musicians and actors as Rubinstein, Schnabel, Bernhardt and Reinhardt; publishers like André Deutsch and Victor Gollancz; Proust, the novelist of the century; Sigmund Freud; painters from Gaudier-Brzeska to Gertler to Bomberg to Chagall; statesmen like Disraeli and Léon Blum . . . none were of any significance whatsoever, even when their contributions were not detested.

'Between the acting of a dreadful thing / And the first motion, all the interim is / Like a Phantasma or a hideous dream.' The final horror prepared itself to which, except in Warsaw, some of the camps, and on the long road out of Europe to Zion, there was little organised Jewish resistance.

We should nevertheless record those Jews who, mostly from the dates of the respective national Acts of Emancipation in the nineteenth century, fought for 'their' countries in causes they judged right, with valour and decency. These men, like the biblical heroes, were in the minds of Herzl, Weizmann and Ben Gurion as they pondered on the future armies of that State of Israel which, throughout two World Wars, was the Holy Grail to which resistance had to be subordinate.

Unlike the fighters of the Old Testament working for their single cause in a single location, united in time and space, these later Jews served many masters in a multitude of regions over two millennia. The causes were various, often separated by countries and huge distances without an apparent common factor, a bewildering variety of states and ideologies. But, in the end, their contributions in the Diaspora merged into the mainstream of Judaic courage leading to Jerusalem.

PART II

22
Khazaria, a Central Asian Jewish state

Dunlop's *History of the Jewish Khazars* informs us that in the eleventh century, a Jew named Solomon ben Duji, aka ben Roy, wrote letters from Khazaria to Jews in neighbouring countries and even further, advocating an armed Jewish crusade to retake Palestine for Judah. He claimed to be Elisha, his son Menahem the Messiah. Nothing seems to have happened for twenty years until Menahem or David Al-Roy, proclaiming himself openly to be the Messiah, took a fortress near Mosul with a force of Khazari and other Jews, with whom he planned to march on the Holy Land through Edessa (Urfa) and Syria.

David Al-Roy (on whom was based Disraeli's novel *The Wondrous Tale of Alroy*) sent messengers to Baghdad ordering the Jews of that city to spend a certain night on the roofs of their dwellings whence they would be taken – 'airlifted', in the modern phrase, presumably on clouds, carpets or other conveyances – to the Messiah. The Jewish leaders in Baghdad, however, took fright and, coincidentally or otherwise, David was assassinated in his sleep by their or another unattributable hand. It has been suggested, without firm evidence, that the shield of David which doubles with the Seal of Solomon as an Israeli national emblem, derives not from King David, but from this adventurer.

Khazaria, the country of the Turkic Khazars, from AD 740 a Jewish state, lay north of the Caucasus mountains between the Azov and Black Seas to the west and the Caspian or 'Khazar' Sea to the east. Khazar fortifications stretched from the Crimea in the Ukraine and the Caucasus to the Urals and the Aral Sea. At their peak in the eighth century, the Khazar military dominated territories which also included Armenia and Georgia; in AD 679 they covered the area of present-day Bulgaria. There seems no reason to doubt that their authority was permanent until the eleventh century, protecting Byzantine and Eastern Europe for almost three hundred years from equally uncouth steppe raiders and, later, from the Vikings or Rus. They broke the Arab armies of the Caliphate attempting the Asian assault on European civilisation, as Charles Martel broke them in Europe at Tours. In the eighth century, after a Khazar victory over the Arabs, the Byzantine Emperor Constantine V was married to Irene, a princess of the Khazars, and their son, King Leo IV, was known as 'Leo the Khazar'.

The Khazars were one tribe of many, including the Huns or Hsiung-nu, known as 'Turkic', forced westwards out of their steppes by the Chinese over four centuries from the first century AD to the fifth. Their name comes either from *qazmak*, to wander, or *quz*, the north side of the mountains. In the fifth century they were identified in the Caucasus, subjects – like the Magyars, Kipchaks, Bulgars, Pechenegs and other barbarians – of Attila and, for a short period after his death, of the West Turkic Empire. They were described as Gog and Magog, wild, white men with the manners of beasts, drinkers of blood, blue-eyed, hair flowing and reddish, insolent, broad, lashless faces, attributes admittedly applied by Arab sources to most unknowns. Thenceforward, from the seventh century, it was the Khazars who ruled the Kingdom of the North: it has been said that the word 'hussar' derives from them.

Their first major campaign, with forty thousand horsemen, was in alliance with Emperor Heraclius and resulted in the defeat of the Persian Empire. The first Muslim armies then prepared *their* assault on the Sassanid Empire – ultimately against Byzantium – but were defeated by the Khazars in the Caucasus and on the banks of the Caspian throughout the eighth and ninth centuries. Khazar military expansion into Georgia, Armenia, the Ukraine and the Crimea, and their defeats of the Magyars and Bulgars did not always have permanent results. But although the Muslims penetrated Khazaria, Khazar Jewish troops holding the Caucasus blocked the eastern route to Byzantium. Complementing Martel in the West, they helped to break the dual Muslim onslaught against Western Europe. Through Justinian, whose wife Theodora was a Khazar, they placed an emperor of their choice on the throne at Constantinople.

At Sarkel on the Don, the Khazar Empire, but not Khazaria itself, ended in defeat by the Rus Prince Svyatoslow of Kiev, the conclusion of the Khazar-Rus (Viking or Varangian) wars of the ninth to eleventh centuries. 'I guard the mouth of the river, and do not permit the Rus who come in their ships to invade the land of the Arabs . . . I fight heavy wars with them,' said the Khazar King Joseph, at a time when he was seeking to avoid hostile Caliphate interference. To this king, tributaries had paid sometimes a sword, and sometimes a white squirrel skin, per hearth.

The Khazars were civilised in comparison with the Volga Bulgars, and with the Ghuzz whose punishments included splitting the accused in two, with the Bashkirs who ate the lice from their underwear, the Rus who hanged people arbitrarily in order to invoke the mercy of God, or even the Emperor Justinian who suspended debtors upside-down over fires. They were, largely through re-export and taxation of transit goods, relatively rich, prosperous enough both to maintain a standing army to form the sheet anchor for Khazar hegemony overseas, and to produce an artistic culture which may have been the ancestor of Hungarian gold and silverwork.

The role of the Khazars in defending the Byzantine Empire would obviously be irrelevant to a work concerning Jewish military commanders, were it not for the unique events culminating in their conversion to Judaism in AD 740. After the collapse of the Sassanid Empire and the West Turkish Confederation, the major powers in West and Central Asia became the Khazars, the Caliphate and Byzantium. To have adopted Islam or Christianity might have secured temporary survival, but hardly independence, a position which the military Khazars were determined to maintain.

Conversion from paganism was, nevertheless, thought essential. The country was no stranger to Jews, who had been expelled in large numbers from Byzantium and to whose beliefs the dual (sacred and secular) leadership of Khazaria was accustomed. This circumstance was not central to the selection of a religion, which both Arab and Hebrew accounts depict as a disputation before the Khazar king between Muslim, Christian and Jewish representatives. (In one version, however, the Jew poisons the Muslim before the conference begins.) In all accounts, King Bulan chooses Judaism for the casuistic and evidently political – *raison d'état* – considerations suggested above, i.e. a Third Force. A Christian source refers to 'Gog and Magog, Huns, the Khazari, who were circumcised and observed Judaism in its entirety', a fully Jewish state.

The Khazars in their capital of Itil or Atil, on the northwest shore of the Caspian, had thus selected the Jewish faith because they intended to maintain their military and political strength, to be submissive in other words to no one. This determination endured until Vladimir of Kiev was baptised in the Orthodox faith and married a princess of Byzantium, when the alliance between Constantinople and Itil against the Rus ended. The alliance between Russia and Byzantium then began with the invasion of Khazaria in 1016 and with the defeat of the Khazar king and army. But Kiev could not resist the nomads who now stepped into the consequent power vacuum: Kumans and Seljuks defeated Byzantium and wrested control of large areas hitherto part of the Byzantine Empire which form modern Turkey.

The last known reference to the once Judaic State is from the journal of the Franciscan monk, de Plano Carpini, on his voyage to Batu Khan's capital in 1245, which does no more than list among tribes in the Caucasus, 'Khazars observing the Jewish religion'. Darkness descends with Genghis Khan's invasion and the establishment of Mongol rule in Khazaria, by which time the Kumans had, anyway, become the Khazars' overlords.

Subsequent Khazar emigration has been claimed, with Kumans, Pechenegs, Magyars and others, to have been mainly westward to the Ukraine, Poland, Hungary and Russia. There are those who assert that the bulk of the Ashkenazi Jewish population in Eastern Europe was not Semitic, originally from the Jordan, forced eastward by anti-Semitic German pressure, but Khazars driven west by the *furor Mongolicus*. Place names, isolated linguistic and trade similarities with antique Khazaria, dress (kaftans and so forth), have been used to make the case, as have massacre, the Black Death, the savage reduction of Western Jewry in Germany, and arguments about German components of Yiddish. It is not a problem capable of resolution, nor is it one in which conventional historians seem happy to engage. There is, nevertheless, anthropological and other evidence of the continued presence in Europe of descendants of the Khazars, including connections between them and Turkic speaking Karaites in the Crimea and Poland.

23
Lambert Simnel and Sir Edward Brampton

One consequence of the Hundred Years War between the British and the French in the fourteenth century was that succession to the British throne during the Wars of the Roses lay more often through violence than through peaceful descent. The pious, weak, but blameless Henry VI was first exiled, then murdered by the Yorkist Edward IV, whose throne at death was seized by Richard III, defeated at Bosworth by the Lancastrian Henry VII. Thus ended the Wars of the Roses, a consummation signalled by the king's marriage to Edward IV's daughter, Elizabeth.

Henry's reign was harassed by pretenders including Lambert Simnel (the 'kitchen-boy') and Perkin Warbeck. Simnel's attempt, impersonating the Earl of Warwick, was backed by the Dutch. Warbeck, whose final landing in England was actively opposed by Irish loyalists was, nevertheless, initially supported by the Earls of Desmond and Kildare when he landed in Cork, splendidly dressed as an employee of a Breton silk merchant. He was then trained in Ireland in his supposed identity as Edward IV's son, Richard Duke of York, the younger of the two 'Princes in the Tower', murdered by Richard III, their usurping uncle. In that capacity, he secured fairly widespread support in Germany, France and Scotland, in the pretence that he had been spared by Edward V's assassin on condition that he lived abroad incognito.

He was, however, according to his confession before execution, born in Tournai of commoner parents (father a boatman) in 1474, living thereafter in Antwerp, Bergen and Middleburg. He left in 1487 in the train of a Lady Brampton for Portugal, where he entered the service of a one-eyed Portuguese knight called Peter Vaxz de Cogna, as well as 'of one Edward, a Jew and godson of the aforementioned King Edward: for my master was on terms of the greatest familiarity with King Edward.'

The Jew, his master, was Sir Edward Brampton, in whose wife's household the boy Peter (Perkin) was serving, 'Edward, once a Jew, but afterwards saved in the sacred font by the King.' In England, the name of Edward *Brandon* is first remarked in 1468, inscribed in the records of the Domus Conversorum, the 'Home for the Converted' for foreign Jews – in this case Portuguese – all formally godchildren of, or 'sponsored' by, the reigning monarch, Edward IV. The 'home' was founded by the devout Henry III and was seldom empty, continually recharged from continental persecution of the Nueves Christianes – converted Jews – the inmates awarded a stipend of $1\frac{1}{2}$d *per diem*. From 1472, he disappears from the Domus, reemerging as *Brampton*, a more English form of his name, and receiving benefits for his 'good service to the king in many battles', perhaps a euphemism for espionage, or for work on the Anglo-Portuguese treaty or, even, for active fighting at Tewkesbury. In that year, he became captain of *Le Garce*, probably a privateer, and in 1473 he was naturalised an English subject by the king at Greenwich, becoming one of the first Jews by birth to attain that status.

He married a rich Northamptonshire widow in 1474, and was granted her property in 1480 after her death; he remarried a few years later. In 1481, in exchange for paying certain sums owed by the king to Portuguese merchants, he received the right to ship wool from English ports to North Africa without customs, acquiring renown in the city and at court. It was perhaps at this date that he began 'the greatest intimacy with King Edward and his sons', later to become so significant.

Edward IV died in 1482, but not before having appointed Brampton as Governor of Guernsey. In this capacity, Brampton was employed at sea to chase and seize the late king's brother-in-law, Sir Edward Woodville, but the latter escaped to Henry Richmond (later Henry VII) in France. Meanwhile, Brampton supported Richard III in his seizure of the throne and in the subsequent struggles against rebels:

Sir William Catesby Bad news, my Lord: Ely fled to Richmond;
And Buckingham, backed with the hardy Welshmen,
Is in the field, and still his power increaseth.

King Richard . . . Go muster men: my counsel is my shield;

> We must be brief, when traitors brave the field.
>
> Shakespeare, *Richard III*

The king awarded him £350 from customs duties on his goods in English ports, and, in 1484, specifically for his work in the field against Richmond and Buckingham, knighted and endowed him with a large estate in Northamptonshire, the first Jew to receive such honour. Soon afterwards, he was given a manor which had formerly belonged to the Duchess of Somerset and, for *undefined services*, received a substantial annuity for twenty years.

At Richard's death, or, rather, after Henry VII's investiture, all Brampton's land and houses were confiscated, and his governorship of Guernsey ended. The world had turned upside-down. Brampton left for the Low Countries where the other Yorkists were sheltering in exile. He did not long remain there, leaving with his family in 1487 for Lisbon. In his wife's train was a Tournai boy named Pierrequin de Werbecque, hitherto working for a merchant of Middleburg. Sir Edward would talk in detail and at length about London and, in particular about the court of Edward IV, at which he himself had been so considerable an ornament; accounts to which de Werbecque listened with rapt attention. 'Old men forget; yet all shall be forgot/ But he'll remember with advantages/ What deeds he did that day.' This course in first-hand history and manners was the basis upon which Perkin Warbeck, for he and de Werbecque were one and the same, was able to speak good English and to simulate what could have been the life of the real Duke of York.

In 1492, Warbeck wrote to James IV, King of Scotland, signing as 'King Edward's son'. In the same year, he went to France as Charles VIII's guest, thence to Flanders where he visited Margaret, Duchess Dowager of Burgundy, who welcomed him as her nephew, 'the White Rose'. Henry VII broke off commercial relations with Flanders, when rioting broke out in England. Warbeck attended the Emperor of Austria's funeral in Vienna: Maximilian, the Emperor's son, recognised him as Richard IV, King of England, while both Maximilian and Philip of Austria ignored Henry's threats and warnings. Warbeck promised to restore to Margaret and Maximilian Yorkist properties torn from them. Conspiracies were launched and a small fleet of ships financed. The fleet landed Warbeck's troops at Deal in 1495; they were repulsed there and at Waterford with heavy casualties. Henry VII bribed one of the conspirators, Sir Robert Clifford, with £500. Clifford revealed the identity of most of the plotters. Many, including Sir William Stanley, the Lord Chamberlain, were executed as a result.

Warbeck married Catherine Gordon, James IV's cousin, but military incursions into Northumberland by him and the King of Scotland were completely ineffective. An invitation by Cornish rebels to land there as 'King Richard IV', although it provided him with about three thousand troops, ended in his ignominious retreat to Beaulieu – after reverses at Exeter and Taunton – where he was arrested, paraded through the streets and sent to the Tower, there breaking parole. A number of degrading and absurd ventures followed before Warbeck was hung from the Tyburn scaffold on 23 November 1499. 'That,' said Sir Francis Bacon, 'was the end of this little cockatrice of a pretender king' – one who would have been very dangerous indeed had it not been for the vigilance and determination of King Henry VII.

As for Brampton, after a visit to Lisbon by a delegation from King Henry in 1489, the knight was pardoned and all his lands and possessions restituted. This Jew had instructed no winner and certainly no champion, but he had played a part, admittedly unwitting, in the adventures of the most vexatious of all Henry VII's military challengers and one who, however unsuccessful in the end, spent six years among the kings and emperors of Europe convincing them of his *bona fides* as the true and proper king of England.

24
The 'New Christians' of Latin America

In the seventh century, because the Visigoth kings brutally persecuted the Jews of Spain, Judaism became a secret thing, its adherents – driven to 'adopt' the Christian faith – known as *conversos*, *marranos* or New Christians.

These, therefore, when the Muslims invaded Spain at that time, hastened to help the invaders. In the process, by their own arts, courage and skill, they created autonomous Jewish areas in a number of Spanish towns, including the Ummayid capital of Cordoba. They prospered, although threatened by wilder Muslims, Berbers, Almoravids and Almohads, who offered the same harsh choices – death, conversion (this time to Islam) or flight to North Africa.

Christian anti-Semitism began again in the thirteenth century with anti-*converso* riots, based largely on blood-libel. It assumed full force with the establishment in the fifteenth century of Torquemada's Inquisition. Those bitter interrogations resulted in poverty, imprisonment and death for tens of thousands of Jews. In 1492, after the Moors too were defeated by the Catholic armies, the Edict of Expulsion drove a hundred thousand Jews into Portugal, and fifty thousand to the Middle East and North Africa; from Portugal, many were similarly expelled to Europe and the Americas.

Several sources believe that if Columbus himself was not Jewish, members of his expedition were, especially Luis de Torres 'who had been a Jew and knew Hebrew and Chaldean'. Certainly advice and instruments were provided by Abraham Zacuto, court astronomer to King John II of Portugal, and by Joseph Vecinho, Zacuto's pupil and physician to the Portuguese king. Charts, sailing directions and so forth were supplied by maritime and hydrographic institutes with Jewish staff in Majorca and elsewhere in the Mediterranean. (Finance was organised by New Christians at the Court of Aragon, Luis de Santangel, Gabriel Sanchez and Isaac Abrabanel.) Columbus, nevertheless, always claimed that his discovery of America was based, however loosely, on prophesy, not on astronomy, specifically Isaiah XI, verses 10–12. Before his fourth and last voyage, he said that his sole remaining objective was to liberate Jerusalem, again on biblical and prophetic, not scientific, lines.

His preferred name was Colón, a common name in medieval times among Jews in Italy but, despite Genoese 'nationality', he spoke no Italian and even fought at sea under Guillaume Casenove-Coullon for Portugal against Genoa. (The *Encyclopedia Judaica* refers also to a disputed claim that he was a *marrano* from Majorca.) Columbus was given to mysterious boasting about his relationship to King David, and displayed a strong liking for Jews and Moors. 'His signature was susceptible to a Hebraic interpretation.'

It is curious, furthermore, that his log of the voyage to America begins with a reference to the expulsion of the Jews from Spain, and, later, refers in Jewish mode to the Second Temple as the 'Second House', dating its destruction to AD 68, the preferred Jewish date for that event. He postponed his departure for the Atlantic to 3 August, refusing to sail on 2 August, the extremely ill-favoured Jewish anniversary and fast-day commemorating the destruction of the Second Temple.

One historian believes that even the great Hernando Cortés – 'stout Cortés . . . silent, upon a peak in Darien' – was a Jew. Various witnesses, including Gonzalo de Mexia, have alleged that the captain general deliberately avoided distribution of the edicts promulgated from headquarters in Spain or Santo Domingo against the descendants of Jews and of Moors expelled from the mother country. He was, indeed, accused of 'sheltering, protecting and providing Jews with country estates', probably not excluding his cousins, the de Pas y Nuñez, descended from Ines Gomez de Paz, one of the sisters of Martin Cortés, in whose house in Salamanca Cortés once lodged. Some assert that the public clerk of Salamanca, who was Cortés' prosecutor in all his court cases, was a 'New Christian'. Cortés also owed a great deal to the merchant Juan de Cordoba, a leading figure among Seville *conversos*, whose money helped Don Hernando to undertake the conquest itself of Mexico, the 'New Spain'.

One of the conqueror's main objectives was to avoid the continual denunciations and counter-denunciations among his people caused by the proclamations of the Holy Office, leading to expulsions, sequestration of funds, death by burning and other horrors, at the hands of the Holy Inquisition. During the government of the first Audiencia, as lax with 'New Christians' as was Cortés, only two men were expelled from 'New Spain', one a trader from Vera Cruz and the other a clerk from Mexico who was eventually readmitted anyway.

It is the case that as many 'New Christians' took part in the conquest of the Americas as in the Portuguese expeditions to Africa and Asia, in regular armies to Goa, Mozambique, Angola and the Philippines, as well as in the capacity of mathematicians, astronomers, chart-makers, sailors and shipbuilders. In sixteenth-century Peru, for example, one of Francisco Pizarro's captains, Rodrigo Orgoñez, was the son of a Jewish cobbler whose wife had been persecuted as a witch. Both parents were *conversos*. His name was taken from a nobleman, Juan de Orgoños, who flatly denied the soft impeachment of fatherhood, despite being bombarded by Orgoñez with presents in the form of gold and silver artefacts, accompanied by the plea that: 'It be understood by whatever means that I am legitimate and could thus have the habit of a Knight of Santiago.'

He fled his birthplace, Oropesa, to escape, like Kenneally whom we shall meet later, the consequences of a brawl. He fought in the Italian Wars, helped to capture Francis I at Pavia and then sailed with his brother, Diego Mendez, to Central America. In 1533, Francisco Pizarro, the governor of Peru, sent him with four other captains to reconnoitre the approaching Inca army under Rumiñavi. They found nothing, 'no fighting men, nor any with arms, but everyone was at peace . . .', so that the governor wept – 'his eyes wet with tears' – that he had in the meanwhile unjustly strangled Inca Atahualpa to death. Orgoñez fought well against the Quitan forces at Vilcas but then, through over-confidence, the *conquistadores* were badly cut about by Indians charging with arrows, maces, battle-axes, javelins and stones at Vilaconga, before Cuzco. It was from Cuzco itself that Pizarro sent Marshal Almagro to explore Chile in the hope that that country would absorb the marshal's ambitions and cupidity. Orgoñez was selected, leading five hundred and seventy Spanish cavalry and infantry, as his second-in-command, also commanding great trains of indigenous porters and twelve thousand non-combatant native levies loyal to the Inca Manco.

By 1537, the Spaniards – Pizarro on one side and Almagro on the other – were heading for civil war, a divide matched by that among the Incas between Manco and Paullu, the first supporting Pizarro's General Alvarado and the second providing ten thousand auxiliaries for Orgoñez and Almagro, spying, digging wells, mounting deception operations, building rafts. Almagro seized Cuzco in April, capturing Hernando and Gonzalo Pizarro, thereafter defeating Francisco Pizarro's forces at Abancay in July.

Almagro then sent Orgoñez with three hundred Spaniards to capture Manco. The dashing and glamorous young adventurer climbed the mountain tracks to defeat the Indians at Amaibamba but Manco himself got away. Next day, Orgoñez looted Vitcos, again failing to catch Manco. He returned to Cuzco with mummies, idols and a golden image of the sun, first rescuing Rui Diaz and other Spanish prisoners, seizing fifty thousand llamas and alpacas and transferring twenty thousand natives.

But at the Battle of Las Salinas in April 1538, Orgoñez was captured by the Pizarrist forces, executed and his head displayed in Cuzco; his will, made before Abancay, left forty thousand ducats, with slaves and horses, chiefly to his brother, but to his parents as well. Hernando Pizarro also killed Almagro by the garrotte but Orgoñez's brother, although in prison, survived. In all these battles, the Incas protecting their gold - and jewel - encrusted stone buildings, 'some black and rough and others seeming of jasper', fought with courage and tenacity, shouting and uttering shrill battlecries against vast Spanish technical superiority.

25
An Italian Jew at the court of Ranjit Singh

A young Frenchman visiting the 'Lion of the Punjab', Ranjit Singh, in the earlier part of the nineteenth century, found himself quartered in a delicious oasis with a parterre of roses, carnations and irises, orange trees and jasmine, where little fountains played. The 'King' of the Sikhs sent him grapes from Kabul, rich fruits and a purse of five hundred rupees which were followed by a dinner in torchlight, served by a host of servants richly dressed in silk. Monsieur Jacquemont, a fairly odious young poseur, complained freely about his host's conversation and mean appearance – 'like a nightmare' – while being offered five Kashmiri girls from the royal seraglio, all seated on a Persian carpet.

Such delights were also enjoyed by European officers recently imported by the maharajah to train his Sikh and other troops. One of these was a colonel of Italian infantry, Rubino Ventura, a Jew from Modena mistakenly referred to as having been born 'Reuben ben Torra', who had fought as an auxiliary under Bonaparte at Wagram (where an Alsatian Jew in Austrian service nearly defeated the emperor) and in the Russian campaign. He had, thereafter, accompanied by a French cavalry colonel of similar experience named Allard, served the Shah of Persia until that monarch's financial unreliability made their task impossible. Together they moved on through Afghanistan to Lahore, ending up at the great serai attached to Jahangir's tomb; Ventura, a good-looking young man, was elegant in person and wore a long beard.

After infantile attempts by the maharajah to trick them into admitting that they were really English, (the Sikh kingdom had not yet been forcibly incorporated into the British Raj) they agreed to train raw troops, but *not* existing formations. Ranjit told them that he wanted to send his armies under their command to 'settle' Peshawar and then to take Kabul and Kandahar in Afghanistan. Ventura and Allard tactfully suggested that those tasks might more properly be undertaken by his own *sirdars* who, indeed, became resentful of the prominence given to the foreigners.

Nevertheless, by 1824, Ventura – his salary beginning at 500 rupees a month and reaching 3000 rupees in 1826, plus subventions of 800 rupees, had raised four battalions of infantry, three cavalry regiments (grenadier, dragoon, and life guards), and an artillery component of twenty-four guns and 835 men. The infantry wore red coats, white trousers, black cross belts, and turbans rather than the British shako. Gurkhas under command wore green faced with red from which the British Rifle Brigade and 60th Rifles' uniforms are said to derive. The maharajah's payments to both officers and men were irregular and, at one period, sepoys could only afford a meal every third day. Men appeared on parade without shoes: in 1836, Ventura was said to be owed two years' pay.

Ranjit, in return for the higher pay he theoretically awarded to European officers, demanded that they abstain from beef, smoking and shaving; that they 'domesticate' themselves through marriage; remain on station unless permitted to quit; and fight *all* the maharajah's enemies, including their own countrymen if necessary. In 1825, Ventura did 'domesticate' himself by marrying an Armenian girl, Elisabeth Marguerite, dark and handsome daughter of a French father. (Her sister married the English commander of the personal guard to the Begum of Ludhiana.) Ventura's wedding presents from the maharajah and the *sirdars* were valued at 40,000 rupees.

The general built a house for his wife, who soon bore him a daughter. It was pillared on the first floor, and the entrance floor was decorated with an enormous mural illustrating his and Allard's reception by Ranjit. The second public room was hung with looking glasses in gilt frames; another carried pictures depicting Ventura's military triumphs, quite without regard to perspective, cavalry wheeling about in the air. A large foyer led to the bedrooms.

Behind the house lay the old tomb of Anarkali in which Allard and Ventura had lived on arrival, and which Ventura retained as his *zenana* or seraglio, with a harem of Kashmiri and Punjabi girls. (It later became a Christian church and, later still, a storeroom for Sikh government archives.) His use of the *zenana*, and other infidelities of the general, eventually led to Madame Ventura's departure for Ludhiana where she died in 1870, deprived at the general's death of his income and existing only on a small *British* pension. Her daughter, Victorine, married a French aristocrat, de

Trazegnies d'Ittre, and spent a lot of time trying unsuccessfully to induce the French ministries of war and foreign affairs to recognise her financial claims on the French state. The latter, in effect, denied all knowledge, despite Ventura's senior membership of the Légion d'honneur: 'Rien aux archives.' But in 1835 Victorine had at least been granted an estate worth 2,500 rupees by the maharajah, as well as a horse with a gold saddle and 12,000 rupees in cash, at the same time as the rulers had given land (*jaghir*) valued at 21,000 rupees to her father.

In 1827, a British officer reported that Ventura's troops had performed in manoeuvres with steadiness, precision, closeness and accuracy. In 1838, the great General Havelock communicated that the drill of seven infantry battalions, four regiments of cavalry and as many troops of horse artillery under Ventura's command was as impressive 'as might be seen in the Champs de Mars'. Another observer said in 1837 that they fired with greater precision than any troops he had ever seen, their light-infantry work as good as East India Company regiments. Others, however, implied that their steadiness on manoeuvre was not always repeated in the field.

Ventura's first action in command of the 'Francese Campo' was at the Battle of Naushera in 1823. By a flanking attack after the failure of Ranjit Singh's frontal assault, he defeated the Afghans – killing four thousand – occupied Peshawar and returned to Lahore after collecting tribute in the Kangra Valley and Derajat. He then successfully besieged the great hill-fort at Kotla, the entrance to the Kangra Valley, by cutting off the river which supplied the garrison. With Jemadar Khushat Singh, he suppressed a rebellion in Gandgarh and took the hill-fort at Srikol from the Pathans, going on to fine Yar Mohammed Khan, who had probably financed the Gandgarh rebellion.

In 1828, Ventura's brigades, under the nominal command of Sher Singh, overcame the forts at Terah, Riah and Pulhar, absorbing Kangra definitively into the maharajah's dominions. Later, the general intimidated a powerful frontier leader, Syed Ahmad Ghazi, into evacuating Peshawar. Ventura destroyed the Syed and his forces at Bala Kot in 1832. His success in raising forced contributions in the Derajat caused Ranjit to make him governor of that region, where he not only 'shook the pagoda tree' but greatly benefited the economy of Multan. Suggestions that he subsequently became governor of Kashmir and chief judge of Lahore do not seem to be corroborated in the records.

In 1837, the general went on leave to Paris without his wife, returning to Lahore in 1839 before proceeding to Peshawar to organise the tripartite (British, Ranjit Singh and Afghan) force preparing to place Shah Shujah on the Afghan throne in Kabul. Unfortunately, not only did Ventura's Gurkhas mutiny, but Ranjit Singh died, requiring the general's return to Lahore. From that base in 1841, he re-established law and order in the Kulu and Mandi districts, capturing two hundred hill-forts, including Kumlargh, a chain of fortified hills extending for twenty miles. In order to deter desertion among his men, he cut off the noses and 'blackened the faces' of some half-dozen recaptured deserters, a punishment repugnant enough but hardly comparable to the multiple hangings enjoyed by his colleague and compatriot, General Avitabile.

Anarchy now broke out in the Punjab and, after the assassination of Sher Singh in 1843, General Ventura left for France, having settled money on his wife in Ludhiana. In 1848, he returned to Lahore in order to turn his property there into ready cash, receiving more than £20,000 from the British Government in cash and annuities for his property. He was awarded the title of Comte de Mandi after the campaign there, dying in Toulouse on 3 April 1858. Ventura's contacts with officers of the East India Company offer presumptive evidence that, between 1837 and his retirement from service in 1843, he may have been engaged by the governor-general or by one of the latter's subordinates as a British secret agent.

He was trusted and liked by Ranjit Singh, if not to the degree achieved by Avitabile and Allard, rougher 'Sergeants' Mess' individuals. (Avitabile was not only a murderer, but vulgar, ostentatious and corrupt. Although in old age he co-habited with at least nine young women, he was betrayed by them all.) Nevertheless, in response to a direct challenge from the ruler, General Ventura succeeded in seducing Ranjit's favourite dancing girl – 'she loves me as much as I love her,' had said the one-eyed, wizened, five-foot Sikh – extracting her from the seraglio under the noses of the royal guards. The nautch-girl soon, however, returned without recrimination on anyone's part to her original protector, eventually joining his corps of mounted Amazons.

Ranjit Singh on one occasion, believing all Europeans to be mechanically omniscient, asked Ventura to make him a paddle-steamer with his own hands. Having secured 60,000 rupees from the maharajah, the general contracted the task to an Englishman in the Lahore service. The two-decked barge with hand-operated paddle-wheels, probably costing only 2,000 rupees, would not navigate further than ten yards or so upstream. But the maharajah was content that Western science had been matched in his own realm by the construction of a vessel without sails or oars, but including gun-ports armed with swivel guns. In the fore and aft cabins he gave a vast, alcoholic *tamasha*, complete with dancing girls.

The general also pleased the maharajah with the provision of cool water during the summer, achieved by filling a well during the winter and keeping on the lid until May. He acquired too a reputation as an archaeologist, discovering gold, silver and copper coins, rings and medals of the Sassanid period through the excavation of *topes* or *dhagobas* and forwarding them to the British authorities at Calcutta.

For truthfulness and meritorious service rendered to the maharajah, General Ventura was granted the title of 'Faithful and Devoted'. Although he was at the same time promised the rank of 'Great General', this honour does not seem to have been ratified.

26
The first Jewish Admiral in the Royal Navy

Dr Meyer Leew Schomberg was a German Jew who settled in England in the 1720s, finding – through friends in the Bevis Marks Synagogue – a lucrative practice in Fenchurch Street, which led on to the office of physician to the Great Synagogue in Duke's Place. He was a contumacious man, accusing Ashkenazis and Sephardis alike of breaking the Mosaic Law, while simultaneously attacking Judaism itself. His children in effect abandoned the faith, in the fifth son's case in order to join the Royal Navy, a service forbidden under the Test Act to all except members of the Church of England.

This son, Alexander Schomberg, first served in the *Deptford* of fifty guns, then in the *Suffolk* for four years from November 1743; in 1744 at Dungeness his ship was involved in an encounter with the French fleet, which in spite of being bloodless caused a French withdrawal. The *Suffolk* then sailed for the West Indies, capturing prizes in the form of twenty-four large vessels before returning in convoy. No doubt the ship's company received prize money, less percentages for Greenwich Hospital and the prize agent himself, from prize agents and 'slop sellers', many of whom were also Jewish, Isaac Levy in the Minories, Abraham and Lewis Moses in Portsmouth. Slop sellers were a combination of loan-shark and clothier who advanced money, uniforms and so forth at discount, against prize orders which might not themselves 'mature' for years.

From 1747 to 1756, he had two periods of half-pay, but served in two fourteen-gun sloops (the *Horner* and the *Speedwell*) and in the *Medway*, of sixty guns, which cruised off Finisterre, looking for French convoys. In 1757, he was promoted post captain from the *Intrepid* (he had qualified for a lieutenant's certificate in 1747) and commanded, first, the *Richmond*, of thirty-two guns, and then the *Diana*, a new frigate with thirty guns and two hundred and twenty men in extremely congested conditions.

The *Diana* sailed for Canada in 1758 to blockade the French at Louisberg on Cape Breton Island; later she was joined by the main fleet under Boscawen. She and six other frigates covered

General Wolfe's landings through the surf under the enemy's batteries, until all troops were safely ashore. She then damaged by gunfire a French sloop while herself taking casualties. In July, six hundred British seamen boarded the *Prudent* and the *Bienfaisant*, seventy-four and sixty-four guns, at which the governor surrendered Cape Breton and Prince Edward Islands. A medal was struck for this action, awarded to those like Schomberg who had fought well.

Back in Portsmouth, Schomberg reported to their lordships that seven of his men had been killed during the battle, twenty-nine had died of fever, and eight older sailors had deserted once they were home. Presumably with the completed complement he had requested, the *Diana* sailed with forty-nine other ships plus troop transports again for Louisberg. When that harbour was free of ice, the fleet embarked General Wolfe and his soldiers, proceeding one thousand miles up the St Lawrence Seaway and anchoring on 26 June a few miles below Quebec. In avoiding collision with a sloop, the *Diana* ran aground and was hit by French artillery. After she had lightened ship – top gallants, top mast, guns, powder, ballast overboard or in the ship's boats – she was pulled off by sister ships, missing the surrender of Quebec.

Nevertheless, she was back again in April, after refitting, to take a French store ship as prize. Ashore, the French Army had defeated General Murray in an attempt to retake Quebec. The British retreated into the city to await reinforcements. The *Lowestoft*, the *Diana* and the *Vanguard* then arrived, forcing six French warships aground. Quebec was relieved and, although the *Lowestoft* sank, the *Diana* took off her entire crew and rejoined the fleet.

Schomberg was unwell and went home on relief, carrying the commander-in-chief, Lord Colville's, despatches. (He left behind in the *Diana*, among others, Midshipmen Isaac Lewis and Samuel Morris and able seamen Francis Silver and John Morris.) He was, on recovery, appointed Captain of the *Essex* (sixty-four guns), part of a large squadron under Keppel which, with ten thousand troops, took Belle Isle. He came ashore in 1763 after the Peace of Amiens when the Seven Years War had ended, married a parson's daughter called Arabella Chalmers and had five children, all of whom he had baptised.

Schomberg returned to sea in temporary command of the *Prudent*, together with his nephew Lieutenant Isaac Schomberg.

In 1771, he commanded the Lord Lieutenant of Ireland's yacht *Dorset*, against the wishes of the First Lord of the Admiralty. ('He is either extremely indigent, infatuated, or may think my situation at the Admiralty not permanent.') In any case, he thereby debarred himself from flag rank or from further active service, but was knighted in 1777 and, in 1789, published *A Sea Manual recommended to the Young Officers of the Royal Navy as a companion to The Signal Book*. In the meanwhile, the *Dorset* carried despatches between Dublin, Holyhead and Milford until his death in 1804. He and his wife were buried at St Peter's, Dublin.

His eldest son (who died in 1850) became Admiral Sir Alexander Wilmot Schomberg, while the younger, Charles March Schomberg, served at the Nile in the *Minotaur* and was later flag captain to Sir Sydney Smith. In 1811, in the *Astrea* at Mauritius, with two other frigates and a sloop, he encountered three large French frigates, of which the *Astrea* obliged the *Renommée* to strike her colours. He became commander-in-chief at the Cape from 1825 to 1832, and then lieutenant governor of Dominica.

Captain Isaac Schomberg, who served in the *Prudent* with his uncle, was First Lieutenant of the *Pegasus* in Dominica when that vessel was commanded by Prince William, later King William IV. The prince was a martyr to gonorrhoea, drank too much, worried incessantly, was always short of money, issued absurdly strict punishments, including flogging for drying wet clothes on deck or for using that 'horrid expression, *Bugger*, so disgraceful to a British seaman'. When Isaac Schomberg protested, Prince William demanded a court martial from Lord Nelson, then on station, who weakly arrested Schomberg, but persuaded William to drop the demand.

As soon as Schomberg arrived back in England, he was posted as first lieutenant to the *Barfleur*, Lord Hood's flagship, which appointment drew a bellow of rage from the prince as 'an attack on [his] professional conduct', equal to Lord Howe's 'disapproval of [his] conduct about Lieutenant Hope', whom William had sent home in disgrace for visiting Schomberg in his cabin under arrest. Schomberg later commanded the *Culloden* at the Glorious First of June in 1794, and wrote a major work, *Naval Chronology, or an Historical Summary of Naval and Military Events from the Time of the Romans to the Treaty of Peace, 1802*.

Also with Schomberg at the Glorious First of June, but as a

master's mate in the *Thunderer*, was a Sephardic Jew named Donald Fernandez. Fernandez had taken baptism, joined the navy in 1790 as a midshipman, and had served in the *Assistance* and the *Thunderer*, with Lord Bridport off Groix, then in the frigate *Lively* in Lord St Vincent's fleet at the Battle of Cape St Vincent. He was subsequently in flagships *Victory, London* and *Princess Royal*, commanding the brig *Speedwell* (fourteen guns) in 1803, thereafter on half-pay as a commander. Other Jewish officers included Captain Maximilian Jacobs, who had been senior officer on the St Lawrence River and captain of the *Defiance*, where he put down a mutiny, later attacking Charleston and Savannah (taking Port Royal) in the *Europe*, then going to pension on the Captains' List.

On the lower deck, only Church of England members could join the navy, although the press gangs did not ask their victims for details of their religion. Many Jews, furthermore, despite the suspicion in which they were often held, still volunteered for a life of hammocks, the lash, salt pork, rum, foul air and low deckheads, intense crowding, brawls. The watch below was shaken at 0400 hours, decks scrubbed, hammocks lashed and stowed, work done until dinner and the tot of rum. Boat, gun and other drills followed; hands went to quarters after supper. Watches were four (hours) on and four off, starting at midnight, with the midnight, morning, afternoon, first and second dog watches (two hours each, between 1600 and 2000), then the first watch of four hours from 2000 to midnight.

Richard Barnett, immigrant Jew, kept a log in the *Vanguard*, recording the events of the Battle of the Nile, where his ship lost 165 men, commenting later without vivacity on the sights of Messina, Palermo and Naples, on the kings of Sicily and Naples, on Nelson, on Sir William and Lady Hamilton. The *Vanguard* paid off in 1800, Barnett receiving £3 14s. in prize money from the Nile. In 1802, he deserted at Portsmouth, one of five hundred a month at that time; he was never discovered, but a certain John Levy was, and was flogged round the fleet. In the *Victory* at Trafalgar was Moses Benjamin, a seaman, and on the *Britannia*'s gun decks were four London Jews, all volunteers, Joseph and Nathan Manuel, Henry Levi and Benjamin Solomon, sweating, blackened and half-naked. Philip Emmanuel in the *Colossus* survived the battle; Emmanuel Brandon in the *Revenge* did not.

A less attractive Jewish enterprise, akin to the activities of the slop sellers who took the sailors' money, made them drunk and then pressed unwanted kit on them, was 'crimpage'. This was defined as the persuasion of seamen to desert from a ship in order to deliver them to another ship for payment, usually to a merchant ship and often to East Indiamen. 'Crimps' were frequently publicans or innkeepers who filled the seamen with drink, and passed them down the line to the next shipowner. In London, the centre of operations was Leadenhall Street, full of lodging houses, hidden streets, petty criminals and prostitutes, where the sailor was made drunk in the evening, put to bed, intoxicated again in the morning and chased off staggering to India House where the crimps got their pay as well as the owner's bounty before sending them down river. Guilty names included Goodman Levi, Asher Nathan (supplying Royal Naval seamen to the East India Company), Lewis Lazarus, Samson Samuel and Henry Nathan . . . But there were Anglo-Saxons too, Phillips and Mitchell and Phipps: the Jews were in the majority, but had no monopoly.

27
Poland

In 1791, King Stanislas Poniatowski of Poland agreed to a constitution which provided some religious freedom, taxed the nobles and instituted the hereditary principle for monarchy. Austria and Prussia acknowledged and, indeed, guaranteed this constitution, but when the Tsarina, Catherine the Great, invaded Poland, those two greedy powers hurried to share the spoils and, in 1794, to help defeat General Tadeusz Kosciuszko's gallant uprising against Russia. In the partition of 1795, independent Poland was extinguished.

Lively debate in country and Parliament (*sejm*) between 1785 and 1792 on the subject of Jewish emancipation had persuaded the Jews to join the Poles against the projected partition of Poland and Lithuania. When Kosciuszko's revolt exploded, he was joined by a light cavalry unit of five hundred Jews formed by Colonel Berek Joselewicz, born in Lithuania in 1765, who had married (Rebeka) and settled in Praga, a suburb of Warsaw. This formation – possibly the first Jewish military organisation since the Bar-Kokhba rebellion or, at least, the Khazars – was cut to pieces in Praga itself by General Suvorov in 1794.

Joselewicz had been the agent or factor of Prince Massalski, Bishop of Vilna, who had sent him abroad on several commissions where he had acquired a knowledge of French. After Suvorov's victory, he escaped to France where, in the Polish legion commanded by General Dombrowski under the Emperor Napoleon, he crossed the Alps, was promoted to captain of dragoons and awarded the Légion d'honneur. On return to Poland, after helping to form the Grand Duchy of Warsaw in 1807, his detachment was incorporated into the Polish army in which he became a squadron leader, commanding two squadrons of Prince Jozef Poniatowski's cavalry in the Austrian campaign of 1809, and received the Virtuti Militari. Although his career was hampered by anti-Semitism, he was respected by Polish liberals and admitted to the aristocratic Masonic lodge, 'United Volunteer Brethren'. He died in 1809, leading a cavalry charge against the Austrians near

Kotzk in Russian Poland. A memorial was raised to him by local people, and his widow Rebeka and son received a pension until 1831. He himself had become a knight of the Polish Gold Cross; his son, Joseph Berekovich, also served in the Polish army.

Nor should the courage of Jewish troops in Marshal Pilsudski's legion during the 1920s Polish–Russian War be forgotten, that awful war against the Muscovites, which brought Russia to the gates of Warsaw and Poland to the outskirts of Kiev. The feats of these Jews were repeated during the Second World War by the soldiers of General Anders' Division, who played so heroic and forward a role in the Allied assault on the German stronghold in the monastery of Monte Cassino, and elsewhere.

Although Poland was occupied by the Germans in September 1939, the Jewish Fighting Organisation (ZOB), an agglomeration of Zionist and other groups with varying political programmes, was not established until August 1942. It consisted mostly of very young men and women, without money or arms except those that could be obtained by theft or persuasion, without training or experience in battle, commanding nothing but remorseless, indomitable courage and resource, in the vilest, most impossible of conditions.

The pre-war Jewish population of Warsaw was three hundred and sixty thousand, thirty per cent of the total, a community leading a rich cultural and professional life. (In Poland as a whole, the Jews numbered three and a quarter million.) In September 1940, by Nazi *ukaz* they were deprived of their jobs; their food and fuel rapidly diminished, themselves seized for forced labour, harassed, bullied and assaulted. The Warsaw Ghetto was established and, on 15 November, was surrounded by a ten-foot wall enclosing four hundred and forty-five thousand people, the original total of Jews plus refugees from outside.

Without medicine, food or heat, sixty thousand died between January 1941 and May 1942. In January 1942, as a result of the German decision at the Wannsee Conference regarding a 'Final Solution to the Jewish Question', three hundred thousand Jews from Warsaw were arrested. Most were sent to Treblinka and other camps, where many of them were murdered by gassing, or to Germany for forced labour where they died from exhaustion, starvation and often execution. Even in Treblinka, there were still Jews in August 1943 gallant enough to stage an uprising.

On 18 January 1943, the entire Warsaw garrison under General Jürgen Stroop moved to destroy the ghetto, that ghost town, its apartments looted, buildings wrecked by the German bombing of 1939, diseased corpses in the streets, those surviving existing on the contents of rubbish bins. The ZOB resisted, five hundred people armed with a few revolvers, iron bars and so forth, killing some Germans and taking their weapons. After three days, perhaps because of this resistance, perhaps because the German action was a rehearsal, the assault was called off. More Jews left the ghetto for shelter in the countryside, or to join fighters in the Wyszkòw Forest; others still could not believe the full extent of Nazi evil: some informed and collaborated against the Jews; many were too terrified to move; others, who took an 'historical' view, put their heads in the sand in the hope that the horror would go away.

The ZOB, in a daring but brilliantly planned coup, raided a prison where Jewish fighters were held preparatory to transfer to the Gestapo, and freed them under fire. They found and set up hiding places and safe houses; negotiated with the (Aryan) Polish Resistance (AK and AL); forged residence, identity and work permits; secured funding for the purchase of weapons from rich Jews, frequently against the latter's will; and tunnelled under the ghetto in preparation for the next Nazi attack. And, in the meanwhile, they sang Zionist songs and, because they were young, they fell in love, while all the time guarding themselves and their lives against the coward and the traitor.

On 19 April, the Germans came in again against the ghetto, this time with tanks, SP guns, artillery, motor-cycle SS troops and thousands of marching infantry. A ZOB mine was blown up under an SS unit at the ghetto gate, bits of bodies in the air, fences, buildings, even pavements collapsing, the SS survivors, their wounded abandoned, fleeing from the pistols, hand-grenades and Molotov cocktails made or acquired in the ghetto. The Nazis thus withdrew, but returned with light weapons and incendiaries. The remaining buildings took fire and the Jews retreated into the bunkers, until they too became untenable from smoke and flame, no air, no water and no food.

By the tenth day, the ghetto had been destroyed but, although there was no chance of further resistance unless all were to be buried alive under the debris, some fighters were still alive. The aim was to rescue those who could walk – many could not and had to be left under the ruins and in the side sewers – and bring them through the tunnels and sewers to the 'Aryan side'. (The help had to be enlisted of drunken, treacherous sewer men, and of such human scum as the 'Blackmailers', whose occupation was to prise money out of Jews in exchange for silence.) Thirty were extracted through the manholes in one operation and taken in lorries supplied by the Polish underground, to the Lomianski Forest. Others, escaping later that day through a manhole, were caught and shot down to a man,.

In August 1943, twenty Jews who had been existing on one potato a day, were 'arrested' in the ghetto by a Polish policeman and released by him to the ZOB who, under their commander for Poland, Antek (Yitzhak Zuckermann) and his deputy Kazik (Simha Rotem), kept the liaison between the Jews and the Polish underground army, Armia Krajowa (AK), and the Communist Armia Ludowa (AL). ZOB's overall tasks were the supply and distribution of money, arms, forged documents, propaganda and weapons in Warsaw and, for example, Czestochowa, and maintenance of the contact with free Jews, the Polish underground and Jews in captivity. Most of the movement had only one ambition, to emigrate after the war to Eretz Israel. A few, who included Kazik, dreamed of personal revenge against as many Germans as they could lay their hands on, especially the SS and the Gestapo.

Meanwhile, the struggle in the cities, with its direct daily contacts, each potentially lethal because of the risk of being discovered to be a Jew, was perhaps even more important and certainly more dangerous than the forest life of a Partisan. The ghetto fighter's role was to 'rescue, protect and save', against German Intelligence, its Polish and, alas, Jewish secret agents, in a city under the continual minute inspection of hostile, frightened eyes. These dangers were clearest to the submerged band of Jewish children called the 'Cigarette Sellers of Three Crosses Square' who, for fear of treachery, avoided contact with any adults at all except on a transaction basis. But by July 1944, Germans were being killed and robbed in the streets. Wehrmacht soldiers began to circulate, not singly, but in groups; an AK fighting group openly seized a German headquarters: the Soviet army was advancing, said to be close to Warsaw. The Polish Uprising, in which the few remaining ZOB fighters joined the AL and the AK, went well for three days, morale high, victory apparently at hand.

Then the German air force began to bomb, the army encircled the resistance areas and the Russians refused to help the rebellion, sitting maliciously outside the city with their puppet Gomulka. (At their base, Praga, Suvorov had destroyed Joselewicz's Jewish cavalry one hundred and fifty years before.) The Poles of the AL used the ZOB to plan the resistance retreat along an escape route from the Old City through the sewers to Zoliborz, thence through the ruins of blazing houses . . . In the destruction of one, which included a Jewish safe flat, the Germans accompanied their artillery and flame throwers with the music of a brass band; the Jews remained in the burning building until driven out to another cellar by smoke, heat and shortage of water. Some were captured by the particularly cruel, thieving and brutal Ukrainian military auxiliaries of the Wehrmacht, but escaped to a transit camp from which one or two opted in despair for forced labour in Germany. Others got away to Krakow, made contact with the Partisans and returned at once to Warsaw. In Warsaw, Allied bombers had attacked the German positions, but it was not until 17 January 1945 that Warsaw was cleared of Germans, a Warsaw in icy cold and Siberian winds, few houses standing, filled with Soviet soldiers bent on rape and pillage.

Perhaps 200,000 Jews survived in Poland in 1946. Even then there was no diminution in anti-Semitism and in virtually uncontrolled pogroms. (Only six thousand are left today and *charges* of Jewish antecedents were still heard in the recent campaigns for local and national elections.) Many Polish Jews, albeit after periods of up to three years, arrived safely in Israel to help found the new state. After journeys of hideous difficulty, frustration, discomfort and near-death, they embraced an active and successful military role against both Arabs and the mandatory power, the United Kingdom.

28
Stephen Lakeman and the Hottentots

Born in 1824, Stephen Lakeman was a British citizen of Dutch descent and Jewish extraction. As a young man, educated abroad at the Ecole de Flèche and the University of Paris, he volunteered but was not accepted for the British regular forces; instead he became attached in 1847 to the French military staff at Algiers and was involved in engagements against Arabs and Kabyles; later he participated in the 1848 risings in Budapest, Paris and Vienna. In Algeria, he became convinced of the virtues of the Minie rifle and, on return to the UK, pressed its qualities on the Duke of Wellington. The latter rejected its employment on the grounds that the rapid twist of the rifling would unacceptably increase the recoil: 'Englishmen take aim, Frenchmen fire anyhow.'

The British authorities in 1851 agreed that he should raise two hundred volunteers against the Kaffirs in the Cape, the clothing to be provided by himself, but pay and rations by London. He decided to recruit in Africa rather than in the UK and, after buying fifty double-barrelled and one hundred and fifty single-barrelled rifles, embarked in *Harbinger* for Capetown. *En route*, in Sierra Leone, he found the governor, Colonel O'Connor, reclining in torrid heat on a couch covered with white muslin. The colonel resembled a 'lump of yellow butter in a basin of ice water', and was being cooled by a white horse-tail fan manipulated through the bed-hangings by a local 'nigger' or 'sable person', Lakeman's sobriquets for blacks. The room was filled with semi-naked blacks periodically placing their hands in their armpits and then slapping the walls. 'If they sit *still*,' explained an attendant officer, 'they stink like rancid cocoa oil.' Lakeman, in parenthesis, noted that when he was later a pasha in the Turkish army, his fan had *two* horse tails.

On arrival at the Cape, Sir Harry Smith, a benefactor, offered a £2 bounty per head in addition to the £2 which Lakeman was already providing. Although most of the kit and all the cartridges had been spoilt on the voyage, fifty men were rapidly 'recruited'. Their 'ringleader' was a former Royal Navy bosun known as

'Happy Jack', who spent nearly all his time in the pubs and generally caused trouble, while the rest, and many of those who followed, were pressed men, drunks, jailbirds, crippled or infirm. 'Happy Jack' had, on one occasion, to be frogmarched from his pub to the barracks by local regulars. To get this troupe on board the vessel that was to take them to Port Elizabeth required a military exercise – a mock-up action with Lakeman's men on the one hand, and police and artillery detachments on the other. Before the reluctant 'passengers' were driven aboard, less twenty deserters, 'Happy Jack' had demanded grog all round, his companions chanting, 'We won't go home till morning', while the police on the road resembled a swarm of bluebottles on a white Cambridge sausage. 'Happy Jack' then fired a cartridge between the coat-tails of Police Sergeant Herridge who 'cut a double shuffle in mid-air like an exploding cracker, and began to bump his backside on the ground in order to stamp out the fire'.

On the veldt, a Sergeant Waine who had been broken as an NCO in the 44th but reinstated, deliberately fired at Captain Lakeman. 'Who gave the order to fire?' 'A magpie,' replied Waine. Herridge took Waine's firelock, tied him up to a gun carriage and gave him three dozen lashes with Waine's own belt. Lakeman rode down 'Happy Jack' and other malcontents. Most of the men ratted at the first sight of Kaffir soldiers with assegais, but soon, tormented by fear and pricked by thorns, returned to their unit. 'Happy Jack' deserted but Waine came to heel. It was a peculiar looking party, mainly ex-sailors with beards and wearing leather helmets: the officers included a gambler of loose habits, a religious maniac and a former regular who had resigned after throwing wine in his superior's face. One of the sergeants was a confectioner and pastry cook.

Lakeman, discovering that the 'sable heroes' were only twelve miles away on the slopes of Water-Klooff, led the advance guard of General Napier's forces up the heights. After his orderly had been shot, he charged the Kaffirs and Hottentots, inflicting casualties and losing only two killed and five wounded. Napier sent his troops in again under an artillery barrage, while the Kaffirs collected shell fragments for use as pestles, or threw them back. The Minie rifles did more damage than the guns or the rockets.

That night, Lakeman threw up a strong night defence. Over the hill, he heard the Christian Kaffirs singing:

'Awake my soul and with the sun,
Thy daily course of duty run.'

The duty, of course, being to cut white men's throats. But the purpose of the war was really to define and demarcate the areas of organised arable and other farming by Europeans and the nomadic slash-and-burn agriculture favoured by the natives. In terms of military tactics, Lakeman rapidly concluded that, since the Kaffirs – lithe, supple and vicious as snakes' in the daytime – dreaded and feared the night, he should operate in a series of night attacks, resting during the day. He accordingly earned praise from Napier for 'discernment, gallantry, bravery and good conduct' because, after a month, so much panic had been caused by these night actions that the Kaffirs evacuated the whole of the Water-Klooff, hiding in the valley and rock recesses below.

General Cathcart then assembled several thousand troops on the heights overlooking the Klooff but, in the event, only assaulted Mundell's Peak. Subsequently, a brigadier told Lakeman that night attacks were 'unethical and irregular', and himself led the 60th Rifles, 74th, 91st, plus artillery and rockets, in an unsuccessful daylight action from which Lakeman had to rescue him. The Brigadier was reprimanded for his interference.

Waine now tried to shoot Lakeman again, the last attempt. He subsequently blew his hand off when cleaning a gun, and died of lock-jaw.

On 11 July, General Cathcart struck again at Water-Klooff, while Lakeman cleared out Hottentot deserters. The general, unfortunately, in his orders failed to mention Lakeman's men – now known as the 'Water Klooff Rangers: Lakeman's Volunteer Corps' – and the captain that evening therefore interrupted the general who was toasting a chop on a ramrod. (Cathcart had no more knowledge of Kaffirs than he had later of Russians at Inkerman: 'A bold soul in a skeleton frame, but without such material vitality.') Although initially furious, Cathcart promised to recommend him to the Horse Guards for a military appointment in India. Nothing further was heard of that assurance.

In Lakeman's view, the Kaffirs combined thoroughness and simpleness of purpose in action with total inertia in defeat or difficult circumstances. Women, when tired, would *drop* their children on the ground and go on without them; a man, with a noose round his neck, mounted on a pony and waiting to be hung from a tree, 'spurred' on the pony and met an almost voluntary end; all seemed indifferent to the sufferings of their wives and children; a little band of Kaffir children led Lakeman in a night attack on their own parents' villages. Elsewhere, women were disembowelled and men mutilated. The British had their own faults. Herridge killed an old woman for her lion- and leopard-tooth necklace, but died with his right arm withered to the bone, a consequence – he was sure – of the crime. One of Lakeman's men concealed a reaping hook in his clothing, with which to cut the throats at night of women and children prisoners.

When Cathcart was victorious in Basutoland, 'grim-visaged war had smoothed his wrinkled frown'. The Transvaal was annexed and Lakeman gave himself up to the chase – leopard, blue-buck, baboons, wild boar, antelopes, hyenas, jackals, pursued by two Scotch deer hounds handled by a St Helenan ('Saint'), known as Napoleon.

On return to England, Lakeman kissed the sand of Brighton beach, then, with a mouthful of sand and his face blacked up by a practical joker, he covered an unnamed lady with kisses mingled with dirt.

Many flattering addresses in his honour from the South African colonists, Cathcart's complimentary reports and strongly favourable recommendation, and the Duke of Newcastle's interest, all had led him to hope that at last the British army would accept him. Raglan and Clarendon seemed his supporters. Entering Horse Guards to be interviewed by the military secretary, he was jostled by another visitor and demanded an apology which he did not receive. 'If,' he therefore said, 'this gentleman is a foreigner' (he was, in fact, a Lord Forth) 'and cannot speak English, let the matter rest.' When Forth was described to him as the backbone of the nation, he later commented: 'He *did* come to the Front, but showed his backbone, not his front, to the Russians at Balaclava.'

The military secretary refused him a commission despite his extensive continental military education and experience, asserting that he had enough money to purchase one. As a palliative, Lord Clarendon proposed him for the rank of knight bachelor. He was driven to Windsor in a carriage between Lord Palmerston and Lord Aberdeen. In an oak-panelled room he knelt, with little pleasure, to receive the accolade from the Queen's sword. This missed his shoulder and hit the cushion.

In 1853, Sir Stephen Lakeman left for Turkey. On arrival, he was sent to Gallipoli by the ambassador, Lord Stratford de Redcliffe, whom he revered, but found that area a useless rendezvous for any English and French endeavour against Russia, a redoubt for Asia, not Europe. In order to repel a Russian invader, furthermore, defences had to be built, but in so doing – preparing defences against retreat – prestige would be lost. He reported thereafter to the ambassador on military preparations on the Sea of Marmora and, from HMS *Valorous*, on fortresses on the Danube to Varna, and on the Turkish army in Bulgaria. After Varna, he left for Schemla, wearing the ambassador's cloak, then rode up the Deona Valley through Peveda and Balschesci. He saw the 'great' Omar Pasha, and watched Turks who had just bolted from harmless Russian scouts, dragging – with frostbitten hands and feet, huge siege guns on sledges . . . 'with death's cold hand upon them'.

In 1853, he went to Constantinople with a sword given him by Colonel Neville Chamberlain. Without his permission, Riza Shah gave it to the Sultan in exchange for command to Lakeman of the Sultan's Rumelian Guard, one of the regiments forming the brigade which Lakeman later commanded on the Danube. He appears to have fought in the Kars campaign against Russia. The battle of Kars in Armenia was fought from 28 June to November 1855 during the Crimean War between twenty-five thousand Russians under General Mikhail Muraviev, and Turks under Major-General Sir William Fenwick Williams, an artillery officer who was a *ferik* (lieutenant-general) in the Turkish army and a pasha. Since the main allied armies were besieging Sebastopol, Tsar Alexander II could operate more freely in the south; he sent an army into the Caucasus and the Turks fell back into Armenia. At Kars, Ottoman troops under Williams made a stand against the Russians, who assaulted the garrison on 29 September; the attack was repulsed and a relief force sent under Omar Pasha. On 28 November, the Russians stormed the town again. This time, the garrison, weakened by starvation, surrendered. The Russian offensive was then halted because of Austria's threatened intervention in the war. The Tsar signed preliminary peace terms with the British, French and Turks, and was obliged to return Kars to the Turks and cede part of Bessarabia to Moldavia.

One of Lakeman's officers at this period was Major Murad Bey, his second-in-command and a renegade Frenchman, another the son of an English prime minister. Lakeman later became quarter-master-general of the Turkish army, obliged in one incident to throw overboard Hallil Pasha, the Sultan's brother-in-law and commander of the Turkish cavalry, for refusing to accept Lakeman's orders about the non-embarkation of Hallil's harem.

Before promotion to lieutenant-general, he served as governor of the Bourgas district. He and Commander Eardley Wilmot of the *Sphinx* built a jetty in the Bay of Bourgas, measuring one hundred and forty-seven by eight yards, in twenty-two feet of water, handling forty-five thousand troops, nine thousand four hundred horses and one hundred and forty field guns embarked for the Crimea. He later became governor of Western Rumelia, where the metropolitan of Adrianapolis sought his permission to celebrate a mass for the dead Emperor Nicholas of Russia against whose successor Turkey was fighting.

In 1855, the Turks, who had made him a pasha (Mazar) as well as a general officer, seconded him to the Roumanian army where, as commandant of Bucharest, he was approached by a deputation of Jewish converts to Christianity. These, deserted by their pastor, who had absconded to sell sheepskin coats to the British army, sought funds from Lakeman. That officer refused to agree and the Jews reverted to Judaism. In Roumania, Mazar Pasha married the Princess Maria Philipescu, renounced his military rank and career and remained in the country for twenty years, eventually returning to England after his wife's death, and buying Grangewood Hall at Ashby-de-la-Zouch, where he died in the 1890s.

A Jew named Fischel-Freind, born in Lodz in (Russian) Poland in 1880, also became a Turkish pasha. His working life began with the repair of watches, but he departed when very young for Budapest, where he became batman to an Hungarian officer. During Kossuth's rebellion in 1908, he acted with courage and was made an officer, fleeing to Turkey when the revolution was suppressed, converting to Islam in the name of Mahmud Hamid, and joining the Turkish army, for whom he fought as an officer against the Montenegrins in 1876; he was 'promoted' to pasha in

1877, and thereafter was appointed governor of Syria, where he rigorously, but with equity, suppressed the tribes.

29
Austrian Jewish heroes, and victims

European Jews in the Hapsburg Empire lost the right to bear arms in the thirteenth century, a sanction maintained in the fifteenth century against suspicion of espionage for the Hussites or, in the seventeenth and eighteenth, for Prussians and other enemies of the Holy Roman Empire. The more relaxed racial policies of Joseph II, conscription and the requirement to end alleged usury, cheating and robbery by Jews and to turn them into 'useful members of the state', led to forms of mandatory military service, beginning first in 1789 with the destitute province of Galicia and, later, in all Hapsburg lands. Service was frequently and massively evaded by payment and, where undertaken, often complicated by religious and other considerations, Kosher, the Sabbath, clothing (no flax), beards and so forth.

In 1809 a Jew in Austrian service, although killed in action, had begun the decline of the dictator, Napoleon Bonaparte. In 1794, Field Marshal Joseph Armand von Nordman, an Alsatian Jew, with his own regiment and with General Dumouriez, abandoned Napoleon and the French army to join the Austrians and to command the Bourbon Legion in many subsequent actions. In 1809, leading twenty infantry battalions and twenty cavalry squadrons, he first broke through between Aspern and Stadlau, taking Aspern and forcing the 2nd French Corps to retreat. In two days of vigorous battle on 5 and 6 July, he held off a counter-attack by greatly superior French numbers, later retreating himself but, on the second day of the engagement, moving forward again until he met a hero's death at the strong-point of Markgrav-Neusiedl.

'Payments' were abolished during the Napoleonic wars when Jews were enlisted in proportion to Christians, fifteen per cent as an annual total for conscription, employed chiefly in supply and infantry, the duration of their service declining between 1802 and 1858 from life to seven years. The first Jewish officers were now appointed. It should here be remarked that Jews were not formally classified as a minority, but by the dominant ethnic group

– Polish, German, Magyar – in which they found themselves. About fifteen languages were spoken within the Austro-Hungarian Kaiserlich und Königlich army, Imperial and Royal. Only 142 of about 400 units were monolingual.

Discrimination continued, more sharply within the regular than the reserve (*Landwehr* or *Honvéd*) armies, excluding Jews from the financial and judicial branches, but by 1859 the army may have contained as many as 30,000 Jews. When his career ended at the end of the nineteenth century, a Jewish major-general and *Ritter* (knight) had had to fight thirty-four duels in defence of his faith . . .

After Solferino and Sadowa, after emancipation and the establishment of the dual monarchy, the Jews were still heavy in the administrative (including medical) services, but light in the *jäger* (light infantry) and cavalry, for reasons as much geographic and local as racial. The percentage of Jewish officers in the reserve armies was 18.7% in 1897, higher than any other European force; even in the regular army it was 12.7%. After 1867, the military had become more liberal and tolerant than the civilians and, on the whole, so remained. As for the officers, 75% served in combat units, of whom some 65% were in the infantry. There were hardly any in the cavalry, but all military schools and academies had been opened to them; there were, however, no Jewish officers on the general staff.

Of twenty-three Jewish generals and colonels in fighting units before 1911, fourteen became baptised. Lieutenant-General Edward von Schweitzer, originally an Hungarian enlisted man, did not convert. He fought in the war against Prussia and in the campaign in Bosnia-Herzegovina, went to staff college, won the Order of the Iron Crown and a knighthood (*Ritter*), became a major-general and commanded an infantry brigade. In old age, he regularly attended a Budapest synagogue and ate Kosher food, a practice the emperor also permitted when Schweitzer dined with him. Baron Samuel Hazai (born Kohn) did convert, becoming a general and, between 1910 and 1917, Hungarian minister of defence, after which he was promoted to colonel-general and appointed chief of mobilisation and supply. Three other Austrian Jews were promoted to major-general in the First World War. It is alleged that, earlier, General Ritter von Eiss, who fought at Magenta, was offered the Order of Maria Theresa, (the equivalent of the British VC) if he would convert, but refused and became a Zionist; three sons fought in the First War.

The infantry contained the highest number of reserve officers. (One artillery regiment, however, was nicknamed 'von Rothschild'.) Acceptance by Gentiles of Jews as reserve officers was greatly sought as a symbol of emancipation. Gentile officers were forbidden to deny their Jewish colleagues the satisfaction of a duel, on at least one occasion requiring a divisional commander's *order* to proceed. Integration was more developed in the reserve than in regular formations, although relations between Gentile and Jew in the *Bundesheer* were perfectly correct and no more peculiar than those between the various ranks of the aristocracy, on the one hand, and between the *Erstegesellschaft* and 'The Rest' on the other. In any case, 350 Jewish families were ennobled in the nineteenth century.

Three hundred thousand Jews served in the Austrian armed forces in World War I, including 25,000 officers. Half the career officers and 7% of reserve officers were awarded the Order of the Iron Crown; seventy-six gold medals for bravery were presented and Jews, at last, were permitted to serve in élite units. But this record was submerged by the consequences of defeat, the end of the monarchy, communist and socialist revolution (in which Jews *appeared* to play a disproportionate part), financial and economic collapse, bankruptcy. The Jews were increasingly accused of bringing about the chaos of the time itself, the famous 'stab in the back', allegedly delivered by Jewish predominance in the supply corps. Anti-Semitism spread.

After the Nazis took over the Austrian government in March 1938 and the country was annexed (Anschluss) by the Third Reich, the *Bundesheer* was absorbed by the Wehrmacht. An unknown number of Jewish soldiers were dismissed as non-Aryan under the Nuremberg Laws, including 238 officers, among them highly decorated officers sent via the 'model ghetto' at Theresienstadt to the gas chambers at Auschwitz. Six generals, twelve colonels, twenty-eight lieutenants-colonels, thirty-six majors, two hundred captains and an undetermined number of lieutenants and first lieutenants were rounded up by the Gestapo. By 1939, in Hungary also, not one single Jewish officer, including converts, was left in the career army, many dying as manual workers on the Russian Front, others murdered in the camps.

Johann Friedlander, for example, was born in 1882 of Jewish parents in Berne, moving thence to Vienna. He joined the army in 1897, marrying a Jewess from Budapest in 1913. In World War I, he fought against Serbia, and against Italy on the Isonzo Front. He was severely wounded, subsequently serving for six months with the Austrian navy in the Adriatic between Pola and Kotor, then moving to the Isonzo, after which he returned to Vienna at the Ministry of War in February 1918. Despite anti-Semitism and the fissiparous political confusion of the time, Friedlander served in Vienna Regiment No. 2 in the Radetsky Barracks and, from 1925, as regimental commander. In 1928, he was director of the army's training, equipment and education departments. In 1936, as major-general, he joined the inspector general's office, retiring in 1937 as a lieutenant-general on a pension of 850 schillings a month.

In March 1938, since his 'case' came under the Nuremberg Laws, he was made to know that because he was only a 'half-Jew', his father having converted, he could better himself by separating from his wife. Although their marital relations were not harmonious, as a man of honour he refused. An officer of the SA then arrived at his house, seizing his sword and decorations. Gold and ornaments were subsequently sequestrated. At his pension office, he was required to complete documents showing proof or otherwise of Aryan birth. It was particularly tragic that his own brother, who had lost a leg in the First World War, was responsible for this department; in 1942, the general's nephew, Hugo, died in Russia aged twenty-two.

Friedlander could still not contemplate abandoning his country. Efforts by former colleagues to make him an exception to Nazi regulations were, however, unsuccessful and, in October 1942, he and his wife were thrown out of their house in Hietzing, in exchange for a dwelling in Leopoldstadt whence, in September 1943, they were transferred to the Theresienstadt ghetto. Leona Friedlander, in the disgusting conditions of that place, died on 21 May 1944. On 12 October 1944, the general, aged 63, was deported to Auschwitz with a number of Polish prisoners, thrown there hugger-mugger in inhuman circumstances. The death march from the advancing Russians began on 18 January, many prisoners being shot by the SS guards as they went. On 20 January, Friedlander knew that he could go no further. His friends had helped and supported him as far as was possible but, finally, he resigned himself to his fate, kneeling by the road, his head in his hands. An SS man, whom Friedlander knew, shot him twice in the back of the neck, laughing: 'The Field Marshal has just acquired two balls at last.'

30
The USA

An English Jewish couple named Benjamin sailed from the Old World for New Orleans in 1811 but, since the Mississippi was blockaded by a British fleet, their vessel put into the then British Caribbean island of St Croix where their son, Judah Philip, was born in the same year. The family settled in North Carolina and, after three years at Yale from which he did not graduate, Judah was called to the New Orleans bar in 1832, then becoming counsellor at the supreme court in 1848, with a practice chiefly in Washington, rejecting a judgeship in the Supreme Court.

In 1852 and 1857, he was elected as a Democratic senator for Louisiana in the Senate of the United States. When South Carolina seceded from the Union in 1861 he publicly defended States Rights, and left both the Senate and Washington in a hurry, to become attorney-general in President Jefferson Davis' provisional government of the Southern Confederacy. In August 1861, he became secretary of state for war and, in February 1862, secretary of state for foreign affairs. In fact, because of his intellect, ability and industry, his workload was so heavy (8 a.m to 1 or 2 p.m. next day) that he was not only a sort of Admirable Crichton, but the 'Chief Man of the Rebel State'. Jefferson Davis' autocratic methods and the secrecy of his procedures make it difficult, nevertheless, to decide whether Benjamin or others were responsible for all the harsh, arbitrary and repressive measures adopted by the Confederacy.

He resigned in 1863 at the criticism aroused by his bill on conscription. As secretary of state from 1864, he was judged by a Confederate general to be an impediment to the prosperous working of the state. He was also criticised for the circumstances of a loan which he raised in France and which was 'connected' with the marriage of one of his partner's daughters to a French banker. In a speech in Richmond, furthermore, he urged his audience to liberate all slaves who wanted to join the Southern armies, asserting that his own slaves wanted to enlist.

After General Robert E. Lee surrendered at Appomatox and

the Confederacy collapsed, Benjamin fled to North Carolina with Davis and his cabinet. Since he was too fat to ride a horse, he had to travel in an ambulance which, on badly pot-holed roads, became separated from the main body. Davis thought that Benjamin intended to join him in Texas via Cuba and Mexico, but his secretary of state could only escape to the Bahamas in an open, leaky boat, then in a sponge fisher wrecked *en route* to Nassau. He was picked up by a British ship which took him to St Thomas, whence he travelled to England by a steamer which caught fire.

He landed in Liverpool with very little money but, through influence, was called to the English bar in 1866. Although retaining his affection for and loyalty to the Confederacy, he never again saw either Jefferson Davis or the country he was accustomed to regard as his native land – 'Accustomed to regard', because Judah Philip Benjamin, born in St Croix, was an Englishman by birth as well as an American. In England, and in Paris where he had married a French wife and was eventually domiciled, he made a reasonably lucrative practice as a barrister, and also wrote classics on the law. He had to sustain the failure of a large investment, and developed diabetes and heart disease: his end was hastened by a fall from a Paris train in 1884. At least, he had *taken* a state, if not held it.

Earlier, in the American War of Independence, Jewish participation was out of all proportion to the size of the population countrywide. One of George Washington's adjutants was Isaac Franks, while the English spy Benedict Arnold had another Franks, David, on his personal staff. Names like Benjamin, Blomfield, Blumenberg – at Antietam – Busoh, Israel, de Leon, Moses, de la Motta and Seixas filled the commissioned ranks. In the war between the states, nine Jewish generals and six hundred other Jewish officers have been noted in the Union and Confederacy armies; seven were awarded the Medal of Honour. A quarter of a million Jews fought in the First World War, six receiving the Medal of Honour, and six hundred thousand (forty thousand casualties and the same number of decorations) in the Second. Over two thousand Jews fought in Vietnam.

Admiral Joseph Strauss was born in 1861 of German Jewish

parents, Rafael and Sarah at Mount Morris, NY. When commanding the northern mining force in the First World War, he was responsible for a mine barrage from the Norwegian coast to the Orkneys against U-boats. (He had earlier commanded USS *Montgomery*, *Ohio* and *Nevada*, had developed smokeless powder and invented deck artillery for submarines and a new turret system in battleships.) The end of the First War on 11 November 1918 arrived before the barrage could be completed but, by then, US minelayers had laid fifty thousand out of seventy thousand mines in the field. Some eight enemy submarines were lost to it between July and October, and several other vessels damaged, the news of which helped to produce a serious diminution of morale, amounting in some instances to mutiny, among German submarine crews. The risks to U-boats ran from 25% to 80%, depending on the 'thickness' of the various sectors of the field. Strauss later claimed that if the northern barrage and another across the Dover Straits had been complete, any threat from submarines between the Atlantic and the North Sea would have been eliminated. Barriers contemplated across the Aegean and Adriatic Seas would have ended submarine operations throughout the European theatre; the hornets would then have been shut up in their nests.

Strauss, a fine-looking old man with an honourable ancestral nose and a moustache like Foch or, perhaps, Kitchener, became commander-in-chief, US Asian Fleet from 1921 to 1922, later writing a number of works on maritime artillery and ordnance.

Hyman G. Rickover was born in Makow, Poland in 1900, then under Russian occupation. Shortly thereafter, his father emigrated to the United States in the flood of refugees fleeing the East European, Ukrainian and Russian anti-Semitic pogroms and other persecutions. In New York, he became a tailor, sending for his family in 1910 and moving on to Chicago once they had joined him. Rickover worked hard at his schooling, subsidised by part-time work, and entered the US Naval Academy of Annapolis with the help of a local congressman. At Annapolis, he was a loner, concentrating on study, shunning social and athletic pursuits. In 1922, he passed out reasonably well in academic subjects, nearly bottom in OLQ (officer-like qualities), and continued rather to shut himself away thereafter in his cabin on *La Vallette* and on the battleship *Nevada*. He was, however, congratulated on improving *Nevada*'s electrical systems before returning to the naval academy, then to a master's degree course in electrical engineering at Columbia, from where he went into the submarine service.

He liked the 'boats', working to improve the backward electronics of the time. But when the navy passed him over for submarine command, posting him instead to another battleship, and then to a gunnery-target towing vessel as commanding officer, he applied in 1937 for permanent shore employment in engineering duty only. During the Second World War, he was chief of the electrical section of the Bureau of Ships at Washington, overcoming tremendous procurement difficulties, moving on to the Manhattan project laboratories at Oak Ridge, Tennessee to study nuclear technology.

Not many in the navy shared his belief in the possibilities for nuclear powered submarines, certainly not on the crash, short-term basis that Rickover advocated in the Atomic Energy Commission where Lewis Strauss, another naval officer, later served. Here, in the nuclear power branch of the Bureau of Ships, and through existing contacts with civilian contractors, he navigated his ideas through congressional committees. He was a superb, Machiavellian, unpopular naval bureaucrat, whose removal through retirement was sought by almost the entire naval hierarchy. But in 1950, his own relentless lobbying and the pressures of the Cold War, added to growing Soviet nuclear strength and US public opinion, persuaded President Truman not only to authorise the construction of a nuclear submarine, but to agree with Rickover that the hull and reactor should be built simultaneously. *Nautilus*, the world's first nuclear submarine, was the result, passing her sea trials in 1955.

Rickover, now a rear admiral, had considerable control – which he exercised with minute attention to every detail – over the naval nuclear programme, at the same time leading the project for the first American nuclear power generating station at Shippingport, Pa, which went on stream in 1957. After visiting Russia with Nixon in 1959, he took an articulate, noisy lead in castigating the whole United States' educational system, a campaign based initially on perceived deficiencies in the nuclear system compared with that of the USSR.

His control over the naval nuclear programme became tighter as well as more extensive over the next few years, although personal tensions were acute enough to exclude him from planning the nuclear-missile submarine programme, Polaris. His retirement, however, was deferred or, rather, elided, and for twenty years he remained, to the irritation of many, as director of the division of naval reactors, a monument in his own time. As is observed by the *Dictionary of American Military Biography*:

> Rickover's reactor programme revolutionised naval warfare. Now warships could remain at sea indefinitely without refuelling and submarines could circle the globe without surfacing to replenish batteries. Whether less abrasive officers might have eased some of the growing pains of the nuclear navy seems less important than the effective leadership Rickover supplied in the birth of a nuclear fleet.

Vice Admiral Hyman Rickover was twice awarded the Legion of Merit, once the Distinguished Service Medal, and was an Honorary Companion of the Order of the British Empire. His publications included *Education and Freedom*, *Swiss Schools and Ours* and *American Education – a National Failure.* Gadfly, publicist, high-handed promoter, he was still the father of the nuclear navy.

Major-General Maurice Rose, a Jew and son of Samuel Rose, was born in Middletown, Connecticut on 26 November 1899. Wounded in the infantry in the First War, he served during the Second World War in North Africa and Europe. In Tunisia, as chief of staff, Second Armoured Division, he personally rallied green troops in their first encounters with an experienced enemy, later taking the terms of unconditional surrender to General Boroweitz, commanding the Wehrmacht. In Europe, as commander, Third Armoured Division, he was usually ahead of his own troops who, in turn, led the van of the First Army through the Falaise Gap to Chartres, across the Seine, through France and Belgium to the Siegfried Line. Rose's division took vast quantities of equipment and large numbers of prisoners, and was the first to cross the German border, driving on to Cologne and the Elbe in a 'cavalry' movement to be compared with those of Napoleon's marshals in their great days. But at Paderborn, the Germans fired on him, well ahead of his soldiers: he was killed on 20 March 1945.

31
Germany

The banker Jacob Mossner and his wife Henrietta Riese-Mossner were both Jews; their son Walter was born in Berlin in 1846 and died at a great age in Heidelberg in 1932. Jacob was of assistance to Prince William of Prussia, son of King Frederick William IV, during the reform movement of 1848 and the rioting and bloodshed which ensued. During this time, the prince, accused of absolutism and reaction, had been obliged to leave Berlin. In fact, the German revolutionary activity, unlike violent radicalism in France, Austria and Italy, took a more liberal course. Republicans were even in a minority. Its main accomplishment was the election of a national assembly, dispersed however by Frederick William, although not before it had decided on Germany's future as an empire under the Prussian king, excluding Austria. The king rejected the imperial crown since it had not been offered by the princes and, using the army to suppress revolution throughout the country, formed a new federal parliament, at Erfurt.

Austria, through Prince Schwarzenberg, refused to be excluded, and an Austro–German War was narrowly averted or, rather, postponed until Bismarck's victories ended in the destruction of the Austrian army at Sadowa on 3 July, in the seven-week war of 1866. King William I had become regent of Germany in 1858 and was crowned first Hohenzollern emperor of Germany in 1871 at the Proclamation of Empire in the Hall of Mirrors at Versailles.

The king was, above all, loyal to his friends and, soon after accession, asked Jacob Mossner for some request by which he could recompense the banker's earlier kindness. Mossner told him that his son, Walter, an excellent horseman, had no other wish than to join the Prussian cavalry. In 1865, William was happy to admit him, aged eighteen, into his personal regiment, the King's (or 'Blue') Hussars, then stationed at Bonn. As the officers of this regiment then refused to elect the Jew as a member of their circle or corps of officers, the king issued an order to the regimental commander of the Hussars that, if they did not comply, his majesty would regard their obstinacy as a personal affront. The officers thereupon ceased their resistance and withdrew their objections. On election, Ensign Mossner fought his first duel, with Ensign Prince Karl Karolath, an anti-Semitic officer who had especially opposed his incorporation in the Hussars, hurting him severely with a heavy sabre blow to the head. (Karolath was chiefly known for his marriage with a great beauty, Gräfin Elisabeth Hatzfeld.) Other duels followed, but his courage in the field, particularly at Koeniggratz (Sadowa), secured his position and reputation as a first-class soldier and cavalryman.

After that battle, he was promoted to lieutenant and served with the regiment as adjutant from 1867 to 1872, in the course of which he fought with distinction in the Franco-Prussian War, being promoted to senior lieutenant and posted as ADC to the commander of the 22nd Cavalry Brigade. In 1872 he went on the general staff and, in 1875, was promoted captain. In 1877, Mossner was named staff officer to the Hussar Life Guards, commanding a squadron in that regiment. In 1882, he was appointed ADC to the commander of the 5th Cavalry Division and, in 1884, ADC with the rank of major to the commander of the 3rd Army Corps.

William I's son, Kaiser William II, 'knighted' (*Ritter*) Mossner in 1890. From 1891 to 1895, as a lieutenant-colonel, Mossner commanded the Hussar Life Guards, becoming the emperor's ADC in 1892; in 1893, he was promoted colonel. In 1896, he served as brigadier-general in command of the 3rd Cavalry Brigade, having commanded the 3rd Division of Imperial Horse Guards in 1895. From 1898–9, he was head of the Cavalry Institute, and in 1889 was promoted to lieutenant-general commanding the Guards Cavalry Division. In 1903 he became governor of Strasbourg. In 1904, he was appointed as general officer commanding all German cavalry formations, retiring in 1910 but acting in the 1914–18 War as deputy commander of an army corps. In that capacity, he may have been the last Prussian general to receive the Order of the Black Eagle, having already been decorated with the Red Eagle after the Battle of Sadowa. He was much admired for his conduct of cavalry tactics and for his horsemanship, both in battle, dressage, on the parade ground and in the more prestigious of the military's races.

Earlier, during the Napoleonic Wars, over seven hundred Jews are known to have fought between 1813 and 1815 for Prussia against the dictator. Of these, about twenty Prussian Jews reached junior-officer status, mainly lieutenants; twenty Iron Crosses were awarded. In the Austro-Prussian War, only one officer, a lieutenant, can be identified out of about one thousand Jewish combatants, and only forty-one lieutenants from some four and a half thousand Jews in the Franco-Prussian War of 1870–1: over eighty Iron Crosses, however, were earned by Jews in this latter confrontation.

Mossner is the only identified Jewish pre-Third Reich general officer of the German army. Bismarck, later German chancellor, then Prussian ambassador, said at the Frankfurt parliament in connection with a report that the number of Jewish officers in the Austrian army was increasing: 'He [the author of the report] lists five hundred Jewish officers in the higher ranks, including several staff officers . . . The remarkable thing is that this is supposed to be something to be proud of.'

At least one hundred thousand Jews fought for Germany in the First World War, of whom four thousand were officers. One thousand five hundred Iron Crosses (first class) and ten thousand Iron Crosses (second class) were awarded to them. No Jew, either then or in the Second World War, was promoted to general's rank. It is, therefore, in order to refute them, and with neither pleasure nor revanchist spirit, that the repellent rumours surrounding Heydrich must be reviewed.

Richard Tristan Eugen Heydrich was born in Halle an der Saale in March 1904 and christened in a Catholic church in that town, where his father (Richard) Bruno Heydrich, a singer and composer, was founder and co-director of a conservatoire. His mother (his father Bruno's first wife), Maria Anna Amalia Elisabeth Kranz, was the daughter of Hofrat Professor Eugen Krantz, himself a director and founder of the Royal Conservatory at Dresden. (It is not surprising that Richard Heydrich was also an accomplished violinist.) Elisabeth's mother, Marie Antonia, a Catholic, was born a Miss Mautsch in Bantzen.

His father Bruno's mother, Ernestine Wilhemina Heydrich, née Lindner, was married again after the death of Bruno's father to a journeyman locksmith named Gustave Robert Süss. Rumours were circulated – 'Jew Süss' – in 1932, allegedly by one of Bruno's musical rivals, that Bruno and therefore Richard had Jewish blood. These rumours were transmitted by the gauleiter of Halle Museberg to Gregor Strasser, a leader of the NSDAP, the Nazi Party, before the Nazis took power. Strasser ordered an investigation. Achim Gercke, the party genealogist, concluded that there could be no possible grounds for the charge: this particular Süss was not a Jew, and anyway, he was not Bruno's father, Bruno having been born before his real (Heydrich) father had died, and before his mother's remarriage.

There was, accordingly, no Jewish blood line, no line of descent between Süss and Richard Heydrich, a view apparently accepted by the party, and certainly by Heydrich's most substantial biographer, Gunther Deschner, in *Heydrich: The Pursuit of Power.*

It was subsequently charged, however, by a British journalist named Charles Wighton, that Gercke's 'public' report had not covered Heydrich's maternal lineage, in other words, the 'dog that did not bark in the night', since it contained no reference at all to Elisabeth Krantz's Mautsch mother and grandmother. Wighton drew the conclusion that these omissions were so glaring as to justify the assumption that they had been deliberately excluded by Strasser and Bormann from the report, and therefore demonstrated Jewish blood in the vital maternal line. The name Mautsch, therefore, and the fact that – according to Wighton – grandmother Mautsch had 'brought money into the family for the first time', were *for Wighton* the keys.

This allegation has been accepted by several commentators. H.G. Adler, the historian of the ghetto at Theresienstadt, has suggested that 'Heydrich sought to conquer his hatred for his Jewish core through the murder of all Jews within reach.' Reitlinger, a British Jew himself, has referred to Heydrich's 'pathological Jewish hatred of his own blood'. Gert Buchheit, the historian of the intelligence service, alleged that 'Heydrich's Aryan passport was a forgery.' Karl Dietrich Bracher, in *Die Deutscher Diktatur,* said that 'Heydrich's Jewish origins had been exposed', and Joachim Fest, 'that he had Jewish ancestors'. Hugh Trevor-Roper has speculated on Heydrich's consequent 'fear of blackmail'. Suggestions were made by a former counter-intelligence worker and pianist named Helmut Maurer that either Heydrich, or Maurer at Heydrich's orders, had removed all records of his (Heydrich's) ancestry from the Halle records. Heydrich is also supposed to have removed his maternal grandmother's gravestone from a Leipzig cemetery and substituted another which read, not Sarah Heydrich, but S.Heydrich. Given that one grandmother's family name was Mautsch, not Heydrich, and that the other's forename was not Sarah, this makes no sense.

To add to all this scuttle-butt, an SS general in the Berlin HQ was reported by Deschner as saying that Heydrich was 'either fully or one quarter Jewish'. Field Marshal Erhard Milch reported him 'one quarter Jewish'. (According to Hannah Arendt, Milch himself was 'half Jewish'). Michael Freund, the Kiel historian, alleged that Hitler and Himmler, aware of Heydrich's Jewish origins, positively chose him for the task of extermination for that very reason. The same comment was made by Felix Gersten, Hitler's masseur and medical adviser, often regarded as an unreliable source and/or a British agent. According to Gersten, Hitler observed to Himmler that 'he will be eternally grateful to us for keeping him rather than throwing him out, and will obey us blindly. Non-Aryans can be kept on a tight rein.' Gersten said that Himmler had referred to Heydrich as 'a half-caste', Gersten himself describing him as 'stained with an irredeemable blemish and in a condition of mortal sin'.

Both Richard Heydrich and his brother Heinz seem to have been teased for 'Jewishness' by fellow students. Richard, because of his weakness and high voice ('the goat'), was greeted by the other boys as 'Isi! Isi!' ('Isidore') at the Halle Reform (gymnasium). (He was once described, incidentally, as having 'pre-Raphaelite lily-white hands as though made for protracted strangling'.) 'Quiet, withdrawn, isolated' was another verdict on the growing boy, who seemed to find release only in playing violin; a school-friend, Dr W. Sommer, referred to Heydrich's 'complex about his alleged Jewish origins'. Certainly something in his childhood produced insecurity and, for some reason, inferiority.

In 1930, he suddenly announced his engagement to Lina van Osten, the daughter of a schoolmaster and, before the German takeover of Fehmarn in Schleswig-Holstein, member of a minor Danish aristocratic family. This action, because of an earlier, serious attachment to the daughter of a dockyard superintendent thought to be leading to marriage, led to his dishonourable discharge from the navy by a German Naval Court of Honour. It was this dismissal, the loss of his career and his officer's (lieutenant's) uniform which, in Deschner's belief, turned him towards National Socialism and the Secret Service.

By the age of twenty-seven, he was already head of the infant Sicherheitsdienst, the Security Service (SD) of the SS (the Blackshirts), under Himmler, at that time Director of the NSDAP's Secret Intelligence Service. In 1936, at thirty-two, he led the Secret State Police, the Criminal Police and the SD. In 1939, he was in charge of the Reich Security Headquarters in Berlin, a Saint-Just unifying all security and police services.

His enemies, as he saw them, were communists and socialists, the Catholic centre, people's and nationalist parties, the political church, Freemasons, Jews and 'Marxists'; he subjected them to the terror of 'protective security', then allowed them to be released, thus producing maximum apprehension. But his principal task after the Wannsee Conference was the execution of the Final Solution to the Jewish Question, to be implemented in the initial stage by forced emigration and, from 1942, by extermination. His next appointment in Prague extended his activities to Eastern Europe.

In September 1941, Heydrich had been appointed to the post in Czechoslovakia of Reich Protector and Hitler's deputy for Bohemia and Moravia. The Czech arms industry, working on behalf of the German armed forces, in particular the arms factories at Brno and the Skoda works at Pilsen, had become the target for active strikes and sabotage by the communists and by the Czech resistance run from Dr Beneš' government in exile at London. Hitler always imagined Prague as the 'centre' of two triangles vital to Germany, Warsaw, Prague, Berlin and Prague, Bucharest and Sofia. He had also been most impressed by Wallenstein's achievements in the seventeenth century, his defection to the Emperor Ferdinand II, suppression of the Bohemian nobility, and the creation in Czech lands of the imperial military power. Perhaps he saw his protégé Heydrich as a twentieth-century version of the Prince of Friedland . . .

In a matter of weeks, by consistent, ruthless terror based on excellent intelligence, Heydrich had seriously disturbed, if not completely broken, the organisations, cells and individuals working against the Reich's industrial interests. He killed, among others, twenty-one Czech officers, six generals and ten colonels. Four to five thousand Czechs were arrested, four to five hundred sentenced, weapons and ninety transmitters seized, five hundred 'criminals' executed.

Beneš, in order to protect – too late – his achievements, and because he knew that the status of his government, already weakened by its communist rivals, was under further danger from Heydrich, flew assassins trained by the SOE to the country. Two, Kubis and Gabchik, ambushed Heydrich in his car in May 1942, wounding him mortally with a Mills bomb. He died on 4 June. The consequences were even more lethal than predicted, reprisals against hostages and prisoners, the massacre of thousands of others, the destruction of all organisations not puppets of the Hitlerian State. All the males in Lidice, a small mining community, were killed, all the women and children sent to the Ravensbrück concentration camp from which very few indeed emerged. Lidice was razed to the ground.

Deschner sees Heydrich as the perfect SS man, tall, fair-skinned, blond, remorseless, a deeply flawed, twisted character. Since he did not believe that Heydrich had 'Jewish blood', he dismisses – as reasons for Heydrich's actions – the theories of those who persisted in believing it. (It seems improbable, furthermore, that Hitler's pathological hatred of Jews would have permitted Heydrich's advancement.) Deschner's own analysis centres on Heydrich's experiences as a child, on the loss of his naval rank and on his extraordinary combination of artist (violinist) and 'control monster'. Giovanni Zibordi in his *Critica sociálistica del fascismo* may have been closer to the mark than the racists in his definition of Fascism as a 'violent revolution of *déclassés* soldiers'.

32
France, and the Dreyfus case

In 1880, there were only eighty thousand Jews in France, of whom perhaps half lived in Paris. Except in Alsace, anti-Semitism was rare. Tsar Alexander II's assassination in 1881 brought a substantial flight of Jewish refugees, but anti-Semitism did not greatly increase until Drumont's exposé in the *Libre Parole* of 'Jewish financiers' and, in particular, of the Panama scandal.

In 1894, a Franco/Prussian military 'convention' was signed, encouraging some to think not only of a counter-blow to the German victory of 1871, but even of the recovery of *La Ligne Bleu des Vosges*. Although General Galliffet, hero of Sedan, was probably the only real senior republican in the Army, the institution was not deeply Jesuit, nor political, nor exclusively aristocratic. It was, nevertheless, a club, regarding itself as something apart and similarly regarded by most of the population. And, furthermore, although the press was becoming increasingly anti-Semitic under the influence of Rochefort and Drumont, the army could not be so defined.

French military thinking concentrated on potential war with Germany. The war office's most secret counter-espionage section in this context was the 'statistical section', an inefficient body headed in 1893 by an anti-Semitic Alsatian, Colonel Sandherr, suffering from creeping paralysis. His principal assistant, Major Hubert-Joseph Henry, closely resembling Oliver Hardy of Laurel and Hardy, was a former peasant, blindly loyal to the army, who had served in Algeria and Indochina, 'brave and astute – with the simple cunning of the uneducated'.

The statistical section's major targets were the German and Italian military attachés in Paris, Colonels Schwartzkoppen and Panizzardi, who appear to have worked almost in tandem. Schwartzkoppen's office was to some extent penetrated by a French maid, called Bastian, who emptied the embassy's wastepaper baskets. The contents, conveyed to Henry, included plans of the French fortifications on the eastern frontier for Schwartzkoppen, and on the Alpine frontier for Panizzardi. One intercepted letter referred to plans of Nice for the Italian attaché, received from 'that scum D'.

In January 1894, Henry learned that an even graver penetration, which he could not identify but which involved the Deuxième Bureau (Intelligence) of the French War Office, was in progress. Later that year, a French officer personally approached the German military attaché, claiming to have been in the Deuxième Bureau. Because he had been reduced by the state of his personal finances to 'suicide or service to Germany', he was willing to pass information. Schwartzkoppen, shocked that an *officer* should sell his country, nevertheless agreed after extensive reference to Berlin. The officer was Major Count Walsin-Esterhazy, son of a French general, a seductive but treacherous speculator, debauchee, debtor to all, and *coureur de femmes*. Esterhazy was married to a rich wife, whom he regularly deceived with prostitutes. He was serving in the 74th Regiment at Rouen and furnished documentary intelligence of varying quality. At the same time, unknown to Schwartzkoppen, in September 1894 he left with the concierge at the German embassy a list (known hereafter as the *bordereau*) of future contributions. This reached Henry via the maid Bastian and was then distributed by him to departmental heads in the war office who concluded that the writer could only have been a 'highly qualified gunner', the first of many professional mistakes made by these stupid and prejudiced men in the long *déroulade* of tragic error.

These officers decided that the source was probably an artillery captain named Alfred Dreyfus, an Alsatian Jew who had served in the Deuxième Bureau as well as in the other three *bureaux*, where he had not been popular. An initial comparison persuaded them that there was enough similarity between the *bordereau* and an example of Dreyfus' handwriting to require further investigation. Although proper examination of the list would have raised doubts in the mind of any competent intelligence officer, Sandherr passed it with his comments to General Boisdeffre and to the minister of war, General Mercier.

The handwriting experts, then and for years afterwards consulted, were completely divided. When, furthermore, Dreyfus was ordered by du Paty de Clam to copy it, the differences were so great that the war office forbore even to show the copy to the experts. Nevertheless, Mercier, although in political difficulty, was so convinced of Dreyfus' guilt that he ordered his arrest and incarceration in the Rue de Cherche-Midi military prison. (It is possible that Boisdeffre disapproved.) From that moment, all concerned at the war office – Generals Mercier and Gonse, Major the Marquis du Paty de Clam, Major Henry, Colonel Sandherr – distorted evidence, suppressed evidence favourable to Dreyfus and illegally failed to show to the defence the evidence upon which Dreyfus was actually convicted. In a word, they lied consistently, and for twelve years.

Alfred Dreyfus came from a well-known, devoutly French cotton-spinning family in Alsace, annexed by Germany in 1871. The family, apart from Mathieu and Jacques who continued to run the Mulhouse factory until shifting part of it to Belfort, moved then to France as French citizens. Alfred was at the Ecole Polytechnique before commissioning in the Artillery, then at the Ecole Supérieure, before becoming a *stagiaire* at the French War Office. He married in 1890 Lucie Hadamard, daughter of a French dealer in diamonds, with whom he had two children; during the marriage, he was thought to have had two passing extra-marital liaisons. He was rich and without financial incentive to seek additional sums from the hated Germans.

Dreyfus' court martial began in Paris on 19 December 1894 before one cavalry and six infantry officers; the court was closed despite the objections of the defence lawyer, Demange. The evidence was thin. Observers and witnesses, including Henry, thought acquittal probable. So Henry lied, falsely alleging an identification of Dreyfus by an unnamed 'man of honour'. The court began to waver. When the documents, including the reference to 'that scum D', were shown to the court illegally, without also being shown to the defence, their views solidified. Captain Dreyfus was sentenced to deportation, forfeiture of rank and degradation. In his cell, he tried to beat his brains out. He also asked for a revolver which his gaoler, convinced of his innocence, would not give him, encouraging him rather to wait for justice. Nor would Dreyfus yield to du Paty's plea from Mercier to admit handing 'chicken-feed' to the Germans in exchange for material valuable to France. (This conversation later became officially perverted into an admission of guilt.) 'If you are innocent,' then cried Du Paty, 'you are the greatest martyr in history.' 'Yes, I am a martyr and I hope the future will prove it.'

Dreyfus, in January 1895, was then marched into a courtyard, at the Ecole Militaire, lined with troops from the Paris garrison. The drums beat. The commanding general bellowed: 'Dreyfus, you are unworthy to bear arms. In the name of the French people, we degrade you.' Dreyfus shouted his innocence, and then: 'Vive la France! Vive l'Armée!' An NCO stripped him of his badges of rank and broke his sword across his knee. On 21 February, after brutal treatment at the Santé, at La Rochelle and at the Ile Mille de Ré, his wife Lucie was allowed to visit him, but not to hold his hand or kiss him. He was taken aboard the ship which carried him to Devil's Island.

On that leper colony, under the pitiless sun, he was confined to a little stone hut with a yard, allowed to walk only on a path two hundred yards long. He had to cook his own exiguous rations. He was not permitted wine, and was forced to endure a lamp attracting innumerable vile insects all night. In the end they even blocked his view of the sea with a high fence. They manacled him to his bed. Here he remained for four and a half years, periodically pestered by bogus letters devised by Henry to create, under censorship, further 'proofs' of Dreyfus' guilt.

Mathieu Dreyfus, now in Paris, began to work on his brother's behalf, but Lucie's application to join her husband was rejected. It was now, also, that Sandherr was succeeded at the section by Marie-Georges Picquart, Dreyfus' ultimate saviour, albeit an anti-Semite and initially convinced of Dreyfus' guilt. Boisdeffre instructed him to look for motive in the case. Nothing emerged. Documents continued to disappear from the staff. In March 1896 Picquart received from Bastian via Henry a letter to Esterhazy, the famous *petit-bleu*, which demanded details in writing on an unspecified subject before the correspondents could continue relations. The letter had not been dispatched and was in the disguised hand of Schwartzkoppen's mistress.

Picquart had Esterhazy followed. The latter twice visited the Germany embassy. He was also discovered to be keeping a registered prostitute, Marguerite Pays, or 'four-fingered Marguerite'. The French military attaché at Berlin, interviewed by Picquart, told him that no one in the German army had ever employed Dreyfus, but that a French battalion commander of about Esterhazy's age had provided gunnery intelligence from Châlons. Picquart knew Esterhazy to have been at Châlons, where he had borrowed money from the colonel, and copied down artillery details. When Picquart reported to Boisdeffre, the general wanted the offender retired 'without scandal, not the centre of another Dreyfus case'.

Esterhazy, with customary impertinence, was currently pulling every kind of string to get himself on to the general staff: the letters he wrote in this regard were passed to Picquart who found the handwriting identical with that on the *bordereau*. General Gonse, when informed, said only, referring directly to Dreyfus' guilt: 'So it looks as if a mistake has been made.' He did nothing. Nor did Boisdeffre, but Picquart was allowed to report to the minister, General Billot. Billot professed to believe that Esterhazy's guilt did not absolve Dreyfus and, instead of facing the cabinet, sought 'further evidence'. The minister told Picquart to put himself under Gonse for the purpose. Gonse said, 'The case can't be reopened. General Mercier . . . is involved.' 'But [Dreyfus] is innocent.' 'That's not important,' said Gonse. 'What,' said Picquart, 'if the Dreyfus family finds the real culprit?' 'If you say nothing,' replied the general, 'no one will know.' Picquart's hands were tied.

Major Henry also saw that for Picquart to reopen the Dreyfus case would ruin himself (Henry), Mercier, other senior officers and damage the army. He started to write the false letters to Dreyfus. He fabricated material for the press. He substituted 'D' for 'P' in old correspondence between the German and Italian military attachés. He blackguarded Picquart behind his back, and forged correspondence not only between Schwartzkoppen and Panizzardi directly implicating Dreyfus, but also between Dreyfus and the emperor, Kaiser William II, himself! Billot agreed to post Picquart, first showing him the forgery and refusing to discuss its authenticity. Picquart left for Châlons, ten days after a young Jew, Bernard Lazare, had caused a reproduction of the *bordereau* to be published in the press with a text describing the contradictions in the prosecution case. Gonse continued to harass Picquart from corps to corps. Henry attacked him by letter with trumped-up charges. Picquart informed his lawyer, Leblois, who urged him to pursue both his own and Dreyfus' causes.

Although an Alsace senator, Scheurer-Kestner, was now sure that Dreyfus was not guilty, he could not move effectively without uncovering Picquart. (Everyone, nevertheless, including Billot, was sure of Esterhazy's guilt.) Meanwhile, Dreyfusist press response to the anti-Semites began to grow. Another photograph of the *bordereau* was published, in which Esterhazy's handwriting was recognised by a banker, who told Mathieu Dreyfus. Mathieu now wrote to Billot a full denunciation of Esterhazy. The case, at last, was in the public domain. Coincidentally, Estarhazy bombarded Picquart – now in Tunisia – with telegrams designed to persuade the censors of Picquart's culpability. The latter returned to a Paris in which the *Figaro* had just republished the *bordereau* opposite extracts from some of Esterhazy's letters to a lady friend: 'If I were told that I should be killed as captain of Uhlans, sabring the French, I should be perfectly happy . . .' and 'The feast I dream of . . . is Paris taken by assault and handed over to pillage by a hundred thousand drunken soldiers.' The anti-Dreyfusist press, of course, said that they were Jewish forgeries.

Esterhazy asked for a court martial. This took place between 8 December and 30 December 1896, and resulted in his acquittal on the *bordereau* charge. Picquart, however, was placed under fortress arrest. But, at the same time, the Dreyfusists were able to demonstrate that Billot was wrong in declaring that the *bordereau* was not the only evidence against Dreyfus. This, together with evidence of the *petit bleu*, now gave the Dreyfusists a clear policy, to which Emile Zola with his enormous readership attached himself in 'J'accuse'. Widespread anti-Jewish riots followed. Zola was tried and convicted – as was Picquart ('for grave infractions of discipline') – in processes as incompetent as they were corrupt. In the middle of them, Esterhazy openly confessed to the *Figaro* to being author of the *bordereau*. In court, Mercier, Pellieux, Boisdeffre, Gonse, all lied or prevaricated. Outside the court and in the corridors, defence witnesses were assaulted and abused. Zola, after appeal and reconviction, took refuge in London.

Outside Paris itself, neither France nor the workers were *much* concerned by the affair, although anti-Semitic rioting occurred. In Paris, it split society wide open and in all directions. The divisions were between those who placed 'order' and the 'honour' of a recently defeated army above justice, and those preferring truth and justice to other considerations. Clemenceau fought a duel with Drumont. Henry, after first refusing to fight a Picquart 'lacking honour', was eventually wounded by him. Picquart refused to answer Esterhazy's challenge. Henry's professional forger hanged himself, or was hung. Henry sowed suspicion between du Paty and Gonse. Picquart learned about Esterhazy's misappropriation of his cousin Christian's loan of fifty thousand francs.

Cavaignac, the new minister of war, instituted military proceedings against Esterhazy as writer of the *bordereau*, which were preempted by Esterhazy's arrest on civil charges. (Cavaignac claimed that Esterhazy's authorship of the list did not, however, exculpate Dreyfus.) The minister then ordered Picquart's rearrest. A lunatic merry-go-round of charges and examinations followed. Du Paty, Esterhazy and 'four-fingered Marguerite' were questioned on the forgeries, Esterhazy's house was searched, Henry begged protection from the examining magistrate and burst into tears. A Captain Cuignet exposed Henry's forgeries and so informed Cavaignac. When interrogated by the war minister, Henry admitted the charge. Boisdeffre resigned; Henry killed himself by cutting his throat with a razor; but Cavaignac still 'held' to Dreyfus' guilt, perhaps only because disclosure of the passage of documents at the 1894 trial would lead to Mercier's disgrace. Esterhazy, summoned before a military court, was dismissed from the service.

A later war minister, Zurlinden, without even considering Henry's probable role, believed that the erasure and reinsertion of Esterhazy's name on the *petit bleu* was Picquart's work. He accordingly ordered the latter's prosecution. Almost the entire foreign press, learning of an admission in London by Esterhazy about the *bordereau*, took the Dreyfusard line, but in a manner which united France against Dreyfus. Strikes broke out in Paris. Sixty thousand troops were moved to the capital. Rumours circulated of military plots. Dreyfusards and the Right fought in the streets. Fears grew of another 1789. The court acceded to an appeal by Lucie Dreyfus but, in agreeing at last to a reinvestigation of the case, did not suspend her husband's sentence.

Picquart's proposed prosecution in a military court – to repeat Dreyfus' fate – was too much for the senate, who ordered a stay of execution. In the Criminal Appeal Court, considering Dreyfus himself, Cuignet was confused and attacked Du Paty for everything from the denunciation of Dreyfus onwards. In so doing, he helped to destroy the case against Dreyfus. (The Court also heard that Dreyfus had positively refused to visit most secret artillery factories.) This court's judgment ended in Dreyfus' release from Cayenne. Almost simultaneously, the Criminal Court found no case against Picquart, who was released with his lawyer, Leblois; two minor charges remained against him, to be heard at the Rennes court martial and, much later, before the appeal court.

When General Galliffet took over as minister of war in the Waldeck–Rousseau cabinet, he told Boisdeffre and Gonse that, although they would never serve again, they would not be 'touched'. Boisdeffre had thought he might be executed.

On 30 June 1899, Dreyfus arrived at Quiberon where he was met by his wife Lucie. He had been very brave, but his privation had rendered him rather inarticulate and unable to concentrate; he was ill, feverish, unhappy and unsure, knowing little of recent events surrounding his case. When he entered the court at Rennes, 'there came in', according to Stevens of the *Daily Mail*, 'a little old man . . . an old, old man of thirty-nine'. Jaurès commented: 'He no longer had the slightest intelligence. He is a puppet.' But Jaurès was no friend.

Dreyfus' lawyers were at cross purposes, Demange seeking precision, Labori drama. The military judges inevitably favoured the prosecution. The 'statistical section', its personnel changed, remained fiercely hostile to the accused and to Picquart. (The charges against du Paty were, however, dropped.) In court, Dreyfus denied charges that he had confessed to his original escort after arrest, and reminded the court of his rejection of Mercier's 'compromise' via du Paty. Gonse repeated his lies. So did the officers of the 'section'. No less than ten handwriting experts were heard. The Sûreté denied the allegations of the 'section'. Wholly contrary evidence was given about Dreyfus' movements, such as his attendance or otherwise at German military manoeuvres. Esterhazy refused to leave London, sending abusive letters. du Paty stayed in bed. Mercier lied, in particular that he, the prime minister and president had waited half the night in the Elysée for the issue of peace and war to be decided by an exchange of Franco/German notes. The president flatly denied this. Hearsay was freely admitted into the farrago of opinions, lies, half-truths, fantasies and speculation, before seven honest but tunnel-visioned army officers. 'The Rennes court martial was not a trial: it was a spectacle, sometimes a farce.'

Dreyfus was again found guilty, by a majority of five to two. On 19 September, the French president, for wholly 'political' reasons, remitted the rest of his sentence and cancelled the order for his degradation. M. Loubet thought that the affair was over. It was not.

Dreyfus infuriated his more intransigent supporters by refusing to echo their violence, seeking only acquittal and restoration to the army. Meanwhile, by 1901, anti-militarism had grown, nurtured by Sorel, Drumont's successors, and Hervé – insulting flag and army, inciting soldiers to mutiny, calling for violence against both civil and military authorities – while the army, especially the officer corps, was undermined by constant changes in the name of 'efficiency, republicanism and democracy'. Morale deteriorated until the appointment of Marshal (Papa) Joffre in 1911.

Picquart had refused to meet Dreyfus and continued to pursue his own case for re-entry, promotion and a command. Dreyfus applied for an enquiry into the *bordereau*, which began in April 1903. Documents suppressed by the statistical section were discovered, further indicating Dreyfus' innocence. Also found were Henry's falsifications of the register, an agent's identification of Esterhazy as the real 'German spy', notes from Schwartzkoppen about purchase of secret material, the revelations of the 'P' to 'D' forgery, and forgery of dates to incriminate Dreyfus. The enquiry led to the Criminal Appeal Court. On 12 July 1906, the joint appeal courts annulled the verdict of the Rennes Court Martial. (The reason for the three-year delay is unknown.) Dreyfus was promoted to major; he refused financial indemnity. Picquart was promoted to brigadier-general backdated to July 1903. In a courtyard of the Ecole Militaire, Dreyfus received the Légion d'honneur, fourth grade, a shabby concession. In 1906, Clemenceau as prime minister appointed Picquart to be minister of war; the latter, while commanding the Second Army Corps in 1914, died from a fall off his horse.

Of the others, Esterhazy in London changed his name to Fitzgerald, writing anti-British articles. His wife had earlier divorced him and he remarried, retiring to Harpenden where he died in 1923 and is buried in the name of Comte de Voilement, having earned a living by selling tinned fish. Schwartzkoppen, on his deathbed in 1917, cried, 'Frenchmen hear me! Dreyfus is innocent. It was all intrigue and forgery. Dreyfus is innocent.'

Dreyfus retired to Carpentras, much settled by Jews and former Jewish soldiers. He was recalled to the colours for the 1914–18 War. It has been related that when a visitor from Paris told him of the arrest on espionage charges of another French Jewish officer, and remarked on the continuing malice of his former colleagues, Dreyfus only commented: 'Oh, I don't know. There's no smoke without fire', which may indicate only that his experience had done nothing to change his unswerving and uncritical loyalty to the French army. The loyalty of the Dreyfus family, and their service to France, continued in succeeding generations with further unhappy consequences for those involved. Ado Reinach (Mathieu Dreyfus' son-in-law) was killed in the Ardennes forest in 1914, leaving his widow pregnant. Jean-Pierre Reinach, who never knew his own father, joined the Free French in England and was killed parachuting into France in 1942. Five months after his death his widow gave birth to a daughter who would also never know her father. A number of descendants of the Dreyfus family were deported to the Nazi camps and Alfred Dreyfus' granddaughter, Madeleine Levy, died in Auschwitz-Birkenau in 1944. The Dreyfus case reverberated across Europe and, amongst other consequences, it prompted Theodor Herzl (in Vienna) vigorously to increase the momentum of his struggle for Zionism.

Despite periodic assertions to the contrary, there is no evidence that Marshal André Masséna, whose name is engraved with others on the Arc de Triomphe, was of Jewish origin. But there are two officers, whose names are also there, who were unquestionably Jewish and were men of distinction; apart from them, the French army has produced at least thirty generals and innumerable other senior and junior officers of that faith and race.

One of those two was inspector general of infantry, General Henri Baron Rottembourg. This officer was born in Moselle in 1769, serving initially as a sergeant in the Royal Hesse Darmstadt Regiment, transferring to the French army in 1792. He was thereafter in the French armies of the North, the Ardennes, Mayence and Italy, fighting under Souchet in 1800 and wounded at Mincio; he was promoted major in 1803. He served as an officer of the Imperial Guard from 1806 to 1807 (colonel in 1806) in Prussia and Poland and was wounded at Wagram. He became a baron of the empire in 1809, a brigadier-general in the Imperial Guard in 1811, general of division in 1814, (commanding the 5th Division of the guard in Oudinot's Army Corps) and engaged in several battles before becoming inspector general. In the Army of the Rhine in 1815, he conducted successful actions at Selz and Honheim. Under Louis XVIII, he was president of the committee of infantry, and commanded the 16th Division at Lille before retiring at sixty-five.

The other was one of Napoleon's cavalry commanders, Lieutenant-General, General Inspector of Cavalry, Marc-Jean-Jerome, Baron Wolff. Wolff, although a convert to Catholicism, was born a Jew at Strasbourg in 1776, dying in 1848, 'the year of revolution'. As a ranker in the 2nd Regiment of Chasseurs à Cheval, he was in the Army of the Rhine from 1794–6 and was wounded at Mannheim in 1795. In 1800, he was aide-de-camp to Louis Bonaparte, the emperor's nephew, serving under the emperor himself from 1805–08 in the Grande Armée, and being wounded at Ostrolenka. Napoleon then seconded him as colonel of the guard to the king of Westphalia, later as commander of Westphalian cavalry before returning to France as brigadier-general in 1812 to command in Russia the 1st Guards Cavalry Brigade of the 8th Corps, then the Light Cavalry in the 6th Army Corps under Marmont. In 1814, he led the Fourth Division of Light Cavalry. Subsequently, he was promoted to inspector of cavalry, becoming a baron in 1819. He was made a lieutenant-general in 1835, but served thereafter in a number of functions.

In 1808, about one thousand of the eighty thousand French Jews were volunteers in Napoleon's army. By 1821, there were only five officers in the army, one of whom was a general, but thereafter, the Lègion d'honneur in all its grades was awarded to a rapidly increasing number of Jewish officers, from lieutenant to general.

33
General Monash, Australian Imperial Force

The Canadians took Passchendaele in November 1917 but that battle, fought over long periods in the trenches, in mud and in cold, almost horizontal driving rain, cost a quarter of a million British and Australian lives. General John Monash, then commanding the Third Division of the Australian Imperial Force, spoke of the deteriorating weather, 'no flying, no photography, no information on the Germans, no effective bombardment' or resupply . . . and 'the whole of the country a sea of mud and, in most places, *waist deep*', not conditions commonly noted in his native land.

Monash was born in Melbourne of Jewish parents from Stettin, Prussia in 1865, the family soon moving to Jerildorie, a bush town on the Billabong Creek in New South Wales. Here, at the local school, he first showed signs of scholarship, as well as of ability to move in rough and broken territory. When he was twelve, he went on to Scotch College, Melbourne, won a mathematics competition, matriculated top in modern languages and mathematics, then entered Melbourne University. He suspended his courses for a while, as he could not pay the bills, working as an engineer on bridges and railways and also joining the Victoria Militia. In 1891, he graduated in engineering and in 1893 as a master of civil engineering; he went on to practise as a patent attorney and consulting engineer, becoming a BA in arts and law in 1895, and then founding construction companies exploiting reinforced concrete. By 1894 he had married.

He rose steadily in the militia, promoted colonel commanding the Thirteenth Infantry Brigade. In that capacity, the inspector general of overseas forces, General Sir Ian Hamilton, speaking later at Gallipoli, remembered Monash holding a conference under an Australian gum tree in Lilydale near Melbourne in 1914, at which he was 'direct, blunt and telling'.

In April 1915, basic topographic intelligence for the landing of the Australians at Anzac Cove, including Monash's Fourth Brigade, was inadequate. Casualties from Turkish guns on the cliffs above were severe. The brigade, nevertheless, supported the defence of the difficult central sector at the head of 'Monash Valley'. In the main offensive in August 1915, against the Aghyl Dere, a junior officer's decision – on the advice of a Turkish guide – to cut corners up a steep, overgrown defile led to dragging, single-file traffic, and to heavy casualties from Turkish rifle and field-gun fire from concealed positions in the Aghyl Dere and Damakjelik Bair. Monash came up a gulley choked with wounded and ordered the stalled columns to move through a passage half a mile long in an advance lasting three hours.

The great Bill Slim, addressing the Fourteenth Army in the Second World War before Myitkina, was assured by his audience: 'We'll *follow* you, sir, we'll be right behind you.' 'Oh no, you won't,' said the future field marshal, with a smile. Nor did Monash try to lead from the front or seek the bubble reputation even in the cannon's mouth. But when all else had failed, as above the bed of the Aghyl Dere at Taylor's Gap, he managed to release and revive the confused troops. Like Gneisenau, or like Moltke who fought the Austrians from within the city of Berlin, where the Prussian general staff was housed, Monash was a detailed planner, a military artist, 'an engineer' who used good staffwork and good intelligence. He preferred a subtle functional plan, the use of brains and deception, to the cavalry charges, confrontation and unremitting slog which some profess to see as the hallmarks of some British generals in the Great War.

For Monash, a musician: 'A perfected modern battle-plan is like nothing so much as a score for an orchestral composition where the various arms and units are the instruments and the tasks they perform are their respective musical phrases. Every instrument must make its entry at precisely the proper moment and play its phrase in the general harmony.' But, also, he added that 'the great essential is entirely to suppress all personal considerations'. He needed to remind himself of this stoic requirement: over eight thousand Australian soldiers were killed and nearly twenty thousand wounded amid the foul conditions of Gallipoli. He wrote to his wife of ' . . . the magnificence of our Australian troops . . .' and went on: 'The British officers are the first to admit that for physique, dash, enterprise and sublime courage, the Australians are head and shoulders above any others.' A German prisoner in France commented, 'I have heard much about the fighting qualities of the Australian soldiers. They are not soldiers at all. They are madmen.' Most of them, including their commanders, the cavalryman Harry Chauvel in the Levant, Brudenell White in Gallipoli and Monash himself, were citizen soldiers, in that regard like British territorials with their loyalties, comradeship and close geographical ties. At Gallipoli they had to face, as well as dug-in Turks, the stink of dead bodies, heat, icy cold, flies, noise, discomfort, and an incompetent leadership at the top.

These Anzac forces and reinforcements were reformed in Egypt in four divisions and two Anzac corps. They fought in Europe between March and November 1916; at the first battle of the Somme Australian losses were tragically large, in particular at the Pozières windmill, now a cemetery like an amphitheatre, crammed with the graves of Australians. General Sir William Birdwood, commander-in-chief of all the Australians, promoted Monash to major-general commanding the Third Australian Division newly arrived in England, which spent from July to November 1916 under training before being attached to II Anzac Corps in a quietish section of the line near Armentières. ('*Mademoiselle from Armentières, parlez-vous . . .?*') Birdwood seems to have been concerned that Monash was getting too fat, but 'abstinence and exercise' on Salisbury Plain reduced this danger and increased his physical and mental fitness.

Haig's high command now began to plan its offensive against the Hindenburg Line, a brigade of the Fifth Australian Division taking Bapaume on 17 March, infantry and tanks of General Plumer's Second Army, British, Canadians and Australians, then moving on to the hard-fought victory of Bullecourt on 12 May. Monash in II Corps under the Second Army now mounted his first divisional attack with Third Division, helping with brilliant thoroughness and organisation to take the Messines Ridge, in a prelude to the great offensive on the entire Ypres-Armentières front.

On 31 July, Third Ypres began with Passchendaele as the goal, I Anzac Corps in the lead against the Ypres ridge from 1 September, getting astride it by 4 October with well over one thousand enemy dead, the same number of prisoners and large quantities of captured artillery and other equipment. Australian losses were heavy, at Polygon Wood and Broodseinde, but corps and army headquarters were both more than congratulatory. It was now that the hellish struggle for Passchendaele began; the Forty-fifth and Sixty-sixth British Divisions, who had succeeded the Third Australian and the New Zealand divisions in the line, were unable to progress more than four hundred yards, so that in the next phase Monash and his colleague were required by the high command to make up the ground they had not covered and, therefore, to advance for one and three quarter miles. After the battle, in which the Third Division reached the outskirts of Passchendaele before being repulsed, all five Australian divisions were joined into one corps, I Anzac Corps, under General Birdwood, later Lord Birdwood.

In March 1918, Monash was on holiday at Menton in the South of France when the Ludendorff offensive began, breaking through on 21 March at St Quentin and thrusting at Amiens. The Third and Fourth Australian divisions were out of the line, sixty miles north in Flanders, but moved south to stop the German advance. Monash drove to Paris, arriving there on 25 March. He went on by car to Amiens, Doullens and Blaringhem, ready to move southward by train and car. British troops were in retreat. Doullens was chaotic, crammed with military and civilian refugees.

On 26 March, Monash called on the commander of VII Corps, Lieutenant General Sir Walter Congreve VC, and his chief of staff, Sir Alexander Hore-Ruthven VC, later Lord Gowrie. Congreve said, 'Thank heaven, the Australians at last.' He explained by candlelight in the blacked-out château that his VII Corps, the right wing of General Byng's Third Army, was holding the Albert line, near the River Ancre, across higher ground to Bray on the Somme. (General Gough's Fifth Army was in place from the Somme southwards.) Unfortunately the VII Corps line was abandoned in error, leaving ten miles of land between the Somme and the Ancre undefended and open to the Germans. The Third and Fourth Divisions had already embussed to Matigny where Congreve ordered Monash to relieve the three British divisions who had been four days in the Albert-Bray line, fighting continuously without sleep or food. The Australians were told to fill the jamb between the Ancre and the Somme, thus stopping Ludendorff's cavalry before they could get through to Amiens from Buire and Morlancourt.

Monash made his dispositions from a small room with a single telephone and, next day, intercepted the Germans, inflicting huge casualties and taking over the Third Army's flank. The recipients of his orders, which were read out to the debussed troops by the light of torches at the side of the road, recognised 'the old man's' touch in their brisk and lucid expression. The German offensive, however, continued, although with reduced momentum. The Third Division held Ludendorff at Villers-Bretonneux. That town and others were later lost by the Eighth British Division, but recovered in a counter-attack on 25 April, Anzac Day. Monash, whose usual principle it was that infantry should be preceded or accompanied by the greatest possible quantity of armour and ordnance, commented on this occasion that 'the counter-attack, without artillery support, is the finest thing done in the war by the Australian or any other troops'.

In May 1918, when Birdwood was appointed to command the Fifth Army, the Australian Army Corps was given to Monash. His first operation, with three Australian infantry brigades and attached Americans, was against Hamel. It ended in victory after ninety-three minutes, so successful and so brilliant that Clemenceau, the 'Tiger', at the age of seventy-seven, on his usual Sunday visit, called not on the usual French units, but on the Fourth Australians near Corbie. The lessons of this battle – attention to detail, inter-arm cooperation, surprise, counter-battery fire, skill and fighting spirit among infantry and tank crews – were distributed in a brochure throughout the British armies on the Western Front.

A German offensive directed at the French began on 18 July, Foch retaliating on the Marne, and Rawlinson's Fourth Army (III British Corps, the Australians and Canadians) assaulting the Somme valley on 8 August (Ludendorff's 'black day' for the German army). The latter retreated under Australian pressure to the Péronne. The Third Division captured Bray and other Somme towns. But the Germans stood at St Quentin, which surveyed from its heights the ancient, embattled, moated little town of Péronne, and dominated the whole position. Monash sought Rawlinson's agreement to take the hill with three battalions transferred by bridges which he had had built across the Somme from the south to the north bank of the river. The army commander laughed: 'And so you think you're going to take Mont St Quentin with three battalions? What presumption! However, I don't think I ought to stop you, so go ahead and try, and I wish you luck.'

The Third Division cleared the enemy from forward positions while, under an artillery barrage, the seventeenth, eighteenth and nineteenth battalions of the fifth brigade, Second Division, 'rose out of their trenches in the cold, pre-dawn darkness, yelling like fiends and keeping up a rapid fire in order to make the Germans think they were being attacked by a larger force . . . they made up for lack of numbers by their speed and savagery'. Only eight officers and seventy-five men survived in the seventeenth battalion, but when the brigade was relieved at midnight by the sixth brigade, the Fifth Division was able to seize Péronne itself. The Australians had lost three thousand men and won six VCs.

The Canadians were similarly successful at Cambrai. The Germans fell back, pursued by the Fourth Army with ten divisions, including the First and Fourth Australian. On 19 September, the Australians were on the St Quentin canal side of the Hindenburg Line. From 26–9 September, the First, Third and Fourth British Armies and the First French attacked between Douai and St Quentin; the First American and Fourth French advanced towards Sedan; the Belgians and the Second British Army marched on Ghent; the Fourth American attacked at Verdun. In late September, the Australian Corps, minus the First and Fourth Divisions and so badly depleted that two American divisions had to be added, took Bellicourt, Joncourt and Le Catelet, the Second Division finally breaking through the German line along the whole Australian front on 4 and 5 October.

On 5 October, in the last action fought by the Australian infantry in the Great War, the sixth brigade broke through the Hindenburg Line and took Montbrelian; the Hindenburg Line, under all these blows, collapsed at last.

The prime minister, David Lloyd George, believed that Monash was the most resourceful general in the whole British army and that, had the war lasted longer, he might have risen to become commander-in-chief. In those days, and since, in the eyes of fashionable iconoclasts such as – most recently – Alan Clark, no one had much to say for the 'attritional' generals, a view which Monash privately shared, but which is becoming less common. He was a first-class, thorough, industrious and flexible soldier, brilliant, cautious, but bold. He himself said, 'From the far-off days of 1914, when the call first came, until the last shot was fired, every day was filled with loathing, horror and distress . . .

the dreadful inefficiency and mis-spent energy of war . . . Yet it had to be.'

In September 1918, the strength of the Australian Army Corps under Monash was, with attached troops, two hundred thousand men, four times larger than the Duke of Wellington's command of British troops at the Battle of Waterloo. On return to Australia, after organising and supervising the repatriation of all Australian troops overseas, Monash became general manager and chairman of the vast Electricity Commission of Victoria. In 1923, he was elected vice chancellor of Melbourne University. He died, to a sadness that was felt throughout the British Empire, on 8 October 1931.

34
The Jewish Legion; the Jewish Brigade

In 1914, a polyglot Jewish orator from Odessa named Vladimir Jabotinsky was given a roving commission to the Middle East by a Moscow daily, possibly with a Czarist intelligence brief. Pogroms in Russia had driven large numbers of Jews to emigrate to Palestine, of whom up to twenty-five thousand had been forced out or even killed by the Ottoman Turkish administration. Jabotinsky therefore decided to try to raise a Jewish 'army' for self-defence, but the British authorities were only able to agree to a Zion Mule Corps under the command of an admired British officer, Lieutenant-Colonel J.H. Patterson DSO ('the *collonél*'), a man with glittering contacts, author of *The Man Eaters of Tsavo*. Patterson's second-in-command was a romantic figure named Captain Joseph Trumpeldor, born in the Caucasus, a lawyer *and* dentist by trade, who fought as a private soldier at the siege of Port Arthur during the Russo-Japanese war, where he lost his left arm. After leaving hospital he went back to the front line, winning four Crosses of St George and becoming one of the Czar's first Jewish officers, before emigrating to Palestine to work as a labourer in an agricultural cooperative.

The Zion Mule Corps did good service at Gallipoli, where it was commended by General Sir Ian Hamilton, the commander-in-chief, and repatriated to the UK at the end of the Dardanelles campaign. Jabotinsky was initially unable to interest His Majesty's Government in the creation of any further Jewish units. Trumpeldor therefore returned to Russia where he successfully persuaded Kerensky to form a Jewish army of between 75,000 and 100,000 men to join the British in Mesopotamia and Palestine and defeat the Turks. The Bolshevik revolution extinguished the project. Trumpeldor himself was killed in 1920, leading a force of young Jews against Arab terrorists at the hill of Tel-Hay.

Jabotinsky left for London in the spring of 1917 and joined the Twentieth London Regiment, forming the sixteenth platoon. As a result of his efforts, and those of Chaim Weizmann, the War Office agreed to the foundation of the 'Jewish Legion', the first component of which was the Thirty-eighth Battalion, Royal Fusiliers, under Patterson, officially gazetted on 24 August 1917. It was despatched to Palestine and sufficient further volunteers now came forward from civilian life and from other British units to make up the Thirty-ninth Battalion, commanded by Lieutenant-Colonel Eleazor Margolin, originally a Russian who had lived and worked in Palestine with his parents before emigrating to Australia where he became captain in the militia, subsequently going overseas in the Sixteenth Battalion of the Australian Expeditionary Force. He, too, had served at Gallipoli, winning a DSO.

After the Balfour declaration of November 1917, the US Government strongly supported the concept of the Jewish National Home. Isaac Ben Zvi and David Ben Gurion in New York, having failed to enlist Turkish support for Zionism, persuaded six thousand five hundred men in the United States to volunteer for service with British units in Palestine. It is not clear how many of them actually reached the 35th, 39th, 40th and 42nd battalions of the Fusiliers, the 40th under Lieutenant-Colonel M.F. Scott, then Lieutenant-Colonel F.D. Samuel DSO, the 42nd under Lieutenant-Colonel J.S. Millar DSO. (James Rothschild was in the 39th and Jacob Epstein in the 38th.) Nine thousand six hundred men in all joined the Jewish Legion which, in the end, numbered five battalions – *schneiders* (tailors) from the East End, Palestinians in the 40th battalion, a hundred and fifty Turkish Jews, ten per cent from Jaffa – forming the basis of the eventual Haganah. There were Russians, English, Americans, Georgians, Argentinians, Moroccans, Uzbeks. Between the wars, the children of the British contingent joined the Jewish Lads Brigade, with affiliation to British regiments in London, Birmingham and Sheffield.

The 38th battalion went into the line near Nablus and then held a difficult stretch in the Jordan valley westwards from Jericho, its principal tasks scouting and patrolling. The battalion earned a reputation for assessing Turkish plans and for effective support of the Australian and New Zealand cavalry, who, with the 39th battalion, helped to outflank the Turks and managed to cross the river toward Ramoth Gilead. The 38th later crossed the Jordan and held the road between Es Salt and Tel Nimrus until the Turkish army collapsed, also holding the railway line from Romani to Ludd and Haifa. General Allenby commended their 'good fighting qualities'.

The battalions were awarded the Shield of King David and the name 'The Judaeans', carrying the Maccabean symbol, the *menora*, the eight-branched candlestick, with '*Kadima*', Hebrew for 'Forward and Eastward'. There is an apocryphal story of three Jewish battalion commanders in boots and jodhpurs, settling after dinner and a glass of port on the legion's motto: 'No Advance without Security'.

Jabotinsky, in British uniform and carrying a cane or crop, was imprisoned by the British in 1920 for military action against militant Arabs. He returned after his release to translation work, but soon re-emerged with plans in the Union of Zionist Revisionists to bring as many European Jews as possible into Israel, and as fast as possible. These attracted much support in Eastern Europe, especially Poland where Menachem Begin was head of Betar, the Youth Wing of the Revisionists. By 1934, Jewish immigration into Israel had reached forty thousand and continued to rise. The British reduced the rates of entry. Partition was proposed, a Jewish state along the coast and inward therefrom, an Arab state comprised of Judaea, the Negev and Ephraim, plus a British mandate from Jerusalem to Lydda and Ramleh to Jaffa, to which the Arabs violently objected. In 1939, a British White Paper reduced Jewish immigration to twenty thousand per annum for five years, and *none* thereafter.

By 1936, Jabotinsky who was, incidentally, a sergeant and honorary lieutenant in the Royal Fusiliers, had already established the Irgun Zvai Leumi, a clandestine, military organisation to fight Arab terrorists and force the British from a potentially independent Palestine. In 1939, he unleashed the Irgun in open harassment of the British, a role in contrast to that of largely defensive Haganah with its 'non-Revisionists' and Socialist Zionists. He wholly disbelieved in the possibility of voluntary 'sharing' with the Arabs, or in the peaceful establishment in Palestine of Eretz Israel: 'only an iron wall of Jewish bayonets . . .' David Ben Gurion called him 'Vladimir Hitler'. It was, indeed, the case that Jabotinsky sought sole Jewish rule and control.

When the Second World War began, one hundred and thirty thousand Jews volunteered for British service. Although about fourteen thousand served in various units in Greece, Crete, Abyssinia, Libya, Cyprus, Iraq and Palestine, it was only after heavy lobbying by Chaim Weizmann and Moshe Shertok that Winston Churchill eventually agreed to the 'independent national Jewish formation' described below. 'I like,' said Winston, 'the idea of the Jews trying to get at the murderers of their fellow countrymen in Central Europe.' It was certainly a likeable idea, but the lessons learned by the Jewish Brigade from their cooperation in Cairo and Italy with the 8th Army had consequences after the war that the prime minister does not seem to have anticipated.

In 1940, fifteen Jewish companies had been created in Palestine and attached to 'the Buffs', the East Kent Regiment. In 1942–3, they became the Palestine Regiment, three battalions being engaged directly in guard duties in Palestine, Libya and Egypt. In September 1944, the British agreed under pressure, as we have seen, to the formation of a reinforced brigade to join purely British fighting units after more comprehensive training. This force of about five thousand men was composed of the three battalions earlier referred to, plus an artillery regiment, Service Corps, sapper, signal, transport, medical and military police units. It was commanded by a Canadian Jewish sapper, who learned Hebrew, Brigadier Ernest Benjamin CBE. The battalion commanders were British and the company commanders mainly Jewish; the men were British, Russian, Czech, Austrian, Polish, Yemeni, Falasha.

After training in Egypt, the Jewish Brigade joined the 8th Army in Italy for further training at Fiuggi before going into the line on the Alfonsini against 42 Jäger Division, and on the Senio where it was opposed by the 12th German Parachute regiment. On the Alfonsini, it attacked twice and took prisoners, while against the paras it crossed the river, securing a bridgehead but losing twenty killed and seventy wounded. Twenty-one men were decorated (MCs, MMs etc. and one CBE) and seventy-eight mentioned in despatches. Passover was celebrated in the line with wine from Palestine and *matsa* or unleavened bread.

In north-east Italy, Holland and Belgium, the Jewish Brigade gave much time and practical help to refugees from the Holocaust, feeding and clothing them, guiding them across borders to safety, even smuggling them into Palestine. The gold Star of David on the blue and white ground was rapturously welcomed in France, in Italy and in all the camps. In the Jewish transit camps, breakfast consisted of only three hundred grams of bread, one ounce of margarine (per week) and acorn coffee; 'lunch' was bean soup and one and a half ounces of horse-meat, sometimes Spam. For supper they had one and a half litres of soup. 'More soup was provided even in concentration camps,' said one victim. It was not the brigade, however, but the British, under General Sir Gerald Templer, who fed the concentration camps, fed the starving Dutch, repatriated two million displaced persons, got in the harvest, restarted the coal mines, repaired the railways.

Growing Anglo–Jewish tensions led to the brigade's disbandment in the summer of 1946, most of the men returning to Palestine to decommission there. Although it was not retained by the putative Jewish authorities as an independent formation, it had gained experience which was rapidly to become valuable to the Haganah and to its 'sharp end', the Palmach, two Haganah chiefs of staff having served in the Jewish Brigade.

Most potential clashes between the Jewish partisan tradition originally established by Jabotinsky, and the systems of an organised, formal, professional army, were avoided in Israel. The War of Independence permitted the integration of the Haganah with a strength of 100,000, of whom 20,000 were armed and trained, and the 'British' ex-servicemen whether *sabras* or exiles. Although the brigade's battle experience was not extensive, its training had covered almost the whole spectrum of strategic and tactical military activities, command, cooperation between infantry, air and artillery and the use and maintenance of most types of equipment other than tracked and armoured artillery and tanks. The former 'British' veterans adapted to the different requirements of the Israeli Defence Forces. We shall learn more of the Haganah in Chapter 44.

35
Italy

Josephus, the Jewish soldier and historian of the war in Palestine between Rome and the Jews in AD 66–70, noted that there were already eight thousand Jews in Rome by 4 BC. This total over the centuries reached fifty thousand, including *marrano* refugees from Spain. The Middle Ages brought to them misery and persecution, mitigated under the Renaissance but renewed in the Counter-Reformation, when Jews faced isolation, poverty and persecution in the ghettos where excessive taxation, bullying and forced baptisms were commonplace.

But in nineteenth-century Italy, Jews served militarily against the French, the Hapsburgs, the Papal power, and with Garibaldi. After full Italian unification and emancipation, they were admitted to parliament, the senate, diplomacy, the law and the bureaucracy, some reaching ministerial rank, including that of prime minister (Luigi Luxatti) in 1910. By the end of the nineteenth century, an Italian Jew had become war minister, and several hundred Jewish officers were in the army list. Anti-Semitism had diminished after emancipation, or seemed to have; it is nevertheless significant that thousands of Jews converted to Catholicism in the 1930s and some ten per cent joined the Fascist Party.

The Holocaust was, however, just as real for Jews in Italy as elsewhere, beginning on a small scale with 'private' gangs, but getting into full swing after the fall of Mussolini in September 1943. Thereafter the SS and the Republic of Saló applied the usual disgusting measures – castor-oil, beatings, torture, murder (mass and individual), deportations from which few returned. The relatively low proportion of Jews liquidated, about a fifth, was owed to the high proportion of non-Jewish rescuers and, above all, to the relatively early destruction of organised German resistance by the Allies.

The names of Levi, Segré, Guastalla, Ottolenghi, Pugliese and Rovighi are among those of Jewish families who fought for the states and kingdoms before unification. Modena, as in the chapter on General Ventura, and Mantua, have been among the nurseries for Italian Jewish soldiers, sailors and airmen. The heroism, incidentally, of Italian soldiers, including Jews, is little acknowledged. Thousands were massacred on Cephalonia and Corfu defending themselves against the Germans after the Armistice of 1943; thirty thousand more died in German prisons; a commander, Don Fernando Gonzaga, refusing to surrender his sword to Germans, was instantly killed; many officers, some of them elderly, retired admirals and generals, died at Auschwitz in horrible circumstances.

Giuseppe Ottolenghi was born on 26 December 1838 in Sabbionetta where his family were bankers to the Gonzagas, Lords of Mantua. The family, probably for political reasons connected with the Risorgimento, moved to Turin towards the middle of the nineteenth century where they opened the Bank Ottolenghi Brothers in the Piazza San Carlo. The mother belonged to the Forto family of Sabbionetta, where the family palace with its tower and two lions still stands.

Lieutenant-General Ottolenghi joined the army in 1859 and in 1860 was promoted to lieutenant in the 17th Infantry Regiment where he served on the staff, and as an instructor at army school until 1871, when he was transferred to the 62nd Regiment. Ottolenghi was decorated for service against France in 1859; he fought at the siege of Gaeta in 1861, where he was wounded, against brigands in Sicily in 1864, in campaigns for independence against Austria from 1859–61 and at Custozza in 1870. He received, partly as a result of service as tutor to the crown prince, later to be King Victor Emmanuel III, the highest Orders of the Crown of Italy and of Saints Maurizio and Lazzaro. He became chief of staff of the Second Army Corps in 1884 and of the First Army Corps in 1886. He was successively promoted to brigadier (1888), major-general (1889) and lieutenant-general commanding the Turin Division in 1895. He commanded the Twelfth and the Fourth Army Corps in 1897 and 1902. In 1902, he was made senator and minister for war; in 1903, he was given the First Army Corps. He died in November 1904 and was buried in his wife's tomb in the Hebrew cemetery in Turin.

Admiral Augusto Capon was gassed at Auschwitz on 23 October, paralysed and carrying a signed and dedicated photograph of Mussolini, eight days after being arrested in Rome. On the morning of 16 October he had written in his diary: 'They say that incredible things are happening here. Groups of Fascists and German soldiers are seizing Jews of every class and condition and taking them who knows where . . . The facts are certain, but not the modalities.'

Capon was born in Venice in November 1872, the youngest of eleven children of Nina Levi and Abram Capon, a businessman. He fought in the Italo-Turkish War, the First World War, as commander of reconnaissance forces in the Adriatic, and chief of naval intelligence. In 1919, he commanded the cruiser *Roma* on a two-year cruise carrying the Duke of Aosta's son, Aimone di Savoia Aosta, to 'show-the-flag' and improve Italian relations with the Latin American states. Capon, whose wife died of Addison's Disease, had four daughters, one of whom married Enrico Fermi, the great nuclear physicist and Nobel prize-winner, who left for the United States after the promulgation of the racial laws, Capon himself had been attacked by a tropical disease in 1923, and was afflicted thereafter with progressive paralysis of the legs.

Other Jewish naval officers included Umberto Pugliese, born in 1880, naval constructor and engineer, discharged as a Jew under the racial laws of 1938. The navy was obliged to recall him on his own terms in 1940, to raise and repair the ships of the Italian fleet torpedoed in port by Swordfish of the Royal Navy, an attack which so impressed the Japanese that it led directly to Pearl Harbor. Pugliese was the inventor of sub-aqueous protection for hulls and a double system of steerage for vessels of the Vittorio Veneto class; he left the navy in 1945 to become president of the Institute for Naval Architecture.

Admiral Aldo Ascoli was born in 1882 in Ancona, the tenth of eleven children and the brother of General Ettore Ascoli. He fought in the Italo-Turkish War of 1911–12, the First World War and the Abyssinian War of 1936, distinguishing himself in all of them. His finest hour was in the war of 1915–18, first as a naval aviator (observer), then in the defence of Venice during the violent Austrian offensive on the Isonzo and Lower Piave. Here he commanded the famous Raganelle, artillery mounted on floating pontoons among the vegetation on the river banks, always in the front line despite exhaustion and malaria. For this task, he was richly decorated with national medals for valour, with the Croix de Guerre and the British Distinguished Service Cross, promoted in the field. Ascoli was dismissed from the navy under the racial laws of 1938, but in 1943, after an adventurous sea-voyage, he found his way to the 'liberated' zone in southern Italy, where he joined his own service and the Allies. He was a strong character, brave, discreet, balanced, with an absolute sense of duty but an open mind, interested in music, the arts and mankind, in particular the young whom he inspired; a modest man, dedicated to the navy and to the highest ideals of country.

General Roberto Segré was the son of a colonel. A Jew, born in Turin on 6 April 1872, he was *de facto* in command not only of the Italian artillery of the 6th Army at the Battle of the Piave in June 1918, but of associated British and French artillery units. The system which he himself had invented, of mass fire with special fire schedules, enabled accuracy and mass concentration of fire without endless adjustments and consequent delays; his German and Austrian opponents referred to him as 'Europe's best gunner'.

Segré had earlier fought in the Italo-Turkish War ('crossing unknown territory infested by the enemy, cold-blooded unshakeable resolution and great physical endurance'), at Goriza, and as chief of staff of the Fifth Corps in the icy highlands. In 1918, he was head of the Armistice Commission in Vienna where he not only pursued the welfare of children and the sick, but recovered many of the treasures removed from Italy by the Hapsburgs. On return to Italy, he commanded the Brescia Division. In 1936 he became a Corps commander but died later in the same year.

When he was fourteen, his mother, having to leave the house, entrusted her other children to his temporary care. His little brother Uderico, aged eight, disobeyed him. The future general hung him out of the window by his heels: 'If you disobey, next time I'll let go.' When older, arriving at a *grand salon* on his horse, Roberto shouted, to his mother's embarrassment, 'I'm sweating like a pig', as if in barracks. At a conference organised by him at his colonel's orders, he answered a very senior hostile critic: 'Your observations are irrelevant' ('impertinent' in Italian) . . . a slight pause . . . 'to the argument under discussion.'

In the last year of the Great War, Segré saw his nephew Luciano at Turin railway station, a volunteer officer in the Alpini, where discipline is less formal than in some regiments. After several battles, he had been released from the front line, taken the train to Turin to embrace his mother, to have supper and a bath, to sleep in his own bed, and return in the morning to his regiment.

'How much leave have you got?' asked the general. 'None,' said his nephew, 'but I'm going back tomorrow.' 'No; go back this instant,' said his uncle, whose sense of duty was even stronger than his affection for his sister and her son. His own son Gino acquired lice during a trip in the mountains. 'You've got crabs,' said the general, as if his son had contracted venereal disease. Another son, Paolo, went skiing at Lake Castel, in the Val Fornazza, but forgot to bring back his sheets to the family's house. The sergeant of Carabinieri sent to recover them upbraided the watchman at the huts: 'You've taken the General's sheets,' he shouted, scowling. The family hardly dared go back to Castel until they had made their excuses. 'Papa is a general. You know what *they're* like.'

His promotion, slow in peacetime (ten years as a lieutenant, thirteen as a captain), became very rapid in war, when he earned several promotions in the field, one of which was cancelled by the personnel bureaucracy since it was contemporaneous with one awarded for simple seniority. Illness or, by that time, convalescence, did not deter him from returning immediately to the front after the defeat at Caporetto.

In Austria, an anti-militarist alliance between Italian socialists and officials of the Ministry of Foreign Affairs in Rome, had contrived a financial scandal which charged all the members of Segré's Vienna mission with 'theft'. The general appeared at the trial in full uniform, orders and decorations, mounting a violent attack against his accusers, demanding and securing not only acquittal for himself and his officers, but promotion with honour.

Polemics, because of the age difference between himself, a divisional general, and Giardino, Marshal of Italy, over Segré's system of fire control, were not easy. They became very difficult indeed when Mussolini, who wanted a monolithic Italian military, forbade the general to publish a controversial article in a military review. Segré's chances of promotion were not forwarded when, instead, he sent the same article as a pamphlet to all corps and divisional commanders, to the War College and to all the professional 'clubs'.

He was not an easy man. In the 1930s, when he had been unemployed for several years, General Gallo Bua, his superior in 1911, but later his junior, took him to see the minister for war, General di Giorgio, a Sicilian like Gallo Bua. After introducing them, the latter soon heard raised voices. The doors of the minister's office flew open and, black with rage, our hero emerged, with the minister behind him crying: 'Segré is impossible.' Out rushed Gallo Bua after Segré, who bellowed: 'Di Giorgio is a cretin.' In fact, the minister had offered the general nothing less than the inspectorate general of artillery, to which the general had responded with an absolute demand for full powers, *carte blanche*, and other *ultra montane* conditions.

His introduction of mass fire with special fire schedules superseded the old system of firing one salvo, then changing altitude and direction 'by eye' at each round, a system with great disadvantages – waste of ammunition, evidence to the enemy of the guns' positions, and no possibility, having reached a new site, of moving instantly to effective fire. Segré was the first European gunner to calculate the principal variables which influenced a shot and which could be the basis of tables enabling guns to fire effectively after the first salvos. But such tables were only the first step. The next thing was to apply them when wind speed and direction were also factors. On 15 August 1918, the Austro-Hungarians and Germans unleashed a battle, 'Solstice', which could have been one of annihilation lasting several days. It ended in a decisive Italian victory due largely to 'Preventive counter preparation' by the 6th Army's artillery. The general's concept consisted in bringing forward the Italian artillery two hours before the encounter, the long-range guns being moved to the front line itself one hour before the assault. (Absolute confidence in Intelligence on the part of the high command was, of course, fundamental.) The 6th Army, which practised Segré's principles, had much lower casualties than the 4th Army, which did not.

36
Leon Bronstein, alias Trotsky

Just before his expulsion in 1926 from the Soviet Union, Lev, or Leon, Bronstein, later known as Trotsky, possibly after a jailor of the name in Odessa, was described by a supporter:

> . . . His gaze clear and direct, a smile unexpected and celebrated: a voice of bronze, modulated between sweetness and rasp . . . His hair already going grey, brushed back high, continuing the line of a forehead steep as a cliff. Jutting jaws, their angle softened by the goatee [beard] . . . The lips, flat and broad, turn the mouth into a moving millstone that breathes, tramples or shatters his words. The moustache is thrown back on both sides with vivacity. In this sculptured face the simple and sky-blue eyes, glinting behind the spectacles, cast a gaiety, even a joyousness that give his whole head an indefinable touch of some intelligent and faithful pride, the very hallmark of courage and self-possession.

It was, unfortunately, at this period also that Trotsky – nearing the end of his *domestic* political career – could still write such fevered rubbish as:

> Having rationalised his economic order, man will totally demolish his present-day warped, debased domestic life. The cares of feeding and rearing children, a gravestone weighing on today's family, will be swept away together with it, and become an object of social initiative and inexhaustible collective creativity. Woman will emerge, finally, from her semi-barbarous state. The average human type will rise to the level of Aristotle, Goethe, Marx. And above these heights still loftier pinnacles will rise.

Trotsky was born in 1879, the son of that *rara avis*, a Jewish farmer, on a three-hundred-acre wheat and sheep farm in the vast flatlands of the Ukraine, north of the Black Sea. The family attended the synagogue regularly. Trotsky always denied unconvincingly that he had ever spoken Yiddish, although that was the language of his elementary school. Whether at his home at Yanovka or later at school in Odessa, it was now that he began to sense what he perceived as the injustice of privilege, despotism and inequality at a time when, although forty-seven million serfs had been liberated, not enough land had been made available to accommodate their abilities. Here was fertile ground indeed for Alexander Herzen's Populism. The assassination of Alexander II and the attempt on Alexander III, his son, by killers of the Socialist Revolutionary Party (SR) followed. The radical movement, allied to Plekhanov's Marxists, spread rapidly among young Jewish students, artisans and intellectuals, eventually organised into the General Jewish Workers *Bund* of Russia, Poland and Lithuania, which advocated national cultural autonomy, but not emigration or Zionism. Those were never advocated by Trotsky who frequently seemed to regard as burdensome his entire Jewish legacy. Marxists at that time envisaged a capitalist stage which the Populists believed could be omitted. The Marxist ethos of universalism, omniscience and the dialectic was tailor-made for Trotsky's questing, theorist, messianic temperament.

His work as a propagandist in 1898 for the South Russian Workers' Union earned him his first prison term. In his Siberian gaol, he married Alexandra Sokolovsky, his first wife. In Siberia too, this 'narcissistic, self-important pedant' as he was once described, had the courage to face down his camp commandant. 'Why don't you take off your cap?' 'And you, why don't *you* take your cap off?' Trotsky replied with dignity before being bundled off to solitary. The exiles in Siberia not only enjoyed substantial liberty and received financial subsidies from government, but were permitted to work, in Trotsky's case as a merchant's clerk. On learning in 1902, nevertheless, of the publication abroad of Lenin's *The Spark* (*Iskra*), with its objective of a professional, revolutionary organisation, he decided to escape. Hiding, first of all, in a cart, buried in hay, and leaving Alexandra to 'cover' for him by putting a dummy in his bed, he reached London by train via Vienna and Zurich, waking up Lenin and his wife, Krupskaya. 'The Pen', as he was called, had arrived. Krupskaya paid for the taxi.

He was then 'a tall, gaunt young man with long hair and yellow shoes . . . there was something in his face that made him like a bird of prey . . . his characteristic mouth, big, crooked, biting. A frightful mouth.' His writing and, especially, his oratory were his path to power. The initial step was at the Congress in Brussels of the Russian Social-Democratic Workers' Party, the first occasion at which a Marxist dilemma became manifest – that between 'the inevitability of Marxist power and the need to *seize* power'. Other problems, the role of Jews, economism, the ideas of dictatorship and democracy, the nature of the proletariat and its role *vis-à-vis* the party, also emerged. And the ultimate contradiction: Trotsky's view that 'Lenin's methods led to the Party organisation (the caucus) substituting itself for the Party as a whole, then the Central Committee for the Party organisation, the Politburo for the Central Committee, and finally a single Dictator for the Politburo', was opposed in 1904 by his own proposal that the Party must seek stability in the proletariat and not in a tiny section of the leadership. It was not until 1917 that, in a complete about-turn, he moved to Lenin's position and formally abandoned both the Mensheviks and his severe language directed at Lenin's policies: 'hideous', 'malicious and morally repulsive', 'demagogical' and so forth.

In 1905 he adopted the theory of 'Permanent Revolution' based on 'Parvus' Helphand's predictions of the Russo-Japanese war and of consequent worldwide revolution, the latter in Trotsky's, but not Helphand's view, to be proletarian, not bourgeois. In that same year, on 'Bloody Sunday', troops guarding the Winter Palace in St Petersburg fired into a peaceful procession led by a priest, carrying petitions, the Tsar's picture, icons and religious banners. In October, his brilliant speeches in the fifty-day Soviet Council of Workers' Deputies broke the St Petersburg General Strike without accomplishing a *coup d'état*.

In a farcical scene, a police officer who came to break up the Soviet was told by Trotsky to give his name before the Soviet would agree to hear him. Only then was the policeman permitted to read his warrant. When it was acknowledged, the meeting then proceeded with its next business, without regard to the warrant.

'Does the meeting wish to have further dealings with the police?'

'No.'

'Then,' said Trotsky to the officer, 'kindly leave the hall.' The policeman left, dumbfounded; but Trotsky went to prison again just the same. In prison, although expressing hostility to Lenin, his contempt for Menshevik inactivity led him towards Bolshevism. Sentenced to life in the Arctic Circle, he escaped in a sledge with a drunk Mongol, joining his second wife, Natalya, in Finland and moving on to Berlin and Vienna. Here, with Natalya and his two boys, he wrote for *Kiev Thought* and *Pravda* – financed by his poor father who travelled frequently to see him – concentrating later on the Balkans, but maintaining always his belief in Permanent Revolution. He remained, however, a propagandist, not an organiser like Stalin, Kamenev and Zinoviev, of whom the latter two were also Jewish.

When the First World War broke out, he was working as a journalist in Paris, professing Menshevism and adopting an 'internationalist' stance to war just short of Lenin's positive support for Russia's military defeat. He was deported from France in 1916, moving to the Bronx where he continued to write and lecture, chiefly among Russian Jews in exile. He left for Petrograd in February 1917, under the impression that the riots there indicated an immediate revolution, spreading far beyond Russia. Arrested by the British in Halifax, Nova Scotia, he did not arrive in Petrograd until Lenin had already reached the Finland Station.

The Tsarist government had collapsed, replaced by a dual provisional government comprising the Duma and the Soviet of Workers' and Peasants' Deputies, the latter more or less in control of practical administration. On arrival, finding that Lenin demanded a Bolshevik seizure of total power which Trotsky equated with 'Permanent Revolution', he dropped Menshevism and was elected to 'Lenin's' central committee, then becoming head of the military committee of the Soviets with authority for the coup in the capital. His oratory, only slightly marred when on one occasion his cuff kept falling off, was as much a feature of the putsch and its 'end to the war' slogan as was revolutionary violence.

The truth about the German 'sealed train' which had borne Lenin back to Russia, and about the huge German financial subsidy to him, now came to light. The common objective of both sides of halting the war – for the Bolsheviks, in order to promote revolution – was seen none the less as the purest treason, although, *à la longue*, damaging to Germany. Lenin had to go into hiding: Trotsky, until he and Lunacharsky were arrested as German agents, took over from him as leader of the Bolshevik Party. Fortunately for the latter, General Kornilov, appointed by Kerensky, now attacked the Provisional government which *included* the Soviet. Kerensky had to call for help from the Red Guards, the Kronstadt sailors, and the other Bolshevik and even Menshevik armed sections. These not only destroyed General Kornilov's forces without bloodshed, but achieved Trotsky's release from prison on 4 September 1917. That day he (Trotsky) was seen as 'a little taller than the average, not corpulent but well-built, with fair skin, an abundant shock of dark hair, a little moustache and a goatee. His pince-nez sharpened his gaze.' He was thirty-eight.

Both Lenin and Trotsky believed in September 1917 that a European revolution would instantly follow a Soviet revolution. They therefore decided, opposed only by Zinoviev and Kamenev, that a putsch should be mounted in October; Trotsky, chairman of the Soviet, would be responsible for the coup's execution as chief organiser and propagandist. The circumstances surrounding the task helped him – peasant rioting and attacks on property, the collapse of both the economy and of the army at the front. First of all, the Petrograd garrison acknowledged the military committee. On 23 October, Trotsky literally talked the vital Peter and Paul Fortress into joining the Bolsheviks. The Central Telephone Exchange, controlling all government communications, and the Central Bank were taken on 25 October. At 18.30 on the same day, the Winter Palace fell, defended only by cadets, Cossacks and a women's battalion. All ministers present were arrested. Kerensky had already fled in a car provided by the American Embassy.

At Smolny, then the Bolshevik HQ, 'nothing but faces slack with fatigue, smudged by a stubble of beards, with circles around puffy eyes. Trotsky's face was drawn: he was pale, exhausted, overexcited . . .' The Soviet Union had been born; Trotsky its 'orator-in-chief', was now first commissar of foreign affairs. No bureaucrat, he demanded the right to propagandise among German troops, and insisted that the revolution should not lead to a German redeployment against the West, seeking, as did Lenin, a separate peace before the Allies could make their own arrangements with the Germans. (In the interior of Russia, the Whites were already preparing to overthrow the Bolsheviks.) But because of his initial refusal to sign a peace agreement with the enemy –

'neither peace nor war' – by February 1918 the Germans were advancing unopposed into Russia. The Treaty of Brest-Litovsk was therefore signed on 3 March, the Ukraine, Finland, Estonia, Lithuania, Courland all carelessly surrendered. The Allies, Japanese, Czechs and Germans, occupying huge tracts of the country, now operated with the Soviet government's own internal enemies to destroy the new state.

Trotsky, in this alarming situation, became commissar for war from March 1918, living at first with Natalya and the two boys in the Kremlin. (His father, over seventy years old and robbed by his son's Bolsheviks of land and stock, visited him there, having crossed Russia to get to Moscow, much of the way on foot.) The army now consisted of a single division of Baltic snipers. Outside the army, the only faintly organised force was that of the Red Guards. Soon, however, he had persuaded many Tsarist officers, NCOs and other ranks to join a new officer corps with a proper chain of command, albeit parallelled by a system of political commissars. These officers and their rawish men, however, were soon in flight from Cossacks and White Guards under Denikin, coming up from the south, holding the Ukraine. Admiral Kolchak from Siberia, aided by the Czech Legion, was moving across the Volga towards Moscow, and General Yudenich threatened Petrograd. Trotsky, in Kazan, from 'The Train' in which he lived in comfort for eighteen months, first defeated Kolchak and blocked the route to Moscow. By September he had retaken Kazan and assumed control over the Volga. He had a million and a half men under command, many provided by conscription organised forcibly by the trades unions; his proposed Revolutionary War Council was, however, impeded by Stalin in the south and the Tenth Army Commander, Voroshilov. Despite political interference from the Politburo, again notably from Stalin, he defeated Denikin at Tula before Moscow (and then regained the Ukraine), and Yudenich in the suburbs of Petrograd, victories largely attributable to his presence, obstinacy and discipline.

The Civil War, although continuing for a long time, was effectively won for the Bolsheviks by the end of 1919. Trotsky's name and reputation as a political and, now, military icon, stood second only to Lenin's and, by success, he had also reduced Stalin's prominence on the southern front.

Unexpectedly, Trotsky now advocated dictatorship, including

direction of labour, as against 'workers' democracy'. His arguments were defeated at the Tenth Congress of the Soviet Communist Party. (At the same moment, nevertheless, he suppressed a revolt by Kronstadt sailors, and sent Tukhachevsky with over twenty-five divisions to defeat a peasant revolt on the Volga.) War Communism was discarded by Lenin in favour of the New Economic Policy, which combined economic liberalism with the totalitarianism implicit in the single, Bolshevik party political system. Trotsky changed course again, to a modified pursuit of (very) modified democracy, but when Lenin died, he lost his main personal ally against the Stalin-Kamenev-Zinoviev *troika*. Lenin's will, proposing the crushing of Stalin, his enemy and the bitter foe of Trotsky, was ignored. Trotsky's fate was sealed.

'It was,' he said later, 'a real conspiracy, comprising all the Politburo but me . . . a special kind of careerism was developed that later on was openly called anti-Trotskyism.' He was denounced and condemned at the Thirteenth Party Congress, replying pathetically: 'Comrades, none of us wishes to be or can be right against his party. In the final analysis the Party is always right, because it is the only historic instrument given to the working class for the solution of its fundamental tasks . . . One can be right only with the Party and through the Party, because history has not created any other way for rightness to be realised . . . My party, right or wrong . . .'

The remainder of his life in Russia was passed in a permanently losing struggle against the cunning, organised and malign Joseph Vissarionovich Stalin. The battle culminated in final defeat in 1927, over, among other issues, his advocacy of world revolution masterminded from the USSR, against Stalin's 'Socialism in One Country'. Expelled from Politburo and Party, in 1928 he was exiled to Alma Ata, capital today of the CIS Republic of Kazakhstan. Expelled even from the Soviet Union in 1929 and his citizenship annulled in 1932, he found asylum in Mexico after unhappy periods in Turkey, France and Norway. There he spoke and wrote persistently against Stalin's policies. Leader and figurehead of the worldwide Trotskyist Fourth International, in 1927 he was cleared by an international commission under the philosopher John Dewey of Stalin's accusations that he had directed armed subversion within the USSR itself.

In 1940, a dashing Catalan Spaniard named 'Jacson' had

urbanely ingratiated himself into the Trotskys' guarded residence through friendship with Leon's secretary; Jacson was, in fact, a Soviet agent named Mercader whose Cuban mother in Paris had close contacts with the NKVD. (In May 1940, an armed attack unconnected with Mercader and mounted by twenty Spanish and local Communists disguised as soldiers and policemen penetrated the household but failed to kill any of its targets.) On 20 August 1940, Mercader stole behind Trotsky's back, and taking an ice-pick from within his overcoat, hammered it down like Jael into Trotsky's brain. The victim struggled furiously, even seizing the weapon from him, before dying twenty-four hours later. Mercader whined as the guards arrested him: 'They made me do it . . . they're holding my mother . . . they've put my mother in jail,' another lie.

As for the Jews, although few – other than Trotsky himself, Kamenev, Zinoviev and Helphand – played significant roles in the Revolution, this was not the universal Gentile view, then or later. Trotsky, the reluctant Jew, and his friends, representing for Hitler 'a Jewish-Bolshevik plot to dominate the world', may have been more responsible for the massacres of their kinsmen in Europe than some have cared to think, unwitting entrepreneurs of Holocaust.

37
Borodin of China

'The star that glowed . . . over China' in the 1920s was born Mikhail Markevich Gruzenberg in the Jewish Pale of the Vitebsk province of Russia in 1884. His family then moved to Latvia where he added Russian and Latvian to Yiddish, before floating logs down the Dvina for a living. His natal village, Yanovichi, was twenty miles from Chagall's place of birth, Vitebsk, town and port.

More than a million Jews fled from the pogroms after the assassination of Tsar Alexander II in 1881. Others stayed in the *shtetls* and in the General Jewish Workers' *Bund* of which Gruzenberg, alias Borodin, became a member. He joined Lenin, however, in 1903 when the leader sent him to Switzerland; he was recalled to Russia in 1905 after Tsarist troops had fired on workers at the Winter Palace on 'Bloody Sunday', his duty to organise the various factions in Riga. But the revolutionary gale blew itself out, and the Party confined Borodin to conferences abroad, where he made his own name.

On return in 1906, he was arrested and, released, fled to the United States. There he married a girl from Vilna, the lumpish Fanya, had two sons, Fred and Norman, and opened and successfully ran a language school in Chicago, drawing away from Bolshevism. Full of doubt, he did not return to Russia until June 1918, long after the fall of Tsarism. Enthused by Lenin, he acted as a recruiter, smuggler and propagandist for the Comintern in Scandinavia after the famine of 1918–19 in Moscow, *inter alia* carrying diamonds worth $500,000 into the US in suitcase linings. They were mislaid. Some were later recovered by Fanya. According to one account, most were not recovered by the Soviets until 1948 when the Irish leader, de Valera, to whom they had been earlier pawned, returned them to the CPSU. Another source alleged, however, that Borodin, for fear of capture, had thrown them into New York harbour.

Visiting Mexico, he met the Brahmin M.N. Roy, an anglophobe Indian socialist, who was richly funded by the Germans after Borodin had converted Roy to Marxism. Together they founded the Mexican Communist Party. Borodin was unsuccessful in establishing a Spanish equivalent, and a conference at Amsterdam of the West European bureau of the Comintern was broken up by the authorities; Borodin had to escape from Holland into Germany hidden in a hay wagon. Berlin took Amsterdam's place for the Comintern, but Borodin was ordered back to Moscow.

'There goes a great man,' was said of him now, and he was firmly in Lenin's 'favour', employed as the latter's propagandist abroad, initially on 'Left-Wing Communist: An Infantile Disorder' and similar theses, travelling frequently to Berlin and elsewhere. In Russia, he cultivated, if not converted, such notables as Enver Pasha, Clare Sheridan and Isadora Duncan, and was the constant companion of the ubiquitous Roy.

In March 1921, the German workers failed to rally to arms while, in Kronstadt, the garrison on the Neva rebelled against starvation under Bolshevism. Consolidation became the watchword, with effects on Borodin's morale. The great conciliator was in 1922 sent to England to reorganise the CPGB after the failure of the miners' strike, helped in that task by Willie Gallacher and Palme Dutt. He was arrested, imprisoned and deported to the USSR in 1923, pink-cheeked, scarred on face and body from logging days, grey-eyed, with brownish hair, about five foot ten inches, not yet with his later Stalin moustache. He was said to have resembled at that time Eli Wallach.

Back in Moscow, frustration with the West led the leadership to turn East for an alternative strategy. Sun Yat Sen was the obvious *point d'appui*, the 'liberal' anti-Manchu revolutionary, now running a shaky local government in Canton, opposing the warlords after overthrowing the Manchu. As the warlords were uninterested in, even opposed to his reform programme, he spent as much time running away from them to the French Concession in Shanghai as in his Canton base. The West could not help him, seeing no alternative to a divided China. Only Russia, despite Sun's suspicions of Bolshevism and fear of penetration of the Nationalist Kuo Min Tang (KMT) by the Chinese Communist Party (CCP), would supply money, arms and training. For the USSR, the KMT was the only visible vehicle for Revolution, certainly superior to the militarists or even the CCP. Borodin was the Kremlin's choice to lead the mission to which Sun eventually agreed, Moscow's objective the transformation of the KMT into Russia's revolutionary creature with a military capacity also provided by the USSR.

On meeting Borodin, Sun emphasised his first priority, to consolidate and strengthen the Canton regime, before undertaking the unity of China through the Northern Expedition. Borodin's aim of a reorganised KMT to revolutionise the people was accepted neither by the war lords and entrepreneurs, nor by the CCP who resented Moscow's requirement for them to merge themselves into the KMT. Nor, although he was able – with five hundred and forty Chinese volunteers – to stiffen resistance against a takeover by warlord Ch'en Ch'iung Ming, could he persuade Sun and the entourage to agree to leftist land and urban reform as a means of uniting the masses. Ch'en, nevertheless, was beaten back, with a consequent gain in Sun's opinion of Borodin.

The latter dominated the First Kuo Min Tang Congress in January 1924, interrupted by Lenin's death. Thanks to Borodin, the CCP was brought at a significant level into the KMT which was itself considerably reorganised; the Whampoa Military Academy was authorised; and the CCP acquired the 'right' to deal with 'workers and peasants'. But the KMT remained, not a real party but Sun's creature, not a mass revolutionary weapon, but a bourgeois association. In the meanwhile, Chiang Kai Shek, Sun's chief of staff, who had been sent to Moscow, returned to command the Academy, which became an ideological jousting ground between Communist agitators and middle-class cadets. Sun, however, needed Borodin, his Lafayette, as much as Borodin needed him, and his relations with the USSR were maintained despite the contradictions between CCP and KMT.

Borodin had little confidence in peasant trade unions as such, regarding the Chinese class system as unpredictable, leading to unreliability; but, with Sun's half-hearted agreement, he helped to unionise half a million peasants in Kwangtung. Sun, on the whole and in the last resort, always supported landowners and opposed confiscations. But Borodin believed that he was holding his own, at least beginning to construct a revolution. Sun, however, was running out of funds, increasingly deserted by wealthy merchants alarmed by the Soviet connection and by widespread strikes. In October, he withdrew his forces from the

Northern Expedition which he had intended should join with his northern ally, Chang Tso-Lin, to unify China. He brought some of his twenty-four thousand mercenaries back to Canton where, with Chiang Kai Shek and his Whampoa and other cadets, he defeated the traders' militia, the Merchants' Volunteer Corps (MVC). At this point, Borodin was joined by General Vasily Blyükher (Blücher aka Galen), a noted Red Army officer whom the West complacently assumed to be a noble German or Austrian, incognito.

In Peking, 'the Christian general' Feng Yiu Hsiang, given to baptising his troops with hoses, called for a unification congress to which he invited Sun. In November 1924, Sun Yat Sen, already very ill, ignored Borodin's advice and left with Ching Ling Soong, his wife, Eugene Chen, his foreign minister, Wang Ching-Wei (head of Government, but Chiang's rival) and Borodin, for the capital. On 25 March 1925, Sun died, leaving no successor. After a substantial military victory in Canton over warlord usurpers, power devolved to a national government under Wang and Borodin's ally, Liao Chung K'ai. While Borodin had been in Peking, Blyükher and the Whampoa troops of the KMT, although heavily outnumbered, had defeated Ch'en Ch'ung-ming's armies. Borodin was now 'dictator of Canton'.

In June, Sikh police in Shanghai fired on student protesters and a general strike began, involving some five hundred thousand workers. In Canton, the 'Shakee massacre' permitted Borodin not only to call a general strike there also, but to proclaim the blockade of Hong Kong, which resulted in a massive strike there too, and a move by fifty thousand Hong Kong workers to join the strikers in Canton. But, gradually, both the strikers and the middle classes tired of strikes which were often hijacked by thugs and armed *goondas*, fearing for their own livelihoods and increasingly suspicious that the Canton government was controlled by Bolsheviks. Liao was assassinated outside KMT headquarters. But Borodin – without Blyükher whose earlier wounds had driven him north – first defeated the troops of warlord Hsü Ch'ung-chih and then, in the Second Eastern Expedition, what remained of Ch'en's army. Bringing them into the National Revolutionary Army (NRA) tended to increase the proportion of cowardice, opium addiction and desertion in the army, but Kwangtung was at peace. Borodin, Wang and Chiang Kai Shek ruled in Canton. Chiang was flattering enough to compare Borodin with Foch. It was plain that many of his accomplishments were recognised in both Moscow and the South.

His military and other victories over the Right had unfortunately caused a bourgeois reaction which was not eased by the Second KMT Congress where the Left, including Mao Tse-tung and Chou En-lai, made noteworthy gains. His achievements had to be considered against the growing defection of the middle class, and the nervousness of the Powers demonstrated by warship movements. The strength of the CCP, the trades unions and the army provided no counter-balance.

In February 1926, before a secret Soviet commission considering future Russian policy in China, Borodin claimed that the old regime could only be overthrown by agricultural reform, but reform would cause the collapse of the only national instrument available to revolution, the KMT. The alternative was to press on with a Northern Expedition obliterating landlord opposition in military liberation a country united by political, economic, peasant, army and Party reform, leftist, and – if necessary – Bolshevik, unacceptable to KMT and landlords alike.

A bombshell exploded on 20 March in Canton, where Chiang Kai Shek mounted his own *coup d'état*, arresting opponents in the Communist missions at Whampoa and the NRA, proclaiming martial law and rounding up the strikers. He declared in April, nevertheless, that the Soviet–Chinese alliance was unaffected and that the KMT would continue to accept Comintern guidance. It was clear that need for aid in his idea of a Northern Expedition ruled out any principled attack on the Soviet presence with the KMT: the Soviets chose to think that the coup only increased the necessity for Soviet cooperation with the KMT in planning the Northern Expedition, while saving their own faces by putting the blame on the wretched CCP for ultramontane behaviour. There was, in fact, no choice for the Kremlin, except perhaps with Feng, but when Borodin met him in Ulan Bator in 1926, Feng rejected advice to return to China in favour of 'retiring' in Moscow.

Borodin, when he got back to Canton, was under orders to accept the strict, even humiliating preconditions that Chiang imposed before cooperation. These excluded criticism by the CCP, CCP leadership of government or of KMT departments,

KMT membership of the CCP, orders to the CCP except through a KMT/CCP committee. Stalin, in order to be involved in the Northern Expedition, felt bound to support the United Front and Chiang, even though the element essential to revolution and reform (the CCP) was precluded.

By July 1926, the NRA of 70,000 men in eight 'armies', under Blyükher's guidance, with Chiang Kai Shek as commander-in-chief, was ready to move north. By the time it reached the Yangtze in September, it numbered 150,000 men in fourteen armies, although these included less disciplined and dedicated warlordists. Chiang, fearing that the left wanted to capture Wuhan, bypassed it but, stopped at Nanchang, had to call for rescue on those of 'his' forces who *had* by then taken Wuhan. There were thus two KMT/NRA centres, almost capitals, at Nanchang and Wuhan, while Borodin in Canton busily introduced measures to reduce rents, form armed peasant units, reinstate 'Prime Minister' Wang, and contact Feng, all countered by Chiang's men *sur place*.

Borodin, Ching-Long Sun, her son, Sun Fo, Eugene Chen and T.V. Soong accordingly left for Wuhan. They travelled initially on palanquins borne by opium addicts who bolted every night, single-file on tracks and footpaths, wading across unbridged rivers, in driving rain. They slept where they fell, in schools, tumble-down temples, police stations, tea houses, eventually meeting Chiang *en route* before going on to Wuhan. On arrival there, Borodin was warmly welcomed by 300,000 striking citizens, and by General T'ang Shen-chih, Chiang's rival. He heard agreeable rumours that General Feng was on his way to join him. But trade had seized up, the United Front was disintegrating, Feng Yiu-hsiang never came, and T'ang was a landowner and capitalist, no soldier.

The mobs were almost out of control. Food and raw materials were running out, unemployment and hunger grew. Although the British concession was invaded and the British withdrew, a visit from Chiang to Wuhan brought no reconciliation with Borodin. Instead it led to resentment among the Powers, the bankers, business, the warlords, the bourgeoisie throughout the country against the Communists, and to support for Chiang. Foreign warships started to close in. Blyükher, on Stalin's orders, was sent back to Chiang. Borodin had few allies, a chaotic working class, a divided and inexperienced party, support for whom anyway alienated potential 'militarist' supporters. More and more middle-class businessmen left for the coast. Borodin certainly could not have armed the peasants and workers or organised mass sequestration, and still maintained the United Front, Stalin's preferred instrument. In mid-February, Fanya was arrested by Marshal Chang Tso-lin, while returning by sea from Vladivostok.

In Shanghai, on the news that Chiang was advancing on the city, three hundred and fifty thousand workers had struck in his name, and on 22 February 1927 there followed an armed uprising when the northern troops in the town began to execute them. Chiang halted his advance. The Third Plenum of the KMT under Borodin's management opened in Wuhan, where a 'Down with Chiang Kai Shek' campaign exploded and resolutions were passed to destroy Chiang's authority. Chiang started two offensives, one against Nanking and another against Shanghai, but broke off the second because he did not intend to share triumph with Communist revolutionaries planted inside the city by General Blyükher. Although Blyükher's 'internal' takeover of Shanghai was completely successful and Shanghai fell to his Fifth Column on 22 March, the NRA entered the city next day. Chiang claimed all credit for the victory, established his own trades unions, police and government, arrested supporters of Borodin, kicked out and/or disbanded all irregular forces and all leftists in his own armies. In Peking, Chang Tso-lin's troops invaded the Soviet Embassy, seizing huge quantities of documents authenticating Soviet support for the CCP and other radicals.

On 12 and 13 April, Chiang's thugs of the Red and Green Gangs attacked trades unionists, CCP members and strikers in Shanghai, killing between eight hundred and five thousand, purges which were repeated all over China. In Wuhan, Borodin tried desperately to settle strikes and conciliate foreign investors, while organising anti-Chiang demonstrations. On 27 April 1927, the Fifth Congress of the Chinese Communist Party opened, attended by no less than M.N. Roy, Borodin, Mao Tse-tung and Chou En-lai. Roy privately spoke in favour of arming the 'workers and peasants', opposed by Borodin who pleaded the inevitable disintegration thereby of the United Front. The Congress compromised on the seizure of all land except that owned by KMT and NRA officials!

Wuhan, under blockade by the Great Powers, had further weakened. Banks, plant and shops closed. More businessmen left. Taxes yielded little and the government printed the money to pay its climbing debts. Unemployment grew. Strikers stayed on strike, shouting and marching. The army was required for 'Borodin's' Northern Expedition. Among the journalists who flooded Wuhan, Borodin was a hero, but one who could control little, as Wuhan collapsed in the increasing winds of bankruptcy and counter-revolution. But even the Chinese respected his organising ability and his magnetism for the people, his feel for China.

Seventy thousand Wuhan troops left for the North. The city was therefore defenceless and came under a siege lifted only on news of a victory for Blyükher's forces in the north. But Changsha, the most revolutionary town in China, which bore slogans and exercised injustice on the scale of the later Cultural Revolution, suddenly fell to the counter-revolution. Borodin, in order to maintain the United Front, did not counter attack, 'waiting for Feng' as usual. At this point, Feng secured substantial victories in Hunan and joined the Wuhan troops who had taken Kaifeng, the ancient centre of Judaism in China. But on 30 May, far from joining Wuhan, Feng united with Chiang against Chang Tso-lin. He also demanded that Wuhan *minus* Borodin and all CCP leaders should join the Chiang Government, now at Nanking. For Borodin, the Chinese Revolution was over. It was not until Fanya was released (the judge bribed with US $200,000) that, leaving his family in Peking to suffer the consequences of his rapid departure for Tokio, Borodin made up his mind to go.

His party left in four Dodges, a Buick with luxurious interior for Borodin, and five trucks, all waiting for them at Shenchow upon their arrival by rail from a Wuhan in which public executions by Chiang's troops were common. The nightmare journey, shedding vehicles as they went, through Shensi, Ningsha and the Gobi in high summer to Ulan Bator, took over six weeks; Borodin flew to Ulan Ude in Mongolia on 28 September to bring back Fanya who had escaped from Peking separately.

Russia's objective for the Borodin mission had been to undermine the West in China, but that aim could only have been achieved had Moscow accepted the unacceptable course of supporting Chiang, without supporting socialism and certainly not the CCP. In the end, the objective became no more than the maintenance of a Soviet presence in China. Even that possibility disappeared.

Back in Russia, Borodin survived failure, even secured paid employment for a long time, first with US specialists, then with Anna Louise Strong's *Moscow News*, then the *Daily News*, and as a wartime liaison with foreign press correspondents in Moscow. In 1949 he was arrested, partly because of his Jewish birth. He died in the Gulag near Yakutsk on 29 May 1951, at the age of sixty-seven, a sad and bitter man.

Another Jew, a German named Otto Braun, also served China. Braun, in the name of Li Teh, commanded Mao Tse-tung's People's Liberation Army. Mistakes made by certain commanders during the Long March, however, enabled Mao to sack Li Teh/Braun as 'a member of the Moscow Group' at the same time (1942) as he dismissed Po Ku, secretary general of the Communist Party. Li Teh was succeeded by Chu Teh.

38
Two-gun Cohen

In 1938, General Morris Abraham Cohen, ADC to the Governor of Kwangtung and 'Lord-High-Everything-Else', was frequently to be seen in Hong Kong and Canton. He had gone on the wagon, losing fourteen pounds under his Chinese general's uniform, a sword at his waist, pockets bulging with revolvers and pistols. On his vast balding head he wore a general officer's cap and, in contempt for the Axis, he cultivated a small toothbrush moustache. This apparition was, of course, 'Two-gun Cohen', adviser to Chinese Governors and Generals from 1923, smuggler, arms dealer, businessman, soldier, spy, Far Eastern legend.

The general was born in Stepney in 1889 to an immigrant Jewish couple from Poland; in 1900 he was sent to an approved school on justified suspicion of picking pockets, and on his release in 1905 he was despatched to relatives in Canada. Here he worked as a farmhand and also learned to shoot, picking up card-sharping and other irregularities on the side. His 'real' life began when, after saving the property and life of Mah Sam, an overseas Chinese in Saskatoon, from a homicidal robber, he was inducted into the Tongs (secret societies) and pledged to the service of Sun Yat Sen and the overthrow of the Manchu. By then lucratively engaged in real estate, he raised money for the revolution, procured light weapons, trained a local Chinese cadet force, and helped Chinese workers to join the AFL. However tough, he was a generous, open-hearted spendthrift.

Cohen revisited his family in 1911, renewing his faith by performing an important Jewish ceremony, the Aliyah. He enjoyed himself in the West End and, on departure, gave the balance of his savings to his father and mother. When he returned to Canada, he found that in China the revolutionaries had overthrown the Manchu and elected Dr Sun as president. He joined the Kuo Min Tang, incidentally organising the Chinese vote for provincial elections, while continuing to gamble and make large sums on the sale of building lots for the National Land Company. Dr Sun invited him to join his staff in China, but the First World War –

in which he played a creditable role before being wounded in the Chinese Labour Corps – broke out before he could consider the offer.

He was demobilised in February 1919. Help given to Canadian Chinese in trades union matters drew him once more to the attention of Dr Sun, now driven out of power and exiled to the French Concession in Shanghai. Sun asked Cohen to negotiate a railway-construction contract, but the latter realised that the services Sun really required were those of a non-political foreigner who would protect his safety. (When he landed in Shanghai, 'he was so top-heavy with artillery that if you'd given him a push, he'd have fallen slap on his arse'.) Cohen knew that Dr Sun had been kidnapped once in London and held in the Imperial Embassy; he had been saved by the discovery in Portland Place of notes wrapped round half-crowns hurled from his window.

Cohen knew some Chinese *people*, but he did not know China. He feared that the rickshaws would break under his great bulk. He walked for the first time through the twisting alleys, smelled the smells of China, saw the character boards, heard music which he never grew to like, followed the lion dance and other processions, and began to fall under China's spell. He also fell in love with Ching Ling, Dr Sun's wife, sister of T.V. Soong, later finance minister, and of Mei-Ling, Chiang Kai Shek's wife. Dr Sun and he together drafted the railway contract, Cohen voluntarily reducing his commission. Then he met the other two ADC's, both Edmonton Chinese. With colonel's rank, he started to develop his extraordinary mental card-index of Chinese personalities, becoming as famous for that as for his marksmanship, the latter resentfully denied as 'mainly attributable to No. 7 shot'.

In 1923, Dr Sun was invited back from exile to Canton by a Kwangsi/Yunnan alliance, the doctor and entourage staying *en route* in Government House, Hong Kong. Here Cohen slightly blotted his copy book by trying to preempt British security arrangements. At dinner, Sun Yat Sen unsuccessfully sought the governor's agreement to the despatch of six Hong Kong civil servants to reorganise a South China divided between the warlords of Kwangtung, Yunnan and Kwangsi. After two days, including a public lecture from Dr Sun organised by the great Sir Robert Ho Tung, the party left for the Pearl River through the fleets of junks that then navigated those waterways. Accompanying Dr Sun to the front against the Kwangtung army under Cheng Chiung Ming, Cohen was hit in the arm by a machine-gun bullet. Back in Canton, two hundred 'wounded' soldiers penetrated the compound in an attempt to raid the treasury, before it was noticed that their 'bloodstained' bandages were faked. That was the first occasion on which Cohen used his 'Two Guns'. The colonel also beat off a riverborne attack from junks on Dr Sun's headquarters, an attack followed 'by a nasty messy business on the execution grounds'. When visiting the Northern Front, finding the train halted in paddy fields with one walled village visible, Cohen, with great presence of mind, foiled an attempt by Northern assassins to blow up the train and kill Sun.

In the late summer, Cheng's army was close to taking Canton, only repelled by Dr Sun's personal excursion to an embattled Pagoda which, if seized, would have opened the city to the Kwangtung troops. Sun, fearing a repetition, sent Cohen abroad to acquire pilots and the means of actually building aircraft in China, the result being a reconnaissance aircraft called the Rosamonde, Madame Sun's name at Wellesley College. Successful in the first foreign mission for his hero, Cohen returned to China calm, healthy, good tempered, confident, with superb memory and a natural empathy with his employers.

Because of the West's arms embargo, Dr Sun invited the Russian missions under Michael Borodin the Soviet Jew who became adviser to the Kuo Min Tang and imported Russian weapons and instructors, and General Blyükher who ran the Whampoa Military Academy under Chiang Kai Shek. The Chinese Communists were permitted to join the KMT. Their first troops roundly defeated Cheng, but the event was overlaid by the customs crisis of 1923, a Soviet attempt to upset Sun's plans for a united China by weakening him in the south. This failed, as did Borodin's attempt to persuade Sun to mount a premature Northern Expedition with the same undeclared purpose. Cohen, using a bogus arms deal as cover, was then sent by Sun to Peking to arrange the defection of a northern general.

Those whom Cohen monitored before giving them access to Dr Sun included overseas Chinese supporters, convicted spies, pirates commanding potential battalions, negotiators from the north, contractors, merchants, whom neither Sun nor Cohen liked, generals, busybodies, foreign diplomats. Sun was a simple man, happiest with coolies, beggars and children, loving the country and its great works of art. His beliefs were less political than functional, centred on development, communications (railways, roads, rivers), technology. His 'ideology was only nationalism, democracy, socialism'. In 1925, he died in Shanghai; at his death Cohen was promoted to general, moving at his own request to the staff of Sun Fo, Sun Yat Sen's son and heir.

Failing decent Chinese leadership, Cohen successfully led a battalion of Whampoa Soviet trained Communist cadets against Yunnanese troops, bearing a vast Red Banner on his shoulder. Later, when the general strikes were called in Canton and Hong Kong, there were many dead in Canton: the Russians, if they had not caused the troubles, were ready to exploit them. Cohen caught a Chinese placing a bomb on the jetty alongside HMS *Onslaught* and, in the nick of time, ditched the sputtering device. But the strikers stayed out, merely inconveniencing most of the British and other employers, but devastating impecunious Chinese employees. Cohen acted as a principal intermediary, bringing the good news of successful negotiations to the British consul general. Notionally 'disarmed' by a civilian on landing at the Shameen, in fact ostentatiously surrendering a small pearl-handled pistol, he restored face at the club by the very slow public removal from his shoulder holsters of two undeclared 45s.

In July 1926, Chiang Kai Shek, clandestinely supported by General Blyükher, began the Northern Campaign which, by the summer of 1927, brought the whole of China south of the Yangtse under his control. By the end of 1928, the 'Young Marshal', Chang Hsü En Liang, had joined his forces to the KMT and China, for a little while, was united. In February 1926, nevertheless, the Russians had mounted the coup in Canton which was bloodily suppressed by Chiang: Cohen was narrowly able to save from the mob the silver in the strongrooms of the Central Bank of China, to which he had been seconded by T.V. Soong. Chiang had also organised a 'Disbandment' Conference preceding loans, equipment and foreign advisers to implement development projects in China Cohen's rewarding role in this enterprise was liaison with 'Hong Kong and all foreign governments in South China'.

Meanwhile, in order to purchase several hundred British mules for the Canton forces, Cohen pretended that they were for piracy suppression at Bias Bay. Too clever by half, he found himself committed to an operation there with the Royal Navy which he had never intended, concluded successfully but with the execution of seventy-five pirates whose end involved sights and sounds difficult even for Cohen to stomach. Nothing, however, matched the pitiless brutality of those maritime criminals, despatching bits of prisoners' bodies to their loved ones in exchange for ramsom.

But suddenly China began to fly apart, Chiang virtually kidnapping Cohen's boss on charges of involvement in 'Southern Separatism'. Peking and Hankow both also broke away. Cohen became ADC to Chen Chi-tong, successor to that General Li who had now been released by Chiang to exile in Hong Kong. Although Chen employed him extensively on the protection of missionaries, requiring contact also with 'lion men' or lepers, Cohen was still adviser for foreign purchases, arranging the purchase for China of arms from almost every European country, two and a half per cent commission paid by the seller. Endless landing problems resulted because of fierce obstruction by the Shanghai authorities represented by Cohen's former friend, T.V. Soong. And dud deliveries, blocked consignments and imaginary deals were manifold, one of which ended in the removal by Cohen of forty-seven thousand Shanghai dollars at stud poker from his swindling interlocutor.

In September 1931, the Japanese attacked Manchuria, while social revolution inspired by Mao Tse-tung's rural agitators troubled north and south. Cohen, although often needlessly provoking the Japanese, negotiated contracts in Europe, especially in a Manchester badly affected by slump, to help the southern armies. The Chinese leadership showed signs of reuniting, but in 1937 Cohen predicted that Japan, unable to tolerate an effective Chinese central government, would move to full invasion within twelve months. In fact, they needed even less time before conquering Shanghai, Peking, Nanking and Canton itself. Back with Sun Fo, Cohen's loyalties led him to organise intelligence networks from Hong Kong against the Japanese, providing a steady stream of order of battle information, maps, aircraft instruments, nose-fuses, tail-fins, and other significant items of equipment, including a sample of Japanese poison gas, offensive enough to create chaos in Kai Tak airport. At the same time, he arranged delivery to the Chinese forces of substantial quantities of gasoline against Hong Kong government permits to deliver sugar to Shanghai on behalf of the organisation providing the gasoline, in a deal covered by one of Asia's most substantial insurance companies.

In 1941, Cohen identified the principal Japanese agents in Hong Kong. The local police were unable to hold them for any length of time. Nor did he achieve much success in coordinating British and Chinese defence activities. He was, however, just before Hong Kong fell and after the first Japanese raid on Kai Tak, able to evacuate Madame Sun and her sister, the wife of H.H. Kung, from the colony. Although his agents damaged the fifth column, the Japanese army soon overwhelmed the small garrison, the British forces surrendering on Boxing Day 1941.

Cohen was arrested in the Hong Kong Hotel, quickly released, and rearrested by the Kempeitai who, maddened by his earlier insolence and conscious of at least some of his more serious anti-Japanese operations, severely beat him up with kicks, fists and bamboo canes. In the next-door cell, some Chinese tried to escape, but were recaptured: the Kempei beat and thrashed them, in full view of the other cells, using guns, bamboo and rope until the Japanese were glutted, blood on the floor, prisoners dead or dying, others noisily and inefficiently executed outside the gaol. The Japanese then carried out a mock execution with a two-handed samurai sword against the kneeling Cohen, who only murmured: 'Hark, O Israel, the Lord is our God, the Lord is one' and, aloud, 'Get on with it, you lousy bastard', until the guard kicked him over.

After two years in Stanley Camp, he was exchanged for Japanese prisoners held by the Americans and Canadians. When debriefed by the Canadian army in Ottawa, he asked for the First World War medals he had never received, the British War Medal and the Allied Victory Medal: they were given to him with a note reading '279259 Sgt. M. Cohen', although he had been reduced to the ranks for going AWOL after Armistice Day 1918.

39
USSR

When the Germans invaded the USSR in 1941, General Lev M. Dovator was a colonel of Soviet Cossack cavalry. (Cossacks in the nineteenth century were, ironically, mainly employed in massacring Jews.) Dovator, a Jew whose parents were neither rich nor part of the élite, rose rapidly to command the 2nd Guards Cavalry Corps which was hurled by Marshal Zhukov in assault against the German rear during the Soviet offensive of the Tula area in December 1941. The cavalry, in temperatures of minus 25°C, with snow storms and blizzards, operated behind the German lines in collaboration with partisans equipped with wireless telegraphy. Their brilliant and flamboyant general was killed on 20 December, being named 'Hero of the Soviet Union' and, it is alleged, figuring on a postage stamp. (There are, on the other hand, materials to suggest that he may have been murdered by the People's Commissariat for Internal Affairs (NKVD).)

But in this terrible war in which Russia had been engulfed through Stalin's ignorant, arrogance, Dovator was not the only Jewish Commander: there were one hundred and thirty-three Jewish 'Heroes of the Soviet Union', including eight generals. The Soviet army included one Jewish colonel-general, nine lieutenant-generals and ninety-two major-generals: the Jewish component was fourth in representation of twenty-five nationalities, after Russians, Ukranians and Belorussians.

Ivan Chernyakhovskii was born of a Jewish family in the Ukraine, his father a railwayman who died when the boy was nine. Until 1917, young Chernyakhovskii, orphaned by typhus, worked as a shepherd. He was then sent by the new state to school in Novorossisk on the Black Sea and to military academy in Kiev, later becoming platoon, company, battalion and regimental commander, with training periods at Frunze and the Motorisation and Mechanisation Academy. In mid-life, at Kiev, he cut a strong, athletic figure, kind and simple, with large eyes.

When war broke out, among the initial defeats, Colonel Chernyakhovskii's 28th Tank Division, although unable to move for five hours because of shortage of fuel, did at least engage the 1st Panzer Division on 23 June 1941 before the great Soviet retreat began. At Voronezh, ten days later, he was already commanding the 18th Tank Corps when promoted by Stalin on the telephone to command the 60th Army, chosen as one of the 'young generals' to replace incompetent seniors and modify the commissar system. In January 1943, his army took part in an operation against the German 2nd Army on the Voronezh–Kasternoe front, with Kursk as the objective and Kharkov the next prize, totally destroying Army Group B.

In August 1943, the 60th Army was engaged in the drive to the Dnieper with General Rokossovski as central front commander, achieving a bridgehead north of Kiev in October. At the time of the first frosts, in pouring rain, the 60th Army and the 38th Army (Moskalenko) broke out under a massive two-thousand-gun, mortar and Katyusha bombardment, the 38th Army fighting by that evening (3 November) in the outskirts of Kiev. Chernyakhovskii, racing southwest, took Zhitomir on 31 December, a town of white churches possessing also a ghetto with a yellow synagogue.

In Moscow, Stalin, although gratified by assurances from Churchill and Roosevelt on the forthcoming allied invasion of Europe Overlord, caused *Pravda* to refer to 'peace negotiations' between the British and Ribbentrop. Concurrently, the Japanese were employed by the Germans to convey peace proposals to the Russians involving autonomy for the Ukraine and other unacceptable clauses. For his part, Stalin took over the Armia Ludowa (AL) in order to subvert the exiled Polish government in London.

Chernyakhovskii had run into serious resistance by 12 January 1944, but had reached Slavuta on 29 February when the front commander, General Vatutin, was gravely wounded by a group of Bandera's Ukrainian anti-Soviet guerrillas. Zhukov then led the 60th Army and other formations on a front one hundred miles wide and twenty-five deep from Ostrog to the Slutch river. In April, at the age of thirty-eight, the youngest front commander in the Soviet army, Chernyakhovskii was appointed to command the Third Belorussian Front at Krasnoe, firstly in an operation ('Bagration' after the general of that name killed at Borodino in 1812), directed at Poland, Czechoslovakia, Romania, Bulgaria, Yugoslavia and Austria, no less than four Fronts. Absent sick from the main planning conference for Bagration at Moscow, he later visited Stalin's *dacha* to seek the dictator's approval for his plan, a centrepiece for the attack on Army Group Centre.

Armies of the 3rd Belorussian Front were to collaborate with 1st Baltic and 2nd Belorussian Fronts after the destruction of German forces at Vitebsk. Chernyakhovskii would then go for the west bank of the Berezina, haunted by the ghosts of the Grande Armée. On 4 and 5 June respectively, Vasiliewski and Zhukov, chief of the general staff and deputy to the supreme commander, arrived at Chernyakhovskii's headquarters, telephoning Stalin in repeated demands for faster rail supply, which they in part secured. On 6 June, the British and American armies crossed the Channel and landed in Normandy, an event reported to Stalin in a telegram from Winston Churchill. On 24 June, Chernyakhovskii attacked against Vitebsk and Orsha, the latter a partial failure due to violation of camouflage discipline, but redeemed when the 39th Army and the 60th Corps next day penetrated the ruins of Vitebsk, then drove on to the Berezina with instructions to take Minsk by 7 July. Minsk, in fact, fell to the 3rd Belorussian Front by 3 July, as empty of people and undamaged buildings as the country was empty of animals. There was nothing for the Germans to do there but give up: forty thousand had died and, deprived of food, fuel and medical care, four Nazi Corps surrendered to Zakharov's 2nd Belorussian Front. By 4 July, the 3rd Belorussian Front was aiming for Vilno and Lida and, soon, Army Group Centre had been liquidated by the combined Soviet armies with losses of up to three hundred and fifty thousand German troops. Fifty-seven thousand prisoners, led by their generals, were marched through the streets of Moscow to make a Roman holiday.

Chernyakhovskii, having taken Vilno on 13 July with support from Polish partisans, drove on with a strengthened 3rd Belorussian Front to break the Niemen Line at Kaunas (Lithuania), Mariampol and Vilkovyshki, killing many Germans and taking forty-five thousand prisoners at Vilno and in the chase thereafter. On 17 August, a Soviet rifleman from a section attached to one of the 3rd Belorussian Front's divisions was the first Soviet soldier to stand – with the Red Flag – on German soil. By October 1944, the 3rd Belorussian Front menaced the whole of East Prussia, aiming to seal Courland from German reinforcement by an assault, which failed temporarily, from Volkovishki against the Insterburg gap. By the end of 1944, the Soviet Armies had destroyed ninety-six divisions, severely damaging many more, with German losses of one and a half million men and huge quantities of *matériel.* In November, Chernyakhovskii's command was given targets in East Prussia to a depth of a hundred and twenty miles, Stalin himself becoming the coordinator for the four fronts involved in the race for Berlin. The 3rd Belorussian Front deployed five armies and an air army, commanding with the 2nd Belorussian Front a strength of over three thousand armoured fighting vehicles and three thousand aircraft. The four fronts comprised altogether thirty field armies, five tank armies and four air armies, against a numerically inferior German mass, the main thrust being along the Warsaw-Berlin axis. Chernyakhovskii, with the German Tilsit–Insterburg group as the initial objective and Königsberg the next, advanced on January 1945 in foul weather, misty and cold, which only on 16 January permitted extensive air support. Tilsit fell on 19 January, when Guards units turned the Insterberg gap.

In the sombrely magnificent language of Professor John Erickson:

> . . . speed, frenzy and savagery characterised this advance. Villages and small towns burned, while Soviet soldiers raped at will and wreaked an atavistic vengeance on those houses and homes decked out with any of the insignia or symbols of Nazism. German officials lay strewn in the streets with a bullet in the head, small-town functionaries and local burgermasters flung about by bursts of automatic fire; some fussily bedecked Nazi Party portrait photograph . . . the signal to mow down an entire family amidst their table, chairs and kitchenware . . .

On 18 February 1945, deploying his men against greatly increased German resistance, Chernyakhovskii fell at Mehlsack in East Prussia and died of wounds. On Stalin's orders, he was buried at Vilna on 24 February to a salute of twenty-four salvoes from one hundred and twenty-four guns. Colonel-General von Schneider, defeated by him on the Kursk salient, had earlier advised his own officers: 'The main thing now is to get clear of him. It won't be easy, as he doesn't even give you any rest. He sticks to your heels', a policy perhaps perfected by Chernyakhovskii's practice of minutely analysing each day's action before retiring for the night.

In contrast to his death in battle, Jewish colleagues Lieutenant-General (Aviation) S.K. Vladimirovich, chief of the Soviet Air Force in 1939, Smushkevich, former Soviet air commander in Spain, and Colonel-General G.M. Shtern, commander Air Defence Command, Far Eastern Front, were all executed on 28 October 1941 by firing squad in Kuibyshev. They had been earlier held in a 'very special prison' in Moscow until it was hastily evacuated in June on the orders of Lavrenti Beria, head of the NKVD, forerunner of the KGB.

Although the chief of general staff, General Antonov, was not made a marshal because he was suspected by Stalin of being Jewish, Jewish Generals Vainrub, Dragunskii, Kreizer, Davidovich and Moisievich all survived the war. None of them were more senior than colonel by 1945, promoted to general thereafter.

40
Admiral Sir Max Horton

These were the men
who were her salvation
who conquered the water and the underwater
who
in storm and calm
taught England to live anew
And fed her children.

Admiral Sir Max Kennedy Horton as Flag Officer Submarines helped to frustrate Hitler's plans for the invasion of England and, in the Mediterranean, drove back Rommel, wrecking his transports and disrupting his seaborne supplies. As commander-in-chief Western Approaches at Liverpool, within six months he had swept the U-Boats from the North Atlantic and, subsequently, ensured that not one Allied vessel was lost to U-boats during the landings in Europe.

Max Horton was born in Wales in 1883, of a rather unsuccessful stockbroker, called Robert Joseph Angel Horton, who had married Esther Maud Goldsmid, daughter of William Goldsmid and cousin of the banker Julian Goldsmid. His Jewish blood – although he told his mother that he wished to join the navy in order to fight for *her* – led him, via cautiousness with authority, to the means of acquiring both power and independence. From his father he inherited a 'speculative' nature, embodied in high-stakes poker and bridge on a daily pay of two shillings and ninepence. He also part-owned a racing car called a Twin-Minerva.

Command in the navy was achieved much younger for officers in submarines than in surface vessels. Nevertheless, Horton's first report in 1907 from his commanding officer in the A1 was not promising: 'While good in the boat, bad socially, insubordinate to the First Lieutenant and troublesome in the Mess. Extremely intelligent but given to bad language.' Bernard Acworth, his first lieutenant in C8 (two hundreds tons), described him as ruthless towards incompetence or slackness, but exemplifying the real warm-hearted fraternity which existed among those who lived in more intimate contact with one another than in any other branch of the service. Others remarked on his extraordinary intuition, bordering on second sight, although admitting that another cause might have been superior command of the facts interpreted by a brilliant mind.

When the 1914–18 War broke out, Horton's then boat, the E9, sank the light cruiser *Hela* with two torpedoes at six hundred yards, later suffering agonising problems in charging batteries under enemy attack. In 1915, off Ems and the channels and sandbanks of *The Riddle of the Sands*, he sent a destroyer and the cruiser *Prinz Adelbert* to the bottom. Under the overall command of a Tsarist commander-in-chief, he sank by torpedo or gunfire – after the prescribed warnings – a number of motor vessels carrying contraband, including iron ore from Sweden to Germany. Ships of the German High Seas Fleet could no longer move with freedom in 'Horton's Sea', the Baltic, also dominated by two other British submarines, one under the lethal Dunbar-Nasmith.

In the Baltic winter, everything froze on the surface or under the ice, so that submarines had to thaw out on the very bottom. When the rum ran out, Horton asked the Russians for vodka, but their navy was 'dry'. The Tsar asked: 'If he's cold, why doesn't he wear two shirts?' Ashore, a beautiful young woman confessed that she had been paid by German agents to poison his coffee. 'Don't drink,' she cried, as he lifted the cup. He gave her an inscribed gold cigarette case, which served her as a passport when later escaping from the Bolshevik Revolution in 1917. Max Horton liked women and was liked by them, his most permanent flame being a rich and vivacious South African redhead, who was by his side throughout most of the Second World War.

The Admiralty increased the number of submarines in the Baltic from two to six as the best way to assist their hard-pressed ally who, in turn, awarded Horton the Orders of Saints Vladimir, George and Anne. He was turned down in 1916 as 'too piratical' to become senior naval officer (SNO) Baltic, partly on account of his ostentatious habit of flying a Jolly Roger carrying the names and numbers of vessels sunk, and because of a conventional distaste in the Admiralty for 'underhand and damned un-English' submarines, as a class. After a period in two experimental submarines, M1 and M2, one of which mounted a twelve-inch gun and the other an aircraft hangar, in 1919, he nevertheless became SNO at Reval during the Russian Civil War, then a submarine flotilla commander in the Atlantic Fleet. These tours of duty were followed by appointments as chief of staff to Sir Roger Keyes, and as captain of the *Resolution*. He was much remarked for meticulous professionalism, a harsh, ruthless, but warm-hearted and understanding commander, spoken of as a 'new Jacky Fisher'.

As Rear Admiral 2nd Battle Squadron in the *Barham*, with nine cruisers, he firmly believed that it was within the capacity of the Royal Navy to have closed the Suez Canal in 1936 and thus cut off Italy's oil supplies. Mussolini's bluff, because the Duce could not then have maintained his army in Abyssinia, would have been called.

Flying his flag in the *London*, he took off four thousand refugees from Barcelona to Marseilles during the Spanish Civil War, shocked by the brutality of the communist *sans culottes*. He was then promoted vice admiral and appointed Admiral Commanding Reserve Fleet, to render one hundred and forty ships effective in preparation for that Second World War which he was not alone in predicting.

His first wartime appointment was as Vice Admiral Northern Patrol with only eight old light (C and D class) cruisers, useless as a blockading force in the Denmark Straits and Iceland and Faroes waters, until the arrival of the forty or so old American destroyers which he eventually received. But on 7 December 1939, he was appointed back to 'his' boats, Flag Officer Submarines (FOSM) at a headquarters selected by himself, 'Northways' at Swiss Cottage, relatively close to the HQ of Coastal Command. At the beginning, he had fifty-seven submarines in five flotillas, one flotilla of which was in the Mediterranean. Through remarkable prescience, he was ready for the Norway campaign when it began, his boats sinking twenty-one ships, including the cruisers *Karlsruhe* and *Brummer*, and severely damaging the battleship *Lutzow*, while in June 1940 the *Clyde* torpedoed the *Gneisenau*. His midget X-boats lifted the *Tirpitz* five to six feet out of the water. Useless as a fighting unit, *Tirpitz* was later destroyed by the Royal Air Force.

Horton did not believe that Hitler would invade Britain, envisaging blockade instead. But he knew nevertheless that command of the sea was paramount, so that if the Nazis had contemplated a crossing, they would have been either deterred or defeated. His main aim was to keep the seaways open so that military strength could rapidly be brought up offensively at the right time and place. As things were, despite grave lacunae in cooperation between Fighter Command and Commander-in-Chief Nore, which cost Convoy 178 its existence in July 1940, FOSM and Commander-in-Chief Coastal Command together caused the Germans to drop the invasion option in favour of unrestricted warfare by bomber and U-boat. Horton's submarines sank two hundred thousand tons of German shipping, the equivalent of two divisions of troops and equipment. By May 1943, with the priceless help of Enigma*, British submarines had sunk one million tons of shipping in the Mediterranean, the *Upholder* sinking three liners in one day, even with a broken Sperry gyro-compass: in September 1942, Count Ciano, the Italian foreign minister, had *already* noted: 'At this rate, the African problems automatically end, because we shall have no more ships with which to supply Libya.'

Max Horton succeeded Sir Percy Noble as Commander-in-Chief Western Approaches in Liverpool on 17 December 1942, British merchant ship losses having reached 400,000 tons in July 1941. In the six and a half months ending in July 1942, Admiral Doënitz's ships had sunk 495 merchant ships, not including 142 tankers. In November 1942, 117 ships, over 700,000 tons, were sunk by 'wolf-packs', while the RAF preferred to concentrate on their own bomber war against the German mainland; the German navy had recognised that the U-boat offered the best hope of averting defeat at the hands of a nation that lived by seaborne supply. Churchill himself remarked afterwards that 'the only thing that ever frightened him [was] the U-boat peril', and, at this point, oil stocks were desperately low, in particular because of the priority given to Operation Torch in the Mediterranean, the North African landings.

Horton, with Enigma to inform him, seized now upon the concepts of self-contained support groups, six frigates (originally corvettes) and destroyers, operating 'independently' of the convoy escort groups and frequently from different directions, their prime

* A device that enabled British intelligence to decode German radio transmissions.

duty not the defence of the convoys, but the destruction of the attacking U-boats, in or out of 'wolf packs'. These methods were supported by escort aircraft carriers converted from merchant ships, and by very large shore-based aircraft from Greenland and elsewhere, Halifax or Liberator, operating against the Gap or 'Black Pit' in the 'middle' of the Atlantic. Training was also conducted with immense thoroughness, under Horton's unremitting eye, by Vice-Admiral 'Pug' Stephenson in the Western Isles. As light relief, when Stephenson flung his cap on the deck, shouting, 'That's an unexploded bomb!', an able seaman kicked it overboard. The admiral said, 'Now its a survivor: jump after it' . . . in the cold November seas.

In February 1943, sixty-three British merchant ships were sunk, and, in March 1943, a tonnage of 627,000. But twenty-three and fifteen U-boats respectively were destroyed in the same months, half by the new groups and half by aircraft. (The carriers did not come into service until May 1943.) By April 1943, the tide was turning. The monthly British shipping losses were down by fifty per cent because of massive escort and support group effort from their brilliant captains and crews, because of long-range aircraft, improved coastal asdic and echo sounders, increased merchant-ship construction at home and the USA, and, above all, because of Enigma. In *one* convoy battle, sometimes described as Trafalgar, six U-boats were sunk and four damaged; by May, Doënitz went so far as to say that U-boat losses were becoming 'unbearable'. The debt to Bletchley and its people was absolute.

On D-Day in June 1944, the German undersea defence effort was swamped by aircraft and escorts; for 1944, as a whole, U-boat losses ran at twenty a month. Horton said on 15 June that there had been no British sinkings since 17 May, but that thirty-four U-boats had gone down in that time, despite the invention of the schnorkel, enabling batteries to be charged below the surface. (But if the war had lasted long enough to enable these schnorkel-equipped boats to be built in quantity, British sinkings could have increased again.) By the end of the war, the Germans had lost 781 boats out of 1173, and 30,000 men out of 38,000.

The prime minister, Winston Churchill, said: 'We who dwell in the British Isles must celebrate with joy and thankfulness our deliverance from the mortal U-boat peril . . . When I look back on the months of this hard and obstinate struggle, which makes ever more exacting demands upon our life's springs of energy and contrivance, I still rate *highest* among the dangers we have overcome, the U-boat attack on our shipping, without which we cannot live or even receive the help which our Dominions and our grand and generous American ally provide.' The Battle of the Atlantic was fundamental to the fortunes of the country.

It was therefore the more fortunate for British survival that Sir Max Horton, before accepting the post of Commander-in-Chief Western Approaches in 1942, should have refused the more senior and prestigious command of the Home Fleet as not sufficiently independent of the War Cabinet, and therefore insufficiently effective as a means of defeating the Germans.

41
The Japanese Schindler

One cause of Fascism in Western Europe was the disillusionment of the returned soldiers of 1918 at finding their jobs irretrievably lost to Jewish refugees from Eastern Europe and Russia.

No such phenomenon occurred in Japan. Jewish immigration there had been confined to a few Jewish traders in the medieval world, and among the later Dutch and Portuguese settlers, more during the 'opening to the West' after Perry, and far more escaping from the Nazis and the Soviets, not many of whom remained in the islands. After the end of the Second World War, a number of American Jews arrived to exploit the lucrative economic opportunities afforded by Japan's circumstances under US protection and support.

Tudor Parfitt in *The Thirteenth Gate*, estimated that, including Japanese converts to Judaism, there were no more than a few hundred Jews in the country in 1987. This figure did not include the Makuya, who are Christian but have Hebrew-speaking members, Israeli contacts and a belief that Jewish and Israeli cultures have common roots in 'the Lost Tribe of Zebulun', symbolised by a golden mirror, part of the imperial family's regalia. The view is also shared by the Campo Hasada group in Kyoto. Another group, the B'rith Shalom, claim twenty thousand 'followers', but most Japanese are interested in one or other foreign culture or religion, without *adhering* to any. Many certainly dispute a 'common origin', and deny 'similarities of phrase' as any more than linguistic coincidence. It is interesting, nevertheless, that even in prisoner-of-war camps between 1941 and 1945, the guards would eagerly question Jewish prisoners about Judaism.

Japanese, in fact, are more interested in Jews than Jews are in Japan. They are particularly keen on the idea that all Jews are rich, deeply impressed by the loan raised to enable them to defeat Russia in the 1904–05 war by an American Jew called Jacob Schiff, who had been enraged by the Tsar's anti-Jewish pogroms. The Jewish record in battle against the Arabs is also a source of great homage and admiration. Nor is the idea of the Lost Tribe quite discredited. Moses is thought by some to be buried in Japan, is claimed furthermore to have brought Shinto to Israel after a visit to Japan, as opposed to receiving the Ten Commandments from God on Mount Sinai. Jesus is 'said' not only to have visited Japan, but to have married and settled down there after his crucifixion, his brother taking his place or dying in his stead in the Holy Land.

The Japanese government, convinced of Jewish financial power, decided in 1938 that they should exploit Jewish wealth and ability in order to fund the Greater East Asia Co-prosperity Sphere, and to settle Jewish managers and technicians in inhospitable conquered territories where they themselves had no wish to live. They forbade any attempts by their German allies to apply the Final Solution to the thousands of Jews sheltering in Japanese-occupied Chinese cities: as further incentive, the powerful Japanese media would present the Jews in a favourable light to their vast regional audience.

This, the Fugu Plan, was allegedly discussed in 1938 at the Five Ministers' Conference, chaired by prime minister Prince Konoye and attended by the ministers for the army, the navy, foreign affairs and finance. The ministers are said to have agreed that it should be pursued without publicity, indeed clandestinely. It is thought not to have been fully approved 'by the Americans', including American Jews, to whom it was covertly passed. What is *known* about this meeting is that ministers decided that the government would be impartial in dealing with the Jewish people, who were 'to be treated fairly in accordance with the law'. Fugu is the Japanese death fish. One mistake in the kitchen renders it lethal. It was, no doubt, in order to make the political dish more palatable that fanciful ideas about Jewish/Japanese ethnic links, linguistic connections, legends about Jesus and Moses, 'monuments to King David, and the Israel well', and the royal mirror were introduced. Enthusiasts even pretended that the imperial family resembled Jews and were related to the Lost Tribe.

Jews in Japan at the outbreak of the Pacific war chiefly consisted of refugees from Russia and the Middle East, and professionals with German passports fleeing persecution in Germany. In Manchuria, when the Japanese invaded in 1931, there were ten thousand Jews who had been there since the Great War and the October Revolution, some even since the nineteenth century, mostly in Harbin. In 1941, there were six thousand. In 1933, the Special Branch of the Kwantung army in Manchuria had recommended that 'the Jews should be treated well . . . their enormous economic power and covert political influence could be harnessed by Japan'.

Although German and indigenous anti-Semitism, fostered by old White Russian and new Nazi influence, flourished, Japan permitted the Jews to remain in Japan and in Manchuria, despite the protests of Ambassador Eugen Ott. So far as Manchuria was concerned, the Japanese said 'the [puppet] Emperor of Manchukuo can do what he likes . . .' In Japan, a German Jewish pianist called Joseph Rosenstock conducted the Nippon Philharmonic throughout the war; the distinction between Jews and Gentiles was not really intelligible to the Japanese.

In 1937, there had been five thousand Jews in Shanghai, ten per cent of the total foreign community, many associated with the great 'Baghdadi' Jewish business houses of Sassoon and Khadoorie. The tens of thousands of refugees from Germany and the German-occupied territories who arrived in Manchuria from 1938, moved on fairly rapidly, seventeen thousand to Shanghai, where they settled in the Japanese-controlled sections of the city. For some time, they even continued to receive US aid. Ben-Ami Shillony, a Jew who lived in Japan throughout the war, does not repeat Dr Parfitt's comments about the Five Ministers' Conference. He does, however, assert that, in the late 1930s, Army Colonel Yasue Norihoro and Captain Inuzaka Koreshige of the Imperial Navy helped Jews to settle in Manchuria and Shanghai respectively. Koreshige designed a plan for attracting Jewish investment 'as a gesture to the US Jews who controlled the US government'.

At a conference in Harbin involving Jews and Japanese, the guard of honour was formed from the Zionist Betar, the organisation to which Begin had belonged. Dr Kaufmann, a Russian Jewish physician in Harbin, was then invited to Tokio where he met foreign minister Arita, home minister Kido and finance minister Ikeda. He was assured by them that Japan not only had no intention of harming Jews within the territories controlled by the Rising Sun but, instead, sought Kaufmann's help in attracting Japanese investment to Manchuria. In 1930, Arita had already declared in the House of Peers that 'the Japanese would not discriminate against Jews in Japanese-controlled areas'. Foreign minister Yosuke said in 1940 that 'anti-Semitism will never be adopted by Japan. We have a treaty with Hitler, but we never promised to be anti-Semitic.' These remarks are similar in kind, if not degree, to those quoted by Parfitt. (Today, on the other hand, Ian Buruma has told us in his enchanting *God's Dust* that some Japanese believe that any adverse relationships their country may have with other countries are due to a vicious Jewish international plutocracy attempting to diminish the Japanese economy.)

In February 1943, the twenty-two thousand Jews then in Shanghai were moved to the Hongkew suburb, a poor, closed ghetto, but one from which the Jews could move, at least during the day. Nor were there labour camps or executions, and Jewish institutions, including Zionist organisations, were permitted to function.

In 1940, the Japanese consul at Kaunas (Kovno) in Lithuania was Sugihara Chiune, the only Japanese diplomat in the country at that time; he was accompanied there by his family. Even before the German Wehrmacht, intent on invasion, reached Lithuania, Jewish refugees escaping from Eastern Europe via Poland began to pour across the Lithuanian frontier, desperately seeking visas for transit through Japan to the United States, Canada and Latin America. Sugihara cabled his Ministry of Foreign Affairs three times for approval, but was refused on each occasion: Tokio's links with the Axis, although not yet confirmed in the Tripartite Alliance, were perhaps too strong for compliance and, more certainly, the Jews' circumstances – lack of money and entry visas for their ultimate destinations – did not meet the Gaimusho's criteria.

Distraught, even heartbroken at the thought of the certain death of innocent people, Sugihara decided not to obey his instructions, although perfectly aware of the penalties for disobedience and insubordination. For twenty-nine days, even after the Gaimusho ordered him to close the consulate and return home, he issued transit visas for Japan, barely halting for meals until the final day when the only alternative to leaving Kaunas was the internment by the Germans of himself and his family. Even then, standing in the corridor of the train as it pulled eastward out of the station, Consul Sugihara went on completing visas by hand and passing the signed documents to refugees running along the platform after him as the train gathered speed.

His charges, who included three hundred members of the Mir

Yeshiva, with long beards and black robes, boarded the Trans-Siberian railway, notionally in transit for Curaçao, to Vladivostock, then travelled via Suraga and Kobe to Shanghai. There, many of them were permitted to remain with US aid until 1941. Sugihara Chiune, the 'Japanese Schindler', went on to posts at Prague and Romania, having saved the lives of more than fifteen hundred Jews. In 1968, one of them asked the foreign minister for his address. More and more of those he rescued got in touch with his widow after his death: she now organises the Sempo Sugihara Memorial Foundation. In 1992, Sugihara's actions were raised in the Diet, and have subsequently been turned into inspiring stories in school textbooks.

Also in Asia but to the southeast, a Baghdadi Jewish lawyer, David Marshall, became chief minister of Singapore in 1955 as leader of the United Front Coalition. His victory, which pleased the Jews almost as little as it did the British, led eventually to the end of British government in the colony. Perhaps Marshall's greatest achievement was to persuade the Chinese prime minister, Chou En-lai, to advise Singapore Chinese to devote their loyalty to Singapore, and not to China. Chou argued that Chinese, when they died, preferred to be buried in China: 'Ah,' said Marshall, 'just as do the Jews, of whom there are five hundred trapped in Shanghai, seeking only to die in Israel.' Chou allowed them all to emigrate.

Lee Kuan Yew, when he succeeded as prime minister of Singapore, modelled his defence policy on the Israeli defence forces, receiving military aid and advice from Tel Aviv. Nevertheless, because of the end of British protection and because of the selfish greed of some rich Singapore Jewish families, there are now only a few hundred Jews, not thousands, left in Singapore, 'two synagogues, a school and a poor house'. There are none at all in China itself, not even in Kaifeng their home for so many centuries, where Liu Shao Chi died, persecuted to extinction by Mao.

42
Sergeant John Patrick Kenneally, Irish Guards

Like 'the youth', perhaps, in Stephen Crane's *The Red Badge of Courage*, 'there came a red rage. He had a mad feeling against his rifle which could only be used against one life at a time. He wished to rush forward and strangle with his fingers. He craved a power that would enable him to make a world-sweeping gesture and brush all back.'

Lance-Corporal John Patrick Kenneally and the First Battalion, Irish Guards, had landed at Bône, an attractive French port in Algeria, on 13 March 1943 and, after the St Patrick's Day parade, had moved into the Mejerda Valley near Medjez el Bab. By then, the moon and stars lit up clear night skies and the days had become sunny and hot. Opposite the battalion lay Recce Ridge, bristling with German mines, covered by heavy machine-guns protecting German positions on the reverse slope, supported by their anti-tank guns, heavy mortars and 88mm artillery. Rommel's Desert Army, after its long retreat, was about to stand and fight.

A British probing attack on the ridge – by No. 2 Company Irish Guards, preceded by a Royal Artillery barrage – had been a catastrophe. The troops climbed the hills through the mines but, instead of the expected rapid reconnaissance, heavy enemy shelling, machine-gun fire and a grenade onslaught ensued. Only five wounded guardsmen out of the original one hundred and three officers and men in No. 2 Company returned to their position. The action should not even have been attempted. To capture the ridge, tanks and a complete infantry battalion were eventually required.

After they had ultimately lost the ridge, the Germans retreated to a line of hills westward of Medjez el Bab beyond which, because of the rocky slopes, Churchill tanks could not penetrate on their own into the plain which led to Tunis and German headquarters. The Scots, Grenadier and Irish Guards were deployed as the infantry contingent, to take the battle across the minefields to the Herman Goering Division, veterans of Stalingrad, with their supporting artillery, including devilish six-barrelled mortars.

On Good Friday, Kenneally and No. 1 Company moved forward in the darkness through the minefields, under enemy flares, rifle and machine-gun fire on the flanks, dangerous slivers of rock thrown up by exploding 88mm shells. The company took its first two objectives and, on Easter Sunday, 23 April, Kenneally with his close friend Dempster, occupied a German weapon pit, and exploited its abandoned blankets, brown bread, and wine with which they toasted earlier occupants. Before first light, the company stood to, then checked equipment, filled water bottles, drew grenades and ammunition. Some wrote letters home.

The assault against the hills known as the Bou was to be a three-company attack mounted at dusk, 6.30 p.m. The target for Nos. 3 and 4 Companies was point 214 on the left, for No. 1 Company, point 212 on the right and, for HQ Company and No. 2 Company, the centre. Support Company with its mortars, machine-guns and carriers would come up from the rear. The Irish Guards *had* to hold the Bou, or the armour could not get through to Tunis. Captain Chesterton's briefing to them 'had a touch of Shakespeare's Crispin Day speech: Guards officers had ever the aura of history about them.'

Before the attack, Kenneally was sent forward on reconnaissance. Ahead lay the valley, points 212 and 214 visible high on the slopes among olive groves. Both were approached by a vast field of high corn marking the company's future line of advance towards German armour and guns at the base of the Bou, gun barrels reflecting the sunlight. He and his radio man came under accurate enemy fire, losing the radio. But before they hurried back to No. 1 Company, Kenneally managed to shoot dead at six hundred yards a German cook stirring his unit's stew in a dixie.

Hot bacon and beans, fresh bread and hot sweet tea were produced for 1 Company; each man was given an orange. Mass was said. But the orders were changed. The attack went in not at dusk but in daylight, the Irish Guards traversing two hundred yards of open country before even entering the relative shelter of the corn. The German barrage was murderous, shells burst all around the Micks, the corn scythed down by machine-gun fire; 'unexploded rockets from the six-barrelled mortars would cart-wheel across the ground, smoking like long torpedoes'; bullets hissed, shrapnel flew. Beside each casualty, his comrades stuck a rifle, butt-up, to mark where he lay. There were many rifles, the thin line was growing thinner, the British army still addicted to Great War frontal attacks.

Captain Chesterton was hit, but staggered on. When No. 1 Company reached the German mortar position, they found it evacuated and holding every kind of resource including water. Kenneally did not have to depend on his orange. (Meanwhile, he and other guardsmen took the time to kill with grenades twenty Germans hiding in a deserted store.) By now No. 4 Company had lost all its officers and senior NCOs. Chesterton led them, and what was left of No. 1 Company, up the slopes to points 212 and 214 and, thus, took the Bou against a retreating German infantry company. As he went down the hill to the aid post, covered in burns and blood, his arm hanging, he asked: 'Ah, Kenneally, are you all right?' a question he repeated forty years on at the unveiling of a statue in Wellington Barracks to Field Marshal Earl Alexander, commander of the army in which both men served.

There were, by this time, one hundred and seventy-three lightly armed guardsmen on the hill, of whom only eighteen members of No. 1 Company under Sergeant Fanning were left. Kenneally and four guardsmen walked down the hill among the festering corpses of British and German dead, to collect water, bread, corned beef, tea, ammunition and two land-mines. Support Company had been unable, however, to get up the steep slope with the mortars, wireless and machine guns.

The whole Bou was under heavy artillery bombardment. German infantry attacked in the section now held by Nos. 3 and 4 Companies at point 214 to which Kenneally and nine guardsmen went in aid, driving back a hundred Germans before returning to point 212. Shelling recommenced at dusk, and the enemy overran Nos. 3 and 4 Companies, the Germans now heading fast along the ridge to point 212. The day had been very hot under a blazing sun, dust from exploded shells filled the lungs, thirst was agonising. Fire from the three-inch-mortar platoon fortunately stopped the German advance at point 214; Nos. 3 and 4 Companies were back in pursuit. The remaining assailants were trapped in the centre where No. 1 Company employed grenades and the bren until the enemy fled. All firing ceased.

In the morning of 27 April, shelling began again and German infantry were seen unloading at the foot of the slopes. Kenneally crawled down the hill amongst the boulders and the scrub. He removed all his equipment to lighten the load. One magazine was on the bren, another in his pocket, when he spotted numbers of enemy in company strength in a gulley, amateurishly hunched around their officer. He charged forward quite alone, firing from the hip, exhausting the two magazines. The Germans either fell 'like nine-pins' or fled in all directions. No. 1 Company then came over the top, 'screaming like banshees', to pick them off. Later that morning he broke up a machine-gun position, and the depleted company also exploded a grenade tied to a land-mine with enough force to persuade a German unit of three tanks to retreat.

On 30 April, however, the Germans had put in what was to be their final attack against the Bou, a thunderous bombardment followed by armour and massed infantry. Kenneally returned to the pit from which he had first observed his targets on 27 April, to find that the enemy had come back to the gulley where he had destroyed their predecessors. With Sergeant Salt of the Reconnaissance Regiment, carrying a sten, he again sprayed the Germans from above with his bren, both emptying a magazine each. No. 1 Company followed up with rifles and, especially, grenades, until the enemy retreated to concentrate against Nos. 2, 3 and 4 Companies. Kenneally was hit deep in the right leg, but after sulphonamidi powder and a field dressing, fought on, hobbling, against the determined enemy. No. 2 Company was overrun, and the battle became close combat, grenades 'flying through the air like snowballs', until the Germans broke, the British in pursuit. Seven hundred enemy dead were counted; only eighty men of the 1st Battalion, Irish Guards, survived to come down the hill.

The citation for the award of the Victoria Cross to Kenneally read:

> The magnificent gallantry of this NCO on these two occasions under heavy fire, his unfailing vigilance and remarkable accuracy were responsible for saving many valuable lives in the days and nights in the forward positions. His actions also played a considerable part in holding these positions and this influenced the whole course of the battle. His rapid appreciation of the situation, his initiative and his extraordinary gallantry in

attacking single-handed a mass body of the enemy and breaking up an attack on two occasions, was an achievement that can seldom have been equalled. His courage in fighting all day when wounded was an inspiration to all ranks.

Kenneally was born on 15 March 1921, son of Gertrude Robinson, daughter of a Blackpool pharmacist, and of Neville Leslie Blond, who loved Gertrude but immediately left her, outside the confines of marriage, one summer day in 1920. His mother, an admitted 'good time girl', earned Kenneally's affection and respect. He only saw Blond once, probably in the late 1920s when his mother secured a maintenance order of £1 a week from him. (Blond later paid to kit him out for secondary school.) He remembered 'a tallish, dark-haired man . . . in a camel-hair coat and with a flashy black and cream saloon car'.

Blond was born at Hull in 1896, son of a Jewish father and mother, Bernard and Rachel. In 1927 he married Eileen Reba, daughter of an Italian Jew named Nahum, remarrying in 1944, Elaine, the daughter of Michael Marks of Marks and Spencer. He had two sons by Elaine, one of them the former publisher, Anthony Blond, once of Ceylon, now living in France. (Kenneally, after an unsuccessful attempt to meet his father who was away in London, claims to have been given £25 by Elaine, who also gave him sandwiches and a cup of tea before he joined the Irish Guards.) He had fought in the Great War, in the Royal Horse Guards, the 'Blues'. He was mentioned twice in dispatches and awarded both the Croix de Guerre and the Légion d'honneur, before joining the family firm of textile manufacturers in 1921. After the Second World War, in which he served in the RAF, he became an adviser to the Board of Trade on North American exports. He was a Freeman of the City of London, member of a livery company, and a senior official in the British Legion. He wrote a book, *The Rubber-Proofed Clothing Industry*, and, after being made a Companion of the Order of St Michael and St George (CMG) in 1950, died at Gotwick Manor, East Grinstead in 1959.

During the first part of his life, at school and in the Boy Scouts, Kenneally was known as 'Leslie Jackson'. In that name he enlisted in the Royal Artillery, a twenty-five pounder Territorial Army battery in which he served until February 1941 when, after involvement in a fight at a dance, he deserted. He then went to work with an Irish contract gang, 'blacking out' premises in Glasgow for relatively good wages. The leader of the gang procured for him, from a labourer who had gone back to Eire, an identity card in the name of John Patrick Kenneally. The card had a National Insurance number and with that and the clothes he bought with Mrs Blond's £25, he enlisted in the Irish Guards; the Anglo-Jewish 'Irishman' had been only a temporary deserter.

After Tunisia, and after various 'domestic' adventures in Italy, Kenneally took part in the terrible Anzio landings when the battalion lost seven hundred and forty-one men and were never to fight again as a unit. On return to the UK, he was greatly lionised in society, received his VC from King George VI at a Buckingham Palace investiture, took part in the Victory Parade and was then posted to the Rhine Army. From Germany, he joined the 1st Guards Parachute Battalion and, after rigorous training, moved to Palestine as part of the 6th Airborne Division, commanding a National Service platoon, not a move approved by his wife who preferred his company at home.

He and this platoon saw a great deal of action in the preservation of order between Jewish settlers and Arab irregulars as well as regular soldiers; but, in these skirmishes, his own platoon diminished over the weeks from thirty-two to eighteen men. His last task was to defend a kibbutz in northern Galilee against Arab marauders armed with grenade launchers. Rachel, the daughter of the kibbutz leader, Joachim, 'wore very short shorts which made her legs go on for ever', and her *froideur* decreased when she knew that Kenneally was Jewish. Joachim begged him to stay in Palestine, defeat the Arabs and help to construct the Promised Land, eventually perhaps as a Haganah captain.

The thought of his wife, of his two children, together with the disgrace of a second desertion, this one from the adored Irish Guards itself, made the offer, at first so glittering, no more than a chimera, although one, as a Jew and Englishman, which he was proud to have been invited to accept.

43
India

Jewish communities in India *today* include the Cochinis, divided into 'White Jews' whose first ancestors are believed to have landed on the Malabar Coast after the destruction of the First Temple, later arrivals – Dutch, Arab, Portuguese – intermarrying with local Keralans; 'Black Jews', locals with their own synagogues; and Meshuhrarim, descendants of manumitted slaves. There are now no more than a few worshippers from these three subdivisions, but some thousands of 'Bene Israel', who claim to have left Israel at the time of the Maccabee/Seleucid wars, still live in Bombay and on the coast. The Baghdadis form the final group, also in Bombay, mainly stemming from the arrival in the nineteenth century of the great Iraqi-Jewish trading family, the Sassoons, who brought their assistants out from Baghdad; after Independence most left and not more than a few hundred remain.

There is little love lost between the three groups, nor indeed between any of them and an alleged 'Lost Tribe', the Kuki in the Chin States of Burma and in North East India, claiming to descend from Manasseh. Some Kuki served well in 1944 with the Nagas in the British First Assam Regiment and the Assam Rifles at the Battle of Kohima. In 1918, however, they had risen against the Raj. Some, but not all, betrayed V Force posts to the Japanese in the Second World War.

The Baghdadi Sephardic community is small in number but has produced one of India's greatest living soldiers, Lieutenant-General Jack Jacob. Jacob was chief of staff, Eastern Command, during the Bangladesh War of 1971 which established the State of Bangladesh. He later raised 16 Corps in Kashmir, ending his career as general officer commanding in chief, Eastern Command, India's most important field appointment, until retirement in 1978. On that day, as he drove out through the Plassey Gate at Fort William with guards of honour and outriders, he remembered that bright day in 1941 when, as an eighteen-year-old, he had bicycled through the same gate for his first interview for the army.

Jews in India had flourished without adverse discrimination.

Jacob, as a Northern Bengal Mounted Rifles cadet at school in the Himalayas and, later at St Xavier College, Calcutta, saw every reason to fight the Nazis, perforce through the old British Indian Army. He had read Livy, Clausewitz, Liddell Hart and General Fuller, studied the campaigns of Hannibal, Genghis Khan, Charles XII of Sweden, Napoleon and Wellington. The interview, and another at Simla had little connection with the war then in progress, concentrating on social background, sport and general knowledge. It is a tribute to Jacob that the British at Simla, although recognising that Jacob was too young for officer training, put a telescope to their collective eye.

As a trainee, Jacob was required to 'volunteer' for the Artillery, qualifying as a second lieutenant. Service followed in Iraq in the 8th Indian Division under Russell Pasha who, on one occasion, rebuked an idiotic plan of attack with: 'Gentlemen, I stopped reading the Brothers Grimm at the age of twelve.' Here Jacob met Anders' Polish Carpathian Division and Glubb's Arab Legion, before returning to operations in the Arakan and, after the Japanese surrender, joining the failed attempt to restore Dutch rule in Indonesia. Neither Indian nor British troops in his division enjoyed this role, nor did they applaud their intelligence officer, the sadistic Dutch Turk, Turko Westerling, whom one of Jacob's havildars felled with a rifle butt.

After the war, Jacob trained at Larkhill in the terrible winter of 1946/7, caught salmon in Scotland and visited Paris. India then became independent. The general reported to Deolali, now commanded by the one-legged 'Fatty' Frowen who told Montgomery that even *he* might have been captured if he had only had one leg. A number of staff and field appointments followed, including his favourite, a mountain battery in Kashmir, where he grew to like mules as well as horses. There was later distasteful association with the Kashmiri Brahmins, B.M. Kaul in the 4th Infantry Division, his brother Tikki Kaul, the foreign secretary, and the wretched Krishna Menon, minister of defence during the China War. Krishna, after an anti-American diatribe, sent Jacob on courses to the US, regretted by the general only because of a prior need to dispose of his MG and a two-year-old leopard cub. The seaborne voyages home in the *Queen Mary* and Anchor Line were agreeable but, as general staff officer (intelligence), Western Command, Jacob disagreed with General Thapar's views on the defence of Ladakh, the ancient, Buddhist, semi-Tibetan mountain state. General Sam Manekshaw fortunately posted him for a happy three years to the Wellington Staff College, after which he commanded an artillery brigade in 'Little Tibet' with its wild ass, sheep, partridge, pheasant and snow leopard. Jacob then successively commanded the School of Artillery, an infantry brigade on the Jammu border with Pakistan in the 1965 War, and an infantry division in Rajasthan where he developed a system of movement for desert warfare still in operation today.

In April 1969, Manekshaw, then chief of army staff, sent him as chief of staff, Eastern Command in the beautiful Water Gate House at Fort William. He was about to meet his destiny as a general officer, faced with emergencies in Nagaland, Manipur and Mizoram, with static, road-bound army resources, with the Naxalite rebellion and permanent threat from China. The East Bengal (East Pakistan) threat, initially no larger than a man's hand, was to be the worst. A separatist Muslim League Government had been formed under the Raj in Dhaka in 1943 and, after Independence and Partition in 1947, the state as East Pakistan became part of Pakistan. Dissent soon accumulated. Urdu had been imposed as the national language; military rule from Islamabad was increasingly resented; Bengalis were underrepresented in the army, the chief institution of the Pakistani state; East Pakistan was inundated by merchants and officials from Karachi, Peshawar, Rawalpindi and Islamabad. Sheikh Mujibur Rahman and his Awami League, with a policy of restricting Islamabad's power to defence and foreign affairs and retaining Bengali resources in East Pakistan, aroused the contentious Bengali middle class. In the 1970 pan-Pakistan general election, although Mujib won all but two seats in both Dhaka assemblies, Yahya Khan, President of Pakistan, refused to accept him as prime minister. Recent flooding compounded discontent. In 1971 the Awami League called a general strike, seized power, and declared the Independence of Bangladesh.

West Pakistan troops under General Tikka Khan restored control of Dhaka on the night of 25 March and arrested Mujib. The Pakistan army had been built up to thirty-five regular battalions, seven wings of paramilitary forces, and seven from East Pakistan, large numbers of irregulars, six artillery field regiments, independent field and mortar batteries, light anti-aircraft, one regiment and two squadrons of tanks, twenty-five Sabre jets, transport aircraft and helicopters, plus a number of naval gunboats. Resistance from five East Bengal regular battalions, the East Pakistan Rifles, irregulars and police ended on 18 April 1972. Refugees began to pour across the borders into India. New Delhi called on Islamabad to transfer power to the elected representatives of East Bengal.

When Manekshaw ordered Jacob to move his army immediately into East Pakistan, the latter pointed out that, since Bangladesh was swampy, riverine, mostly quite flat and short of road networks, and since his own troops were mountain divisions, the instruction was impracticable. Training, the monsoon and, not least, the need to educate international opinion in the squalid brutalities of Pakistani occupation would rule out action before 15 November. The bureaucrats and politicians in New Delhi instantly accused the army of cowardice. In the meanwhile, Jacob was rebuked for not beforehand informing his Sikh army commander, General Aurora of a coup, the defection of the entire Pakistani Consular Mission in Calcutta: neither Aurora nor Manekshaw, however, accepted Jacob's offer of resignation.

On 29 April, Eastern Command was ordered to assist 'the Bangladesh forces' in their liberation struggle. One hundred thousand Mukti Bahini were trained in India in subversion, harassment, explosives, and guerrilla warfare, although many of the trainees were formed into *regular* units by the extraordinary and lovable Colonel Osmani, commander-in-chief Bangladesh forces. This tiny figure, with ramrod back and vast moustache, enjoyed a personal formation which had been exclusively British and, later, Pakistani. In his 'constitutionals' through Dhaka, right up to his death in the 1980s, old soldiers snapped instantly to attention on every street corner.

Jacob improved the intelligence system by placing all signal intelligence directly under Eastern Command. (He lost the naval traffic when New Delhi insisted on indicating to the Pakistanis that they were aware of a movement that could only have been identified by Sigint.) His strategic assessment was that the capture of Dhaka, across rivers miles wide, was the main, if difficult, objective, together with the seizure of communication centres, not that of towns. The campaign had to be very fast, on subsidiary tracks, by-passing, not confronting Pakistani positions.

At least six Indian divisions and several smaller formations had to be set aside against a potential Chinese intervention which the Soviets had incorrectly predicted, only some seven divisions available for East Pakistan. In discussion, the generals opposed the priority given to Dhaka, Manekshaw saying: 'Sweetie, if we take Chittagong and Khulna, Dhaka will fall automatically.' Acrimonious exchange followed. No troops were allocated to capture the capital. Jacob had to earmark HQ 101 Communications Zone, a parachute battalion, and the Mukti Bahini under 'Tiger' Siddiqui, much reduced by Osmani's depradations, but whose operations had gradually began to demoralise the Pakistanis. The logistic task – weapons, signals, transport, equipment, hospitals, artillery – was substantial, but was solved. A hundred and twenty air-support sorties were planned. The navy's main tasks were blockade and attacks against ports and shipping.

On 3 December 1972, Yahya Khan inexplicably 'declared war' on India by ineffective bombing campaigns against her airfields. Indian forces were unleashed and, by 9 December, were successful almost everywhere against General Niazi and the Pakistan commander's gallant but misguided 'fortress strategy'. The enemy began to surrender in quantity. Dhaka lay open from the Meghna river. It was at this moment, when troops were on the outskirts of the capital, that New Delhi told Aurora to capture all the towns in Bangladesh that had been by-passed, possibly because the Soviets could not have vetoed any further Security Council calls for a ceasefire, unhelpful to Bangladesh at that stage. Jacob immediately contacted General Niazi on the radio-telephone link, urging him to surrender and telegraphing a draft instrument for approval to Delhi. The Chinese then started a series of Sigint deception operations, 'confirmed' by an American military attaché in Katmandu, but not by any other observer. The US sent a naval task force into the Bay of Bengal, allegedly shadowing a Soviet squadron, but in reality intended to divert Indian air and naval strength from East Pakistan.

On 9 December, Dr Malik, governor of East Pakistan, advised Yahya Khan by signal to accept a ceasefire and, at noon, called a meeting in Government House. The Indians intercepted both cables and Jacob, *pour encourager les autres*, promptly bombed Government House. Malik took off his shoes and socks, washed his feet, put a white handkerchief over his head, knelt, prayed, and the Government of East Pakistan ended. On 14 December, Yahya Khan told Niazi to cease operations and, on 16 December, General Jacob flew to Dhaka, where he had to deter the belligerent Mukti Bahini from lynching any available Pakistanis. Niazi argued about the surrender terms, but ultimately accepted Jacob's documents. Lunch took place in a Pakistani mess, full of silver, officers laughing and chatting as if it were peacetime.

When General Jacob went with Niazi in the latter's car to Dhaka airport to meet the army commander, he was intercepted by 'Tiger' Siddiqui, intent on murdering the Pakistan commander-in-chief. Jacob ordered two Indian paratroopers to protect Niazi. Siddiqui, dressed as a major-general, drove off angrily in a truck. (A few days later, he invited international camera crews to witness his louts bayoneting Pakistani prisoners.) The surrender was signed on the racecourse. Niazi had no sword to give up and handed over a dirty revolver and lanyard, the property of another rank; Jacob could not help thinking that, in his own way, Niazi had got a little of his own back.

In this war of fourteen days, the Indians liberated approximately 150,000 square kilometres of territory, and secured victory over a well-trained army fighting on difficult terrain suited to the defender. Superiority in the field was 1.8:1 in favour of the Indians, well below the 3:1 strategists consider to be essential for the offensive. The estimated casualties killed and wounded among Pakistani forces were 8,000, an estimate based on the total strength of the Pakistani regular and paramilitary personnel, as well as attached police elements, given to Jacob by the chief of staff, Pakistani Eastern Command, as 93,000; 84,160 were sent to prisoner-of-war camps. Approximately 3,000 prisoners of war were taken during the fighting but, after the surrender, the number rose to 91,549, including 7,565 civilians of West Pakistan origin. During the campaign, the major items of Pakistani arms and equipment destroyed or captured included 41 tanks, 50 guns/heavy mortars, 104 recoil guns, 18 F86 aircraft lined up at Dhaka airport, and a large number of water craft. Indian casualties were 1,421 killed, 4,061 wounded and 56 missing, presumed killed; 24 tanks were destroyed and 13 damaged. Aircraft losses were 14.

PART III

44
Persecution in Europe; Zionism

> 'By the waters of Babylon, there we sat down and wept. Yea, we sat down and wept as we remembered Zion.' From the time of the Diaspora and the destruction of the First Temple, through the Crusades and the horrors of the Spanish, Russian, Central European and Muslim oppression, Israel had always been the place where Jews everywhere prayed to be: 'Next year in Jerusalem,' and, 'Zion, shall I not seek thee?' Thereafter, it was perhaps only under Ottoman rule in the sixteenth century that some Jewish prosperity returned to Israel. In Europe, on the contrary, Luther urged that the Jews be driven out of his country and other domains, 'so that we may be free of this insufferable, devilish burden, the Jews'.

A few hundred Hasidim, a zealous sect, following their leader, Baal Shem Tov, settled in Galilee in the eighteenth century, but it was Napoleon who, until beaten by Sydney Smith at Acre, invited the Jews of the Diaspora to unite under the Tricolor and recreate the Jerusalem of the Jews. In England, Marlborough's grandson, Colonel Charles Churchill, advocated Jewish sovereignty over Palestine to Moses Montefiore, who then bought agricultural land throughout the Holy Land. His work was supported by the Rothschilds, and by some who even proposed the use of Hebrew and advocated Palestine as a Jewish state. 'Lovers of Zion', from Romania and Russia, began to emigrate to Israel: 'With weapons in their hands, Jews will declare that they are the masters of their ancient homeland.'

But the United States, not Israel, was now becoming the preferred destination of the persecuted Jews of Central Europe. (Only eighty thousand out of two million Russian Jews emigrated to Palestine between 1881 and 1914.) An English supporter of the Jews, Laurence Oliphant, wrote in the *Jewish Chronicle* that Jews should choose Palestine, not America, 'where Judaism, scattered and dispersed . . . threatens to disappear'. A Russian Jewish doctor named Pinsker made the point crystal-clear: so long as the Jews were in a minority, they would always be persecuted and, until they had *a country of their own*, they would always be a minority. In Russia, a little boy called Chaim Weizmann wrote a letter in which he said the same thing: 'In conclusion, to Zion! – Jews – to Zion! Let us go.'

Theodor Herzl, much affected by the results in France of Emile Zola's *J'accuse*, believed that assimilation among the Gentiles had failed. Anti-Semitism drove the Jews to the historic concept of a national home, Palestine, where they could live and die as free men, not in the material or spiritual misery of their condition in Africa, Central Europe and even the West. At the first Zionist Congress in 1897, Congress resolved to encourage the Jewish settlement of Palestine and to seek the agreement of governments to that end. 'At Basle,' said Herzl, 'I founded the Jewish State . . . the foundation of a State lies in the will of a People for a State.' Weizmann, when twenty-six, wrote: 'Israel awaits its children.' Others joined in the appeal for a Jewish home and the Hebrew language. Herzl pleaded before the British Royal Commission of 1902 for the recognition of Jews as a people and for their migration to a national home, thus diverting the Diaspora from countries where Jewish residence, prosperous or otherwise, sooner or later generated anti-Semitism. Herzl's definition of a nation as a group of men held together by a common enemy – in the case of Judah, anti-Semitism – was heard with interest by the commission.

From 1903, serious attacks began in the Russian Pale, beginning with the Kishinev blood-libel pogrom when fifty Jews were killed, hundreds of businesses and homes destroyed, and two thousand people left homeless. In Odessa, under Vladimir Jabotinsky, about whom we have heard, the Jews at least defended themselves. Herzl went to Russia to plead with the Russians, who appeared to agree to an independent Jewish state to be negotiated through the Ottoman sultan. The pogroms continued. An offer from Britain of Uganda as a national home came to nothing at a time when more than six hundred Russian villages had been victimised and over eight hundred Jews killed. By 1907, the Jewish population of Jerusalem had reached more than forty thousand, and of Palestine as a whole about one hundred thousand out of four hundred thousand. Winston Churchill, then a junior minister, declared that Jerusalem was the only ultimate goal. Meanwhile, to compound

Russian brutality, the smell of Viennese Jews 'often used to make [Hitler] feel ill . . . that eternal fission-fungus of humanity, Jews and again Jews'.

Zionism was growing. The first cooperative was established on Lake Galilee, work begun on the first Jewish town, Tel Aviv, the Palestine Industrial Syndicate was established, the first agricultural experimental station opened, the first ground purchased for the Jewish University. The eyes of the future independent Jewish state opened for the first time.

In 1914, however, Britain and Russia declared war against Turkey. All that the Zionists had so far accomplished in Palestine seemed in jeopardy. Most Zionist companies were linked to, if not registered in, London, while numbers of Jewish settlers were still Russian citizens, liable to deportation – indeed deported – by the Turks. Even if Britain and Russia were to defeat Turkey, the establishment then of a Jewish state against the wishes of a majority of hostile Arab inhabitants seemed ludicrously premature. Nor were opponents of Zionism lacking within the British cabinet to vilify the dream of a Jewish state. Various alternatives were discussed, including French, British, Russian, US, even Anglo-Egyptian administrations. In the meanwhile, the Zion Mule Corps had been formed under Colonel Patterson; the fiercer the action at Gallipoli, the more Captain Trumpeldor enjoyed it. 'Ah, it is now *plus gai*,' the one-armed hero used to cry.

With Bulgaria's entry into the war on Turkey's side, defeat of the Allies at Gallipoli could only be balanced by an Arab rising behind the Turkish lines in Arabia, Mesopotamia, Syria and Palestine, guaranteed or paid for by subsequent Arab independence. Sir Harold McMahon always denied that, in his communications with Sherif Hussein, Palestine had been included within the negotiations and, indeed, no mention was ever made of that entity as such or its constituent towns in the correspondence. The Sykes/Picot agreement took note, however, of the interest of the Jewish community worldwide in the future of Palestine, while at the same time referring to possible French, British, Russian and international 'spheres' and enclaves.

The director of the Palestine Zionist Organisation, Arthur Ruppin, a founder of the Kibbutz Movement, wrote in December 1916: 'I have drawn up a settlement programme for the next thirty years . . . I want to settle about one million Jews in Palestine within thirty years.' In June of the same year, the Emir Hussein had declared war on the Turks. Later that month, Jedda fell to his son Feisal and, in July, Mecca surrendered to the Arabs. During 1916 too, the Jewish espionage network, NILI, based on the settler family of Aaronsohn, started to produce important order-of-battle intelligence on the Turkish forces; when Aaron Aaronsohn reached London, he was able to add the locations of wells and to advise on the most vulnerable Turkish points of defence. NILI were very brave indeed. 'In my view,' said a British officer, 'nothing we can do for the Aaronsohn family will repay the work they have done, and what they have suffered for us.'

The anti-Zionists, especially Edwin Montague, denying the impracticality of assimilating Jews into their adopted countries, opposed the creation of a nation state. The Zionists sought public British support for a Jewish Palestine under British Protectorate and, *inter alia*, to enlist Russian Jews, proposing the raising of a Jewish Legion. (Russian participation was, as we have seen, later excluded by the Bolshevik Revolution, despite proven Jewish support worldwide for Zionist policy.) A great deal of negotiation followed between Jabotinsky and Weizmann – through Lord Rothschild – and the British government, about a government declaration. These discussions were held under the shadows of approaching Russian defeat, allied setbacks at Passchendaele, alarming *pour parlers* between Germans and Zionists, the Italian defeat at Caporetto, and Curzon's opposition, ably countered by Mark Sykes' superior knowledge of Palestine's agricultural capacity.

On 31 October, General Allenby, equipped with NILI's intelligence, advanced on Beersheba and, the way to Gaza open, launched an attack on Jerusalem from the south.

On 2 November 1917, the Balfour Declaration by A.J. Balfour, prime minister of the United Kingdom, was sent to Lord Rothschild, who acknowledged it two days later:

> His Majesty's Government view with favour the establishment in Palestine of a national home for the Jewish people, and will use their best endeavours to facilitate the achievement of the object, it being clearly understood that nothing shall be done which may prejudice the civil and religious rights of

> non-Jewish communities in Palestine or the rights and political status enjoyed by Jews in any other country.

The cabinet minutes, however, made plain that

> the Declaration was made from a purely diplomatic and political point of view . . . that some declaration favourable to the aspirations of the Jewish nationalist should now be made. If we could make a declaration favourable to such an ideal, we should be able to carry on useful propaganda both in Russia and America . . . 'national home' [meant] a real centre of national culture and focus of national life. It did not necessarily involve the early establishment of an independent Jewish State, which was a matter for gradual development in accordance with the ordinary laws of political evolution.

Hopes that the Declaration would attract Russian Jews to the immediate battle were, of course, overthrown by Lenin's end-to-the-war proclamation of 8 November, a blow softened by the surrender of Jerusalem to Allenby on 9 December, the day of Hanukkah when Judas Maccabee had taken the Temple from the Seleucids.

Although it was clear that Balfour had an eventual independent Jewish state in mind, many steps were necessary: investment, development and immigration, none of which were necessarily in Arab interests and many of which would be bitterly opposed by the Arabs. But, in 1918, Feisal and Weizmann had developed good personal relations which, it seemed, might even lead to Arab acceptance of the national home. Prince Feisal told T. E. Lawrence that his preference among scenarios was for British and American Zionists in a Syria ruled by himself, and in a British Palestine. Lawrence declared himself as 'in favour of Zionism'. The Weizmann–Feisal Agreement encouraged large-scale Jewish settler immigration, provided that *Arab* farmers were also encouraged and protected.

The Agreement coincided with more hideous pogroms in Russia and Eastern Europe. Four hundred thousand Jews fled westwards from Galicia alone. Dr Weizmann accordingly sought an annual immigration into Palestine of seventy to eighty thousand Jews, to 'make Palestine as Jewish as America is American or

England English'. The aim was supported by Feisal in a letter to Felix Frankfurter, on condition that the Arabs of Syria obtained independence: unfortunately, although in 1922 he was made king of Iraq, Feisal had been deposed in Syria by the French in 1920.

In 1919, anti-Semitism grew. *The Protocols of the Elders of Zion* was published in English for the first time. Hitler denounced the Jews in Munich. British consuls in Eastern Europe reported in strong language on Jewish hygiene and Jewish conspiracies. Lord Curzon, then Secretary of State, criticised – in the Anglo-Muslim strategic interest – Zionist pretensions. Edwin Montague continued to attack Zionism from the viewpoint of a non-Zionist assimilated British Jew. The British ambassador at Paris referred to 'a Jew State in Palestine as a gathering together of all the scum of the Jewish populations of Russia, Poland, Germany, Hungary and what had been the Austrian Empire'. Balfour had already said – contrary to the assessment above – that a claim for the Jewish *government* of Palestine was inadmissible. Even Winston Churchill described the Jews as the progenitors of Bolshevism, if only because he sought to advocate Jewish resettlement in the more healthy circumstances of a national home in Palestine. Arab anti-Jewish riots broke out in Jerusalem.

In April 1920 at San Remo, Prime Minister Lloyd George, who 'put the Jews first and the Scots second among nations', displeased his entourage and some in his cabinet by accepting a British mandate for Palestine as a Jewish national home. Lolling in Monte Carlo, Sir Henry Wilson observed: ' . . . the whole lot, Arabs, Jews, Christians, Syrians, Levantines, Greeks etc., are beastly people and not worth one Englishman' – hardly helpful comment. Although Iraq and Jordan were excluded as components of the Jewish national home, Arab violence under the British appointed Mufti of Jerusalem, Haj Amin al-Husseini, was considerable. Jewish immigration was temporarily suspended. A Palestinian Arab delegation to London demanded a total ban on all Jewish immigration and an end to the creation of a national home for the Jews. These demands were not met, but Weizmann still commented that the aim for Palestine was now 'an Arab National Home with a few Jews inserted in it . . . what the Jews need is not an airy nothing, but a local habitation, not a spiritual sophistication, but a solid surveyable territory'.

But in July 1922, the House of Commons, by reversing an

anti-Zionist vote in the House of Lords, enabled the League of Nations to approve the British Mandate for Palestine. The articles of the Mandate authorised Hebrew as well as Arabic and English among the official languages, recognised Weizmann's organisation as the 'appropriate Jewish Agency toward . . . the establishment of a Jewish National Home', and authorised the administration to facilitate Jewish immigration and encourage close settlement by Jews on the land. When, however, someone said to Arthur Ruppin, 'now we are in our own country', he was much less euphoric. 'One is not allocated a fatherland by means of diplomatic resolutions . . . if we do not acquire Palestine economically by means of work, *and if we do not win the friendship of Arabs*, our position under the Mandate will be no better than it was before.'

He was right. The Mandate did nothing to mollify the outraged Arabs, nor did it improve the position of Jews in the USSR or Germany. Even the Jewish immigration quota into the US was reduced. Arab-Jewish relations deteriorated – at the Holy Places, throughout Palestine, in Jerusalem, Safed and Hebron – with Jews and Arabs killed and homeless. (Haj Amin al-Husseini, if not the originator, was certainly involved.) In 1925, the British cabinet rejected a request from the Jewish Agency for an official loan.

In September, the Arabs warned British officials in Palestine that there would be an armed uprising if the National Home were not modified to take into account Muslims from outside Palestine, in Jordan and Syria. A British government commission of enquiry published findings in 1930 that the Jewish authorities had departed from the Zionist principle that Jewish immigration would be in proportion to the 'economic capacity' of Palestine. There was not enough land to meet Jewish demands. The consequent White Paper curtailed immigration again at a time when traditional refuges in other countries – except the Argentine and Brazil – were also closing. Weizmann, in a rational but emotionally framed appeal, illustrated the historical disadvantages for the Jews of minority status. The UK prime minister, now the socialist Ramsay MacDonald, cancelled the harsh immigration provisions of the White Paper, provided that the Jews did not confine themselves to the employment of Jewish labour. The Jews did not believe that this implicit acknowledgement of the dependence on Arab goodwill of Jewish security would either guarantee that security or attract potential settlers from Russia and Eastern Europe.

1933 in Germany saw the beginning of overt persecution of Jews, starting with economic boycott, dismissals of employees, judicial theft and the first concentration camps for the nurture of legalised torture and murder. Thirty thousand Jews landed in Palestine, making a total Jewish population of over two hundred thousand, or twenty per cent of all inhabitants including indigenous Arabs. The latter accordingly called for their own boycott of Jewish enterprises, also mounting physical assaults on both Jewish and British institutions. Further Zionist demands for increased immigration followed, as did actual illegal seaborne immigration from Mediterranean and other ports. Over sixty thousand Jews entered the country in 1935.

The Peel Commission found that immigration *increased* economic capacity which, however, because of Jewish Agency policy over the exclusive use of Jewish labour, was of little benefit to the unfortunate Arabs. (Emigrant Jews in Europe before departure for Palestine were specifically *trained* as manual labourers.) *In petto*, a mirror image was being created in Palestine of the Nuremberg Laws in Germany. The Jewish dilemma was therefore to maintain Palestine as a refuge for those against whom sudden, unexpected, brutal discrimination by Germans was accelerating, while themselves not discriminating in degree or kind against their Arab co-citizens. But under the heartbreaking suffering of European Jews, Zionist policy turned less covertly from that proclaiming a Jewish national home, to the advancement of a Jewish nation state. And in the cause at least of increased immigration, to escape 'every form of concentrated human wickedness cast upon these people by overwhelming power, by vile tyranny', Winston Churchill remained a principal protagonist. He spoke against the views of the British government itself, which sought to evade the Nazi charge that it was fighting only for its 'Jewish paymasters'.

Churchill, of course, believed that there would be no injustice to Arabs, even in a Jewish state because – he professed to believe – injustice lay only in Arab failure to make the desert bloom. Meanwhile, a British official told the Peel Commission that 'only two thousand' Arabs had been displaced by Jews. The Arabs, for their part, began a general strike against a policy which by 1936 led to the presence in Palestine of nearly four hundred thousand Jews, one third of the total population. This protest was accompanied by attacks against Jewish agricultural and other property, and individuals. During the British response to this violence, thirty-three British soldiers, one hundred and forty Arabs and eighty Jews were killed. Weizmann's evidence to the Peel Commission concentrated on the plight of six million virtually homeless Jews of Eastern Europe who had never forgotten Palestine, whether after the Babylonian or the Roman destructions, and who had 'carried Palestine in their hearts and in their heads wherever they went'. 'Can you,' said Lord Peel '. . . take the responsibility of bringing in Jews without proper protection?' Dr Weizmann replied: 'The Jews "protected" in Poland would prefer to live unprotected in Palestine.'

Ruppin claimed that Jewish immigration, not only because of the market created, but also of its technology, had brought wealth to the Arabs as well as to government in irrigation, construction, drainage. Weizmann, fearing after Abyssinia that Britain would always give way to force, suggested that the only alternatives were to admit three hundred thousand Jews over a short period, or to discard 'economic capacity' as a criterion. He provisionally, however, favoured an idea put to him by the commission, for the partition of Palestine between Jews and Arabs, not a project accepted by the Mufti of Jerusalem.

David Ben Gurion, while agreeing that the Arabs had the right 'not to be at the mercy of the Jews', declared that the aim of the Jewish Agency was 'to make the Jewish people master of its own destiny, not subject to the will and mercy of others – to make it like any other free people'.

The Royal Commission published its report on 7 July 1937, deciding on Partition. A Jewish state would lie chiefly along the coast, but covering the western bank of the Sea of Galilee in the north, excluding the Negev, and the water resources to the east of Galilee. Jerusalem, Mount Zion and a corridor to Jaffa would remain under British control, the remainder would go to the Arabs. The commission recommended an annual Jewish immigration limit of twelve thousand souls *per annum* for five years.

These decisions, clearly, were taken against an imperial and strategic need to avoid unnecessary provocation not only of Arabs, but of Islam in India and elsewhere. The Arabs in and out of Palestine, nevertheless, opposed the entire concept of Partition. Zionists in the persons of Ruppin and Jabotinsky for their part regarded the Jewish 'state' as not large enough to absorb the volume of refugees, and as indefensibly small against concerted Arab pressure from Cairo, 'Aleppo, Basra and Sinai'. Arab terrorism directed from Damascus began, as did protests from that city, Tripoli, Cairo, Jedda and from Muslims in India. Oil, and Britain's imperial communications to India, thereafter became increasingly set against the possibility of a Jewish state which, the Foreign Office considered, might militate against both these considerations. The first step in the formulation of a new reactive policy was to limit immigration to eight thousand between August 1937 and March 1938. Weizmann said that the reduction, which he now foresaw, of the Jews to permanent minority status was to reduce 'a martyred people to ghetto status in the land where it had been promised national freedom'.

From 1938, British policy indeed moved to establish minority status for the Jews, reluctantly accepted by the Jewish Agency, but opposed by Jabotinsky's Revisionists. Weizmann himself stood out firmly for self-government in a national home at a time when immigration was still further restricted. Arab murder and violence increased and, in March 1938, the Jewish Agency's armed force, the Haganah, including the future Generals Moshe Dayan and Orde Wingate, defensively fortified a terrorist infiltration site at Hanita on the Lebanese border. But Arab attacks continued, despite the Mufti's expulsion.

In Europe, the horrid catalogue of beatings, forced dispossessions and evictions, imprisonment, torture, bullying, intimidation and murder led to demands for settlement in Palestine of one hundred thousand Jews a year from Russia, Poland, Germany, Rumania, even Czechoslovakia, Hungary and, now, most shameful, Austria. At Evian, only three out of thirty-two countries had agreed to admit refugees without restrictions; the Australians said that, since they had no racial problem, they did not want to start one; between 1933 and 1938, Britain admitted 65,000 Jews into the UK, a small proportion of those refused. Illegal seaborne immigration to Palestine recommenced. Those few who reached the Promised Land *really* 'made the desert bloom'.

After *Kristallnacht*, the orgiastic madness triggered by Grynszpan's murder in Paris of a German diplomat, London again had to choose between strategic defence and the Muslims of empire, on the one hand, and a Jewish majority in Palestine on the other. Weizmann asked if Iraq could not absorb three hundred thousand Jews on riparian development schemes. Six million Jews, that fateful figure which was the total of those whom Hitler eventually murdered, were, after all, at risk. That figure excluded Jews confined in Soviet camps and often executed, equal to, if not larger than those similarly mistreated in Germany.

But the British, hypnotised by the horror which many glimpsed of the deadly years immediately to come, had lost *élan*, determination and confidence, temporising and compromising before the menace of the dictators. 'Safety first' was an official slogan, affairs in the hands of appeasing politicians. On 18 January 1939, the Colonial Secretary, Malcolm MacDonald (Ramsay's son and, post-war, the Commissioner General for South East Asia), laid before cabinet a new policy which denied the *right* of Jews to enter Palestine and limited their population to thirty-three per cent of the total. He told Weizmann that 'in the choice between Jewish and Arab support, valuable as Jewish assistance would be, it would [not] make up for what would have been lost by the lack of vital support from the Arab and Muslim world'. Alternatives in other countries and in the colonies, Angola, Australia, Burma, British Guiana, the Rhodesias, were either excluded or limited to so few Jews as to be useless.

At the March Round Table Conference in London, Arab States neighbouring Palestine had said that they would be prepared to contemplate immigration of seventy-five thousand Jews over five years, knowing that further entry thereafter could then be voted to retain the thirty-three-per-cent quota. 'Never before,' said Dr Weizmann, 'have I left England with so heavy a heart.' After he had left, Prime Minister Chamberlain emphasised the strategic importance to Britain of the Muslim world: 'If we must offend one side, let us offend the Jews rather than the Arabs.' British ministers and ambassadors humiliated themselves and shamed their calling by their zeal, for example, in urging governments to interfere with refugee ships. ' . . . The passengers tore off their clothing and screamed that they would rather be killed than sent back to sea . . . the filth and congestion had to be seen to be believed.'

Government produced the new White Paper in May 1939. It contained a proposal for an Arab veto on all Jewish immigration into Palestine after 1944, condemned by Churchill as 'the violation of the pledge, the abandonment of the Balfour Declaration, the end of the vision, of the hope, of the dream'. The White Paper restricted Jewish immigration to one hundred thousand over five years. It was rejected by both Jews and Arabs, a 'balance' upon which MacDonald congratulated His Majesty's Government, although Churchill pointed out that *Arab* immigration had increased until their population, drawn to Palestine by its new-found prosperity, had increased more 'than even all World Jewry could lift up the Jewish population'.

British policy thereafter appeared again to concentrate on stopping the illegal traffic, by persuading governments not to allow the refugees to embark from their ports. This attitude, combined with the measures – seen as betrayal – outlined in the White Paper, only increased Jewish determination to achieve their goal, alone now if necessary. And the baiting of the Jews of Slovakia, a new feature on the anti-Semitic scene, which drove many Slovak Jews towards Palestine, was now eclipsed by the Nazi-Soviet pact and the almost certain destruction of three million Polish Jews.

Dr Weizmann concluded his address to the Twenty-First Zionist Congress: ' . . . Perhaps a new light will shine on us from the thick black gloom. The remnant shall work on, fight on, live on until the dawn of better days. Toward that dawn I greet you. May we meet again in peace.' In England, Duff Cooper, who had resigned after Munich, denied that Arab land losses, however serious, 'could be compared with the long torture that is being inflicted on the Jews'. He begged the government, who had opened Palestine to the Jews, not to close it to them now: 'If I forget thee, O Jerusalem, may my right hand forget its cunning.'

A request from Dr Weizmann for the admission to Palestine of twenty thousand Jewish children from Poland was rejected by the British Government on the grounds that it would 'prejudice the successful prosecution of the war'. Pressure intensified to halt the flow of illegal as well as legal immigrants. Jewish land purchase in Palestine was severely restricted. Proposals to establish the Jewish Brigade, to which Chapter 34 alluded, were delayed for four years in a further effort to maintain Arab sympathy for the war effort, a concept which seemed less grotesque at the time than in hindsight.

In Poland, more than one hundred thousand Jews had died in the first months – beginning in September 1939 – of Nazi occupation. Where the Nazis did not decide to destroy synagogues – and hundreds were burned down – they desecrated them by conversion to secular public use, including that of urinals. They burned the books and the *incunabulae.* They forced Jews to submit to public humiliation, dancing to whips, branding with the *hackenkreuz*; made them fight one another, wash out lavatories without cloth or brush. They organised foul games, then beatings, torture and, everywhere, mad and terrible massacres. To these last, despite their courage, the Jews submitted without tears, without crying for mercy, or in any mode except stoic, decent passivity, a consequence of real helplessness, shock, lack of alternatives, submission to Jehovah, or in the hope of heaven. Many even died, without anaesthetic, under the bloody knives of the experimental surgeons.

In January 1942, German officials at Wannsee met in conference to discuss and decide the 'Final Solution to the Jewish Question' – in other words, the deaths of six million Jews. In response to these disgusting events, the requirement for Arab and Muslim support in the war against the dictators led the British government, even Churchill now, to do little to help towards Palestine. In April 1943, however, Churchill declared his refusal 'to contemplate an absolute cessation of immigration'. But, in May, he would not permit the emigration of four thousand Bulgarian Jews, even though the gassings, injections and shootings at the concentration camps were by then well known, indeed promulgated in the House of Commons by Anthony Eden. At that announcement, the House at least stood in silence for the first time in recorded history. From 1939–42, only ten thousand Jews entered Palestine legally and nine thousand illegally. Although Churchill had initially continued to support a Jewish national home with 'a Jewish majority', in 1944 he moved toward Partition, an Arab and a Jewish state. In the same year, he also agreed to the Jewish Brigade, which Chapter 34 described; Haj Amin al-Husseini countered with his plan for an Arab army which, however, even the Nazis felt unable to support. The Shertok-Stanley agreement of March 1944 by-passed the 1939 restrictions on Jewish immigration to Palestine, admitting any Jew to that entity who managed to reach Istanbul. The beneficiaries were numbered in thousands.

When the war in Europe ended in May 1945, Churchill told Weizmann that the matter of immigration had to be deferred until the Peace Conference. Two months later the British electors threw him out. David Ben Gurion, the future prime minister of Israel, warned that if London still wished to enforce the White Paper, it would have to use 'constant and brutal force'. The policy of the White Paper continued. Only thirteen thousand of one hundred thousand Jews were allowed into Palestine in 1945, less than had been permitted to enter in 1944. Few were allowed into Britain either. The US refugee quota was filled – without increase in permitted numbers – for 1939, 1940 and 1941, but only thirteen thousand landed between 1945 and 1946. In 1945, His Majesty's Government seemed once more to have abandoned itself to begging foreign governments to reduce Jewish emigration, even seeking to persuade the Polish and German authorities to keep their own desperate and terrified Jews within their hated borders. Immigrants were returned from captured vessels in the Mediterranean to displaced person camps in Germany, the British also assiduous in incarcerating in prisoner-of-war camps former concentration-camp victims caught at European frontiers. In Poland, persecution – including cases of ritual murder – began again. In the USSR it never stopped. In Palestine, Ben Gurion authorised a *merivri* or Hebrew revolt which led, *inter alia*, to sabotage of the railway system in one hundred and fifty places.

Ben Gurion rejected a particular British plan for Partition, since it gave the Jews only seventeen per cent. The Arabs and the Americans had already refused it. Neither he nor Weizmann rejected Partition as such, provided that it included *control* in the form of a Jewish state. But Weizmann's motion at the 22nd Zionist Congress in 1946 for a halt to 'anti-British acts of terror and violence' by Jews was defeated.

The British foreign secretary, Ernest Bevin, favoured a form of Partition in the shape of a bi-national unitary state, Arab and Jewish, as the only course which could safeguard both the West's Middle Eastern oil supplies and the British strategic position in that region and further East. A Jewish state would not be acceptable to Muslims, nor an Arab State to the Jews who still read the Mandate and the Balfour Declaration as the promise of a Jewish sovereign state, at least when a Jewish majority should have been achieved.

Britain, then, exhausted by war, penurious, its imperial will in startling decline, submitted the entire problem to the United Nations, whose delegation to Palestine in 1947 eventually proposed two states, Jewish and Arab, with Jerusalem under international control. The Jewish Agency agreed, but the Arabs rejected these proposals. They were accepted by the General Assembly of the

UN in November 1947. Arab terrorists immediately went into action and anti-Jewish atrocities occurred throughout Palestine and all over the Middle East. They were met, to the disapproval of the Haganah, the armed component of the Jewish Agency, by similarly violent reprisals from the Irgun Zvai Leumi (Jewish National Organisation or IZL) and from the Lehi or Stern Group (Stern Gang), the 'Fighters for the Freedom of Israel' (FFI).

The Haganah had been formed between the wars directly from the British body known as the Jewish Supernumerary Police, established as a Jewish self-defence force. It became responsible later, not to the mandatory power, but to the Jewish Agency in whose service, incidentally, Moshe Dayan was caught by a British patrol, marching with forty other armed and uniformed Jews. His defence was that he and his men were 'training against Germany, the common enemy'. In 1941, Ben Gurion referred openly to the Haganah as 'the backbone of the Yishuv' (the Jewish community of Palestine), 'the instrument of Zionist struggle and a force for achieving settlement'. While admitting that the formation was illegal, 'there was a higher law than British law', to which this armed force – 100,000 men in 1941 – was subject.

They were later that year trained by MI4 and SOE (Special Operations Executive) officers, including the brother of Lawrence of Arabia, against Axis targets, with the approval of the Jewish Agency and the active collaboration of Abba (Aubrey) Eban, later foreign minister. Those same British also trained the Palmach, the 'sharp end' of the Haganah, which included Yigal Allon and Moshe Dayan. Dayan helped to guide the victorious British advance against the Vichy French in the Lebanon and Syria, Allon taking part in this and other actions. In exchange, the Haganah received arms from an Australian officer subordinate to the British commander in that campaign, which were used against the British in the post-war years. For their part, the British received Jewish interrogation reports on Jews arriving in Palestine from occupied Europe.

After 8th Army under General Montgomery had defeated Rommel at the Battle of el-Alamein, the British requirement for armed assistance from the Haganah and the Palmach obviously declined. The British therefore removed the Palmach's arms, whereupon Allon's men stole them back again. Theft, often with British other-rank connivance, was widespread and a show-trial was mounted from which neither side emerged with credit, lies and hypocrisy especially evident from Ben Gurion and Golda Meirson (Golda Meir).

In November 1944, Lord Moyne, minister resident in Cairo was murdered by two Lehi terrorists. Because the Zionists believed that the assassination was as damaging to their cause as to the British, they determined to suppress or, at least, control the Irgun and the Lehi. The Haganah was instructed to collaborate with the police and the armed forces against both these bodies. It obeyed, rather less than completely, in a collaboration which lasted until July 1945 when the British seemed likely to impose new and rigorous restrictions on immigration.

In October 1945, the Haganah forcibly released nearly three hundred Jewish detainees from a camp at Atlit, killing and wounding policemen. They began increasingly to cooperate with the Lehi and the Irgun and, in late October, set off bombs and other devices all over the country. Troops of the British Sixth Airborne Division, which had earned glory at Arnhem, were stoned by a crowd in Tel Aviv upon whom they eventually opened fire, killing six and wounding forty. The Haganah then blew a number of bridges on the frontiers of neighbouring Arab states in 'the night of the bridges'. The Lehi unsuccessfully raided a workshop near Haifa, and the Irgun kidnapped British officers from a hotel in Tel Aviv. In July, Moshe Sneh, commander of the Haganah, agreed with Weizmann's request to suspend his own raid on a British arms depot, and to instruct the Irgun to postpone the planned King David Hotel assault until the Jewish Agency's meeting in Paris. The Irgun went ahead notwithstanding.

In response to British raids on Jewish Agency and Histadrut buildings on 29 June which secured large quantities of documents, the Irgun on 22 July drove a lorry containing seven milk cans loaded with explosives into the King David Hotel. Fighting in the basement took place between a Captain Mackintosh of the Royal Signals, and Irgun terrorists, disguised as Arabs in *jellabas*. The bombs, when they exploded, destroyed all six floors in the southwest corner of the hotel, including those housing the secretariat. Forty-one Arabs, seventeen Jews and twenty-eight British were killed. One telephoned warning was received two minutes before the explosion, and two after the event.

On 30 July, the Irgun hanged two British sergeants,(and mined the site where they had left them hanging, in retaliation for the hanging of three Irgun members in Acre gaol. Anti-Semitic rioting took place in UK cities, while British police and soldiers assaulted Jews in Palestine and broke up shops.

Although thirty British policemen were killed between December 1947 and Independence, violence was henceforth chiefly conducted between Jews and Arabs. The ostensible disapproval of the Haganah, to which we have referred, over Irgun reprisals was not always confirmed by their own actions. Arms smuggling and illegal acquisitions continued, but the Haganah now turned to *razzias* against Arab villages, killing and wounding their inhabitants, and to paramilitary action against the security forces. On the whole, though, the Haganah was content to concentrate on illegal immigration, regarding the *Exodus* (q.v.) as the one event which turned world opinion, especially American opinion, in the direction of a Jewish state. They saw their own sinking of the *Patria*, with its cargo of refugees, as an unfortunate 'technical error'.

The Irgun were a different kettle of fish. Ready from 1927 to conduct retaliation against Arab terrorists or even Arab 'civilians' on behalf of Jabotinsky's Revisionist Party, they mounted a number of lethal bomb attacks in Haifa, Tel Aviv and Jerusalem. Some of their people, including Begin and Shamir themselves, were born in Poland where they had been armed and trained by the Pilsudski government and its successors. In May 1939, on the announcement of the MacDonald White Paper, the Irgun blew up the Palestine radio station and planted explosive devices in Arab and government buildings. In August they killed two British police inspectors. But, in June 1940, believing that British policy was back on course for an independent Jewish state within the empire, they agreed, until their leader David Raziel was killed by a German bomb, to stand down operations, thus securing the release of Abraham Stern, later leader of the FFI. They had gone so far as to agree to join Britain against the Rashid Ali revolt in Iraq but, again, Raziel's death ended that plan.

The IZL saw themselves as the descendants of Joshua, even of Moses. Their methods were brutal, even indiscriminate, a charge to which they would not have greatly objected. Begin and his wife after escaping from Poland via Lithuania, then enduredimprisonment in Wilna by the NKVD, and enlisted in General Anders' army in Prussian exile. They made their way to Iran and on to Palestine, whence most refugees, but not Begin, went on to Britain. The Irgun had until 1943 placed more emphasis on terrorism against the Arabs, but Begin was convinced of a deliberate plot by London in association with Berlin to destroy Eretz Israel by killing as many Jews as the British and the Nazis could manage.

His tactics, therefore, since at least Britain was *fighting* Germany, were to attack, not the military, but police stations, inland revenue, immigration and other administrative offices as part of a liberation war against an unjust occupier. The Haganah and the Jewish Agency opposed these activities, but did not seek *openly* to involve their own constituents in anti-Irgun police activity; the press called the Irgun 'criminal lunatics . . . despised by every member of the Jewish community'. In the meanwhile, an informer brought about the arrests of fifty Irgun members and, during the period when the Palmach and the British worked together against the Irgun, the number of suspects reached eight hundred and fifty.

But, from May 1945, Begin started again with mortar attacks, the distribution of propaganda, bridge blowing, raids on Lydda station, on Jaffa and Jerusalem police headquarters and on RAF aircraft at their airfields. The Anglo-American Commission's recommendations in 1946 for the admission of only a hundred thousand Jewish immigrants was the trigger for a reversion to serious Irgun terrorism, which included the blowing up of three railway trains, bombs at Jerusalem railway station, severe damage to the British Embassy in Rome, the kidnapping of a British judge in open court and a British major at his tea-table. Including the victims of the Irgun's devastating bombing of the King David Hotel, two hundred and twelve people, Arab, Jew and British, died at the hands of the IZL in 1946. In May 1947, the Irgun blew holes in the walls of Acre fortress, releasing not only twenty-seven of their comrades but two hundred and fourteen Arab prisoners as well. (It was now that Ben Hecht made his celebrated comment about 'the little holiday in their hearts' that the Jews of America made at British reverses.) Acre Fort had not fallen to Napoleon in 1799, which added an extra challenge to the Irgun when planning the assault on Palestine's central prison, the site of the recent hanging of four convicted Irgun detainees. The operation included four 'units' of prisoners within the gaol and six outside it. Unfortunately for the Irgun and FFI, many of them were caught when retreating at extempore road blocks set up by soldiers of a paratroop battalion who were swimming at a nearby beach.

On 18 June, the Haganah sealed off a potentially murderous Irgun tunnel under British military headquarters, killing the Haganah team leader, and infuriating the Irgun by this evidence of collaboration with the occupying power. In July, the bodies were found of the two British sergeants hung by the Irgun, Jon Kimche commented: 'If there were such a thing as a *Streicher* medal, the Irgun leaders would surely deserve it for services rendered to anti-Semitism,' and Ben Hecht was asked whether he had had a little holiday in his heart. No one put this question to him when the Irgun killed two hundred and fifty Arab civilians in Dir Yassin village in April 1948. This massacre occasioned the panic-stricken departure from Palestine of three hundred thousand Arabs to the refugee camps in which they rotted for so long.

In June 1946, the British released most of their Haganah prisoners. The Haganah was not thereby deterred from organising further ships carrying illegal immigrants, the *Exodus* (the *President Warfield*), the *Ocean Vigour* and the *Runnymede Park*. (The Haganah also mounted armed operations on land and concerned themselves with the paraphernalia of clandestine networks.) Boarding parties from a British destroyer flotilla eventually overwhelmed the *Exodus*'s gallant and ingenious Jewish crew; the three ships, carrying over four thousand men, women and children, finally docked at Hamburg in the Germany which had murdered their co-nationals, after a nightmare voyage of harassment through the Mediterranean and Atlantic.

Before this operation, the *Exodus* (previously the *President Warfield*) could make twenty knots, but she was accustomed as a ferry on Chesapeake Bay to calm water; a lot of work was needed in Norfolk, Virginia to stop her shipping water on the high seas and to secure the superstructure. Bunks, eighteen inches wide with two feet of headroom, were installed at La Spezia, and subsequently their occupants, according to the Haganah commander, were 'stacked day and night like sardines in a tin'. The refugees embarked in the South of France on 9 July. The captain's intention was to make for Tel Aviv, evade the escort and go full speed ahead for beaches crowded with Haganah Jews. The British destroyer flotilla, ordered to follow and board her, managed to get forty sailors on board by using homemade platforms, followed by the liberal use of noisy but harmless Chinese crackers. They took the wheelhouse, under heavy bombardment from tins of food, bottles and crowbars, but the Jews disconnected the rudder from the wheelhouse, steering the ship from the emergency steering compartment. The British could not penetrate that space, nor the engine and boiler rooms. The captain of the *Childers*, Lieutenant Commander Tony Bailey, wrote: 'The *President Warfield* certainly presented a fantastic spectacle as she steamed at full speed through the night, two enormous Star of David banners streaming from her mastheads and illuminated by our twenty-inch searchlights. A wailing siren gave the impression of a wounded cow bellowing through the night, as if it fled from some unknown terror.' In the meanwhile, the crew of the *Chequers* hurled 'tear-gas grenades and fearsome pyrotechnics into every opening in the ship as we drew alongside, to wear the buggers out'.

After the Haganah had eventually transferred control of the vessel to the British, the press and, even more effectively, a Swedish and a Yugoslav representative from a United Nations delegation were present in Haifa harbour to witness this argosy's arrival. The *Childers* and the *Chieftain* entered first, their decks black with oil hosed from the Zionist vessel, their hulls stove in, guard-rails gone, rafts, lifeboats and external fittings battered. British sailors were photographed after battle, covered in blood and bandages. Children peered sadly out of port-holes. Three Jews were dead or dying and twenty-eight were wounded. The stretchers bore them ashore under the cameras' gaze. The remainder of the refugees re-embarked for France where thirty-one of them accepted asylum from the French government. On 8 September, the ships arrived at Hamburg. The refugees were disembarked, again under full publicity. As they walked down the gangways, *en route* to a camp near Lübeck, they were able freely to describe British soldiers and Red Cross officials as 'dirty fascists'. The Haganah had thus achieved a series of immense propaganda victories, which increased the emotional support already afforded by the 'free world' to the Zionists, in no way diluted by the legitimate economic, political and military concerns of a government to whom that world owed its very survival.

Lehi (FFI), led by Abraham Stern, had advocated assassinations or, at all events, a more 'individual' approach than the 'institutional' destruction practised by the Irgun, accompanied also by ideological (Russian Social Revolutionary) leaflets and posters. Stern himself wanted to persuade Axis contacts to ship Italian Jews to Palestine, an idea not favoured by the Jewish Agency or even by the Irgun. Two Lehi terrorists shot two Jewish bank clerks dead in January 1942 and, later that month, Lehi bombed two Jewish policemen. Stern himself was found hiding in a cupboard by a brilliant British police operation: he died escaping, while trying to blow up the house. By February, eighty Lehi operators were under arrest. The death sentences passed usually ended in reprieve. (It is interesting that despite the damage they did between 1942 and 1944, Lehi were so distrusted by the Haganah in 1944, and the October 1944 decisions for Partition were so popular, that the Haganah was on the point of denouncing and betraying the Lehi.) But Lehi fighters escaped from their prisons, killing two policemen in February 1944 and three more in March, when they also blew up three police stations. The Haganah, who believed British assurances about a post-war Jewish state in Palestine, were outraged, still more so when the two Lehi gunmen assassinated Lord Moyne. (These assassins, after execution, were reburied with military honours in June 1975 and, in 1977, the Lehi leader, Yitzhak Shamir, was made speaker in the Knesset. Both he and Begin were later to become Prime Minister. But Lehi were exempted from joint British-Haganah measures against both them and the Irgun, whether because they lay low or, as Lehi claimed, because they had threatened to kill Haganah leaders one by one. They had, of course, earlier that year attempted on more than one occasion to kill the High Commissioner for Palestine, Sir Harold MacMichael.

In April 1946, when the Anglo-American Commission recommended the immigration into Palestine of one hundred thousand Jews, Lehi only saw the likely consequent swing away from their own tactics to those of the Jewish Agency. (Apart from the actions taken by Lehi already described, a Lehi platoon attacked tents of the 6th Armoured Division guarding a soldiers' car park. In stealing rifles, they killed seven British soldiers.) In the event, His Majesty's Government rejected the commission's recommendations as likely only to infuriate the Arabs to the point of attacking Jewish agricultural settlements.

The Lehi now decided to increase the toll of British soldiers by setting electrically fired mines at the roadside, placing suitcase bombs and employing other techniques which imposed curfews, prevented men moving off-duty, except in disciplined bodies, and deprived them of freedom of action or even entry into Tel Aviv. The effect on the soldiers' morale, their increasing desire to 'go home', their distaste for their duties, was exactly that sought by Lehi. In March 1947, Lehi arsonists set fire to the Haifa oil refineries. In April, an assassin killed the Haifa CID chief. Lehi's experts nearly succeeded in blowing up the Colonial Office in London by gelignite hidden in a women's lavatory. In November, Lehi murdered eleven British subjects in Haifa and Jerusalem, wounding twenty-three.

If the measures taken after the murders in March 1947 at Goldsmith House, the officers' club, had succeeded in a substantive reduction of dissidence, which they did not, the hanging of the two sergeants (and the mining of the site) would not have had the significance that it did for public opinion in Britain. That action, combined with less than total cooperation on the part of the Jewish Agency, continued violence from the Haganah, the Irgun and FFI, the drain on Britain's weak economy, the absence of convincing US support, lack of British will and vision, all overwhelmed the British military view that collective and capital punishment, plus martial law, could maintain security under the Mandate. That view anyway ignored the probable reaction in Washington at a time when the British economy was dependent on the US administration's goodwill.

What were the alternatives to 'scuttle'? An Arab state permanently opposed by a Jewish military resistance, the latter almost certainly preeminent over time, and with incalculable strategic implications on a more than regional scale? An imposed solution which Britain had neither the will nor the strength to enforce, a view dazzlingly illuminated eight years later on the Canal? Partition, regarded as a hostile act by the entire Islamic world? Surrender, followed by civil war in Palestine, and the loss of British face and empire everywhere, at a date when such concepts had barely entered imperial minds?

Who, then, among the Lions of Judah of those days, bears the most credit for the victory? Was it really the Haganah, whose organisation of settlements, immigration and even departments of state provided the numbers and infrastructure on which the new state could build? The great Yigael Yadin believed that the violence of the Irgun and Lehi 'complemented' the political and administrative genius of the Haganah. Some even believe that the two 'halves' hastened the British abnegation of the Mandate by as much as twelve months.

If that were so, as Lord Bethell has suggested in *The Palestine Triangle*, they might have changed the course of history.

> The events of 1948, the communist takeover in Czechoslovakia, communist victories in China, Stalinist purge trials in Hungary, the Berlin blockade, and Stalin's quarrel with Tito, effectively converted American policy from the belief, which many held, that the world's future would be based on cooperation with the Soviet Union . . . Had Palestine's year of decision been 1948 rather than 1947, Congress and President might have felt it necessary to stabilise the British Empire along lines suggested by the State Department. And this would have meant supporting Britain over Partition, switching to an anti-Zionist policy.

Much ended on 14 May when the British departed, but a great deal more began. The problems, and the wars have never ceased. They are, however, the Jews' own problems and, if the Jews fail to solve them, the blame and the solution lie as much with the Jews as they lie in similar circumstances with any other independent state. The point is that no one, any more, can bully, hurt, insult or slander a Jew with impunity. Eighteen hundred years of ignorant, self-indulgent and arrogant contempt are over.

'The dream,' said Golda Meir, 'had come too late to save those who had perished in the Holocaust, but not too late for the generations to come.' David Ben Gurion reminded his people on 19 May 1948 that 'the Jewish community in Palestine had been built with our own flesh and blood: so too we built, so too we shall guard the state . . . Our own exertions, our own capacity, our own will, they are the key.' And Golda Meir added: 'Now we were a nation like other nations, masters – for the first time in twenty centuries – of our own destiny.'

Nemo me impune lacessit

Acknowledgements

I am indebted to all those writers, living and dead, listed in the bibliography below; to the Public Records Office at Kew; the Imperial War Museum; the Jewish Museum, London; the Centre of Near and Middle Eastern Studies (Chairman, Professor Tudor Parfitt) at the School of Oriental and African Studies (SOAS), London University; the Ancient, Near East, Semitica and Judaica Section, SOAS Library, London University (Peter Salinger and Ellis Weinberger); School of East European Studies (Professor Michael Branch), London University; the British Museum and the British Library; the Warburg Institute; the British School of Archaelogy in Iraq; the Royal Society for Asian Affairs; the Regimental HQ of the Royal Regiment of Fusiliers; Dr Erwin Schmidt and the Austrian Jewish Museum, Eisenstadt; the Office of the Military Attaché, German Embassy, London; the Regimental HQ of the Irish Guards.

My thanks are also due to His Excellency Jean Guéginou, Ambassador of France; His Excellency Moshe Raviv, Ambassador of Israel; His Excellency Mr Hiroaki Fujii, Ambassador of Japan; R. Alatri, Elena Ascoli, Barone Piero Ascoli, Giovanni Ascoli, Joan Ashton, Georgio Avezzu, Maria Pia Balboni, Carolyn Balfour, Prudence Balfour, Bruno Beer, Adrian Bruck, Barbarina Capon, Bernard Cazenove, Emilia De Angeli Diena, Barbarina Digby-Jones, Professor John Erickson, John Guiness, John Hemming, Christian Lady Hesketh, Michael Hastig, The Reverend Roger Holloway, Lieutenant-General JFR Jacob, Indian Army, Contre-Amiral Yves de Kersauson, Peter Kirkpatrick, Cameron La Clair, Dr Alastair Lamb, Patwant Singh, Dottore Giulio Richetti, Aurelia Sacerdoti, Dottore Vittorio Sacerdoti, Count Charles de Salis, Edgar Samuel, Benno and Sue Schwarz, David Scott, Dottore Silvio Segre, Desmond Seward, Basil and Tammy Sherman, John Sterling, Tom Troubridge, Brigadier David Webb-Carter, Stanley Weiss, Dr Frances Wood.

Especial gratitude is owed to my publisher, Naim Attallah, to Quartet's agreeably stoic editor, Jeremy Beale, and to Gaye Briscoe who put it all in legible form.

Bibliography

ALDERMAN, Geoffrey. *Modern British Jewry.* New York: Oxford University Press, 1992.

AMERICAN MILITARY, Dictionary of, Vol. III (Q–2); Roger J Spiller.

ANDERSON, Bernhard. *Living World of the Old Testament*; Longman.

ARTS OF ASIA, Vol. 23 No. 1. (Synagogues in India).

BABEL, Isaac. *Red Cavalry*; Knopf, 1929.

BALBONI, Maria Pia. *Ventura*; Aedes Muratoriana, Modena, 1993.

BALY and TUSHINGHAM. *Atlas of the Biblical World*; World Publishing Co. NY, 1921.

BARNARVI, Eli, (Ed.). *A Historical Atlas of the Jewish People.* New York: Knopf, 1992.

BARNETT, R.D. *Illustrations of Old Testament History*; British Museum, 1996.

BARON, S.W. *Social and Religious History of the Jews*; Columbrian University Press, 1966.

BARON, Salo W. *A Social and Religious History of the Jews.* 2nd ed. Vol. 8, *Philosophy and Science.* Philadelphia: Jewish Publication Society, 1971 (1958).

BARR, William. *Journal of a March from Delhi to Peshawar to Kabul*; James Madden, 1844.

BATCHELOR and HAYSON. *The Children's Bible*; Lion Press.

BEGIN, Menachen. *The Revolt*; Henry Schumann, 1981.

BELLER, Steven. *Vienna and the Jews 1867–1938: A Cultural History.* New York: Conn.: Cambridge University Press, 1989.

BETHELL, Nicholas. *Palestine Triangle*; Deutsch, 1979.

BLACK, Matthew and ROWLEY, H.H. Peakes Commentary, 1964.

BONAVIA, David. *Chinese Warlords*; Oxford in Asia Paperback (OVP).

BRANDON, S.G.F. *Jesus and the Zealots*; Manchester Univ. 1967.

BROOK, Stephen. *The Club*; Constable, 1989.

BRUCK, MIRIAM. Miriams Story: Britto Press, 1996

BURNS, Michael. *Dreyfus*; Chatto and Windus, 1992.

CALVOCORESSI, Peter. *Top Secret Ultra*; Cassell, 1980.

CALVOCORESSI, Peter. *Who's Who in the Bible*; Penguin, 1987.

CAMBRIDGE ANCIENT HISTORY. Cambridge Univ. Press, 1976.

CANTOR, Norman. *Sacred Chain*; Harper Wilkins, 1994.

CARMICHAEL, Joel. *Trotsky*; Hodder and Stoughton, 1975.

CARVER, Lord. *The War Lords*; Weidenfeld, 1971.

CASPER, Bernhard, The Reverend. *With the Jewish Brigade*; Edward Goldston, 1947.

CENTURY Magazine. November 1983.

CHALMERS, Peter (Rear Admiral). *Sir Max Horton and the Western Approaches*; Hodder and Stoughton, 1954.

CHAPMAN, Guy. *The Dreyfus Case*; Hart-Davis, 1955.

CLARE, George. *Last Waltz in Vienna*; Macmillan, 1981.

COHEN, Shaye J.D. *From the Maccabees to the Mishna*. Philadelphia: Westminster, 1987.

COHEN, Stuart, Centre for Jewish Studies, Jerusalem; Lecture at SOAS, 1996.

COTTON, J.J. *General Avitabile*; Calcutte Review, 1905 (pp. 515–585).

CULLIS. Michael. *Austria 1945–50*; Geschichte Zwischen Freiheit und Ordnung; Festschift for Gerald Stour, Verlag Styria, 1991.

CUTLACK, F. *War Letters of General Monash*; Angus and Robertson, 1934.

DAVIES, W.D. *Territorial Dimensions of Judaism*; Berkeley, 1982.

DAVIS, Jefferson, Interview with; *Manchester Guardian*; August 1884.

DAVIS, Jefferson. *Rise and Fall of the Confederate Government*: D. Appleton N.Y., 1881

DEAK, Istvan. *Beyond Nationalism*; Oxford Univ. Press, 1990.

DEBRETT, *Peerage, Baronetage and Knightage, 1876.*

DESCHNER, Gunther. Heydrich, The Pursuit of Power; Orbis, 1981.

DEUTSCHER, Isaac. *Prophet Armed, Prophet Disarmed, Prophet Outcast*; 1954, 1959 and 1963; Oxford University Press.

DIMONT, Max. *Jews, God and History*; Simon and Schuster, 1962.

DOV MIR. *New Guide to Israel*; Ward Lock, 1973.

DRAGE, Charles. *Life and Times of Two-Gun Cohen*; Funk and Wagnall, 1984.

DRAPER, John William. *History of the American Civil War*; Harper, 1867–1870.

DRIVER, S.R. *The Book of Genesis*; Methuen, 1909.

DUBNOV, Simon M. *A History of the Jews in Russia and Poland From the Earliest Times*. New York: KTAV, 1975 (1920).

DUNLOP, D.M. *History of the Jewish Khazars*; Princeton U.P., 1954.

EBAN, Ebba. *The Story of the Jews*; Random House, 1968.

EDWARDS, H.B. *Lahore Political Diaries*; Vol. V: Allahabad, 1911.

ENCYCLOPEDIA BRITANNICA. 1994.

ENCYCLOPEDIA JUDAICA. 1993.

ENCYCLOPEDIA of Military History; Dupuy and Dupuy; Jane's, 1968.

ENGLANDER, David, (Ed.). *The Jewish Enigma: An Enduring People.* New York: Braziller, 1992.

EPISTLE to the HEBREWS.

ERICKSON, John. *Road to Stalingrad; Road to Berlin*; Weidenfeld, 1983.

FANE, Henry (Sir). *Five Years in India*; Henry Colburn, 1842.

FAST, Howard. *The Jews*; Laurel, 1968.

FAUR, José. *In the Shadow of History: Jews and Conversos at the Dawn of Modernity.* Albany, N.Y.: State University of New York Press, 1992.

FOX, Robin Lane. *The Unauthorized Version, Truth and Fiction in the Bible.* New York: Viking, 1991.

FRIEDMAN, Richard Elliott. *Who Wrote the Bible*: New York: Summit, 1987.

FULLEYLOVE and KELMAN. *The Holy Land*; A. and C. Black, 1912.

GANDZ, S. and KLEIN, I. *The Code of Maimonides*; Yale Univ. Press, 1961.

GASTER, Moses. *Samaritans, History, Doctrine and Literature*; Oxford Univ. Press, 1925.

GILBERT, Martin. *Exile and Return*; Weidenfeld, 1978.

GILBERT, Martin. *The Most Horrible Crime*; T.L.S. (June 7, 1966).

GOITEIN, Solomon D. *A Mediterranean Society.* 6 vols. Berkeley: University of California Press, 1967–1993.

GOLB, Norman. *Khazarian Hebrew Documents of the 10th Century*; Cornell University, 1982.

GREEN, Geoffrey L. *The Royal Navy and Anglo Jewry*; G.L. Green, 1989.

GREENBERG, Louis. *The Jews in Russia: The Struggle For Emancipation.* New Haven, Yale University Press, 1965 (1949–51).

GREY, Charles. *European Adventurers of Northern India*; (1929 H.L.P. Garrett, Lahore).

GULCHARAN SINGH. *Ranjitsingh and his Generals*; Sujlana Jullundur, 1976.

GURION, David Ben. *Israel, Years of Challenge*; Blond, 1964.

HARRISON, R.K. *Introduction to the Old Testament*; Eastmanns, 1969.

HEAZY, Mark. *Warriors of the Old Testament*; Firebird, 1989.

HEMMING, John. *Conquest of the Incas*; Macmillan Papermac, 1993.

HERTZOG, Chaim and GICHON, Mordecai. *Battles of the Bible*; Weidenfeld, 1978.

HERTZOG, Chaim. *Heroes of Israel*; Little Brown, 1989.

HILBERG, Raul. *Perpetrators, Victims, Bystanders: The Jewish Catastrophe 1933–1945*; New York: Harper Collins, 1992.

HIRSH, J. Ben. *Jewish General Officers*; Mil. History Society of Australia, (Victoria Branch).

HOLY BIBLE. *Apocrypha.*

HOLY BIBLE. *The Authorised King James* Version; (C.U.P.)

HONIGBERGER, Johan Martin. *35 Years in the East*; H.A. Bailliere, 1852.
JACOBS, Dan N. *Borodin*; Harvard U.P., 1981.
JACQUEMENT, V. *Letters from India*; Oxford Univ. Press, 1979.
JAPANESE Embassy, London. (Japan Society) *Gaimusho Materials on Chiune Sugihara.*
JOHNSON, Paul. *History of the Jews*; Weidenfeld, 1987.
JOSEPHUS, Flavius. *Antiquities of the Jews*; Oxford University, 1975.
JOSEPHUS, Flavius. *The Jewish War*; Penguin, 1981.
KADOURIE, Elie (Ed.). *Spain and the Jews. The Sephardi Experience 1492 and After*; New York: Thames and Hudson, 1992.
KENNEALLY, John Patrick. *Kenneally VC*; Kenwood, 1991.
KHILAL, Samir al. *The Monument*; André Deutsch, 1991.
KHUSHWANT, Singh. *Ranjit Singh*; George Allen and Unwin, 1962.
KIMCHE, John and David. *The Secret Roads*; Farrer Strauss, 1954.
KOMAY, Joan. *Temple of Jerusalem with History of Temple Mount*; Oxford Univ. Press, 1975.
KUNG, Hans. *Judaism: Between Yesterday and Tomorrow*; New York: Crossroads, 1992.
KURZMAN, Dan. *The 1st Arab Israeli War*; World Publishing, NY, 1970.
LAKEMAN, Sir Stephen. *What I saw in Kaffir Land*; Blackwood, 1880.
LANSING, Elizabeth. *The Sumerians*; Cassell, 1974.
LAQUEUR, Walter. *History of Zionism*; Weidenfeld, 1972.
LAWRENCE, H.M. *Adventures with Ranjit Singh*; OUP, 1975.
LEWIS, Bernard. *The Jews of Islam*; Princeton University Press, 1984
LIDDELL HART. *The Other Side of the Hill*; Cassell, 1948.
LORCH, Natand. *The Edge of the Sword*; Massada, Jerusalem, 1968.
MACCABEES, The Book of.
MACCABEUS, Judas. OUP, 1989.
MACKENZIE, Mrs C. (Aden). *Six Years in India*; R. Bentley, 1853.
MAHLER, Raphael. *A History of Modern Jewry*; New York: Schocken Books, 1971.
MALLOWAN, Max. *Noah's Flood Considered*; Periodical 'Iraq' 26, 1964. (London)
MASSIE, Alan. *King David*; Sceptre, 1996.
MENORAH CLUB. *The Jews in the Palestine Campaign*; Menorah, 1936.
MICHENER, James. *The Source*; Secker and Warburg, 1965.
MILITARY HISTORICAL MUSEUM AT SCHLOSS RUSTAT SPECIAL EXHIBITION, *German Jewish Soldiers 1914–1945*; 1981.
MINISTRY OF DEFENCE, Paris. (Service Historique de l'Armée de Terre). (Marshal Massena, Generals Wolf, Rottembourg, Brisac, Valabresque.) 1996.

MORTON, H.C.V. *In the Steps of the Master*; Rich and Cowan, 1934.
MORTON, H.C.V. *The Middle East*; Methuen, 1941.
MORTON, H.C.V. *Through Lands of the Bible*; Methuen, 1938.
NAGLER, Commander D. Exhibition of German Jewish Service Personnel 1808–1945; Austrian State Archives, War Archive.
NARAIN, Pandit Shee. *General Ventura*, Selections from the Journal of the Punjab Historical Society 1982, Journal of the Punjab Historical Society 1917, Vol. VI, 2: pp. 149–158.
NOTH, M. *History of Israel*; Black, 1958.
O'BRIEN, Conor Cruise. *The Siege*; Simon and Schuster, 1986.
O'NEILL, H.C. *The Royal Fusiliers in the Great War*, Heineman, 1922.
OATES, Joan. *Babylon*; Thames and Hudson, 1979.
OSBORNE, W.G. *Court and Camp of Ranjit Singh*; Henry Colburn, 1840.
PARFITT, Tudor. *The Thirteenth Gate*; Weidenfeld, 1987.
PAWEL, Ernst. *The Labyrnth of Exile: A Life of Theodor Herzl*; New York: Farrar, Straus, 1988.
PEAKE's Commentaries. Black and Rowley; Nelson, 1965.
PEDERSEN, R.A. *Monash as Military Commander*; Melbourne UP, 1985.
PERRY, E.W.O. *Stand To* (Australia); Vol. I No. 8, Oct-Nov 1950.
PIEROPAN. *Storia della Grande Guerra sul Fronte Italiana*; Mursia, 1988.
PRINSEP, H.I. *Origin of Sikh Power in Punjab*; Calcutta, 1834.
RAPHAEL, Chaim. *The Road from Babylon*; Weidenfeld, 1985.
REVEILLE. Vol. 24, Feb. 1, 1951, p.7 (London)
ROBERTS, David R.A. *The Holy Land*; Studio Editions, 1982.
ROSE, Norman. *Chaim Weizmann*; New York: Viking, 1986.
ROTEM SIMHA. *The Past within me*; Yale UP, 1996.
ROTH, Cecil. *Perkin Warbeck and his Jewish Master*; Jewish Historical Society, Vol. 9, Spottiswoode Ballantyne and Co., 1922.
ROWLEY, H.H. *Joseph to Joshua*; Pharaoh, 1950.
RUBIN, E.F. *140 Jewish Marshals, Generals and Admirals*; Revero.
SACHER, Howard. *History of Israel*; Blackwell, 1972.
SADKA, Saul. *Blood in Zion*; Brassey, 1995.
SALT (Australia), Vol. I, No. 11, 8 Dec. 1941. pp. 19–21.
SASSON, Bar H.H. (Ed.). *History of Jewish People*; Harvard, 1976.
SCHMIDL, Erwin. *Jews in the Hapsburg Armed Forces 1788–1918*; Studio Judaico Austriaca XI, 1989.
SCHMIDL, Erwin. *Military History of Austria*; 3 vols, Austrian Army Museum.
SENEKOWITSCH, Martin. *Johann Friedlander, a Forgotten Officer of the Army*; published in 'David' (Vienna), 1986.
SERLE, Geoffrey. *John Monash*; Melbourne UP, 1982.

SEWARD, Desmond. *The Monks of War*; Penguin. 1995.
SHILLONY, Ben Ami. *Politics and Culture in Wartime Japan*; Clarendon, 1981.
SINCLAIR, Andrew. *Jerusalem*; Century, 1996.
SIRAT, Colette. *A History of Jewish Philosophy in the Middle Ages*. New York: Cambridge University Press, 1990 (1985).
SMITH, Morton. *Palestinian Parties and Politics that Shaped the Old Testament*. 2nd ed. London: SCM, 1987.
SMITHERS, A.J. *Sir J Monash*; Pen and Sword, 1973.
SOMAN and BYRNE, (Eds.). *A Jewish Colonel in the Civil War*; University of Nebraska.
STAND EASY, Vol. III, No. 1, July/August 1945; 3rd Regt. RHA.
STEINSALTZ, Adin. *The Essential Talmud*; New York: Bantam, 1976.
STEPHENS, Alexander Hamilton. *A Compendium of the History of the United States*; W.J. Duffie, Columbia South Carolina, 1885, and S.J. Hale (N.Y.) 1883, 1872.
STEWART, Desmond. *Theodor Herzl*; Quartet, 1978.
SVERDLOV, Feder Davydovich. *Ustroyu Otvazknykh*; Moscow, 1992.
THOMAS, Hugh. *The Conquest of Mexico*; Random House, 1993.
TIMES Atlas of the Bible.
UCHANY, Eva. National University of Mexico, 'La Vida entre el Cristianismo y el Judaismo eu la Nieva España 1580–1606; Studias de Historia Nova España, 1992.
VLADIMIROV, Peter. *Vladimirov Diaries*; Doubleday, 1975.
VOLCOGONOV, Dimitri. *Trotsky, The Eternal Revolutionary*; Harper Collins, 1996.
VOGEL, Rolf. *German Jews in the German Army 1813–1976*; Haser and Koekler, 1977.
WHEATTEROFT, Geoffrey. *The Controversy of Zion*; Sinclair-Stevenson, 1996.
WOLFF, J. *Mission to Bokhara*; printed for the Author, London, 1845.
WOLFF, J. *Travels and Adventures*; Saunders Otley, 1861.
WOOLLEY *et al. UR Excavations*; British Museum, 1954.
YAMASHITA, Sujji. *The Japanese Version*;
YIGAEL YADIN. *Bar Kokhba*; Weidenfeld, 1971.
YIGAEL YADIN. *Massada*; Massada, Tel Aviv, 1961.
YIGAEL YADIN. *The Art of Warfare in Biblical Lands*; Weidenfeld, 1963.
YURIEV, Lt. Col. Mikhail. Army Quarterly Vol. 2, April–July 1938.
ZAMOYSKI, Adam. *The Polish Way*; John Murray, 1987.
ZUCOTTI, Susan. *Italians and the Holocaust*; Peter Halban, 1987.
PUBLIC RECORDS OFFICE. The Raglan Papers; The Cardigan Papers; Operation Anthropoid and associated documents: H.S. 4/211, 4/39, 4/249, 4/156, 4/137 and 158.

Index